Hi,

Thank you for the purchase of this workbook. Doing simple drawings with pen and ink is a very relaxing and enjoyable hobby, and with this workbook, you will soon discover how easy it is as well.

Pen and ink drawing books usually start with detailed explanation of pen choices followed by different pen strokes and so on and by the time beginners get to actual drawing part, they are sufficiently discouraged. This workbook takes a different approach.

Main aim of this workbook is to help you get started quickly with fully illustrated explanations and hands on exercises. Text is kept to minimum. Key pen stroke and technique to render different elements of nature is clearly demonstrated and this is followed by hands on exercises for you to attempt.

Do try different activities in the workbook. You can supplement it by additional practice on your own drawing book. If the initial attempt is not to your liking, then try again. Don't get discouraged in the beginning and take break between attempts if you need to.

Once you start, you will discover the joy of putting pen on paper and creating simple pleasing landscapes from your imagination. Do feel free to reach out to me to share any questions, comments on the workbook or even your attempts along your pen and ink drawing adventure.

Happy Drawing,

Rahul Jain

www.pendrawings.me

I0504019

# Why Landscapes?

Any new comer to art often struggles with the question of 'what to draw?'. While all of us have some intrinsic interest in some subjects, it is usually helpful to start with subjects that are more 'forgiving' in that they can take variety of shape and form without feeling 'wrong'. Human and animal forms, especially faces, are least forgiving in that there are specific relationships between say location and size of nose and eyes that need to be followed and our eyes are very perceptible to any deviation between the expectation and what is drawn. This causes beginners to get frustrated very quickly in the beginning when starting with such 'unforgiving' subject.

Landscapes on the other hand are very forgiving as there is no 'right' size of a tree. Most elements of nature come in limit less shape and sizes and as long as simple principles are followed (like simple tapering of trunk), any beginner can easily attempt them without learning extensive set of ratios, proportions, different views in perspective etc. In subsequent pages, I will show step by step how to draw different elements of nature and once the stroke and manner of usage is understood, you will be able to create your own limitless variations on it with ease.

Once you learn to draw different elements individually, you can easily put them together to create a drawing from your imagination. I cover some of composition themes you can use with different elements and once these are practiced, you will never be short on 'what to draw'. By combining these elements in limitless ways, you will enjoy putting a landscape on paper from your imagination.

As you progress, you will also find yourself observing nature more closely. Often we pay very little attention to our natural surrounding with our mind internally occupied with myriad things. But a great benefit of learning to draw nature is the appreciation and awareness that comes from learning to draw it and you will soon find yourself looking at the beauty of nature in a new light.

# On Pen and Ink Drawing Style

If you had a chance to look at pen and ink drawings by different artists, I am sure one thing you would have noticed is the different 'style' of such drawings. The 'style' of a drawing is a loose term that generally refers to the way pen strokes are used to lay down tone and overall feeling the drawing evokes. In one aspect, Pen and Ink appears to be a very simple medium as a simple 'line' is used to lay down tone. But with this simplicity comes immense possibilities as there are limitless ways in which a 'line' can be drawn and used. At one end, there is 'Stippling' or 'Pointillism' where instead of line, multitudes of small dots are used to lay down tone. At the other end is use of bold brush strokes, usually used for drawing comics. In between, there are limitless ways in which lines can be drawn and used to create different feel for the drawing.

My 'style' and the one I present here is based on the use of simple pen lines to create what I call a 'pleasing' drawing. The size is often around 6 by 4 inches or less and is something that can be easily done in a small sketch book that can be easily carried around. What I recommend is to carry a pocket sketch book and pen with you and attempt these drawings in between your small breaks or whenever you feel like it. I don't aim for 'realism' in my drawings or instructions here. Such drawings are often done at much larger scale in a studio setting in slow deliberate manner. While you may eventually get there, my aim with the techniques and style presented here is to help you adopt pen and ink drawing as a relaxing and creative hobby that can be enjoyed anywhere. This means that my style and one presented here is aimed at use of simple pen lines at a small reasonable drawing size that can be attempted anywhere.

As you attempt the techniques and experiment with drawing with pen, you will develop your own style. Your drawings will look different than mine and that is completely fine. Indeed, your own 'style' might evolve over time as well. The key point is not to copy my drawings but instead to understand the key aspect of stroke as illustrated and then use it in your own manner.

If you feel frustrated, then take a break and try again. Persistent daily practice is key to improvement. Soon you will develop your own style and discover the joy of putting pen on paper and bringing to life the imagined or real landscape on a piece of paper.

Lets start the journey.

# Note on Pen and Paper:

So, what is a good pen for drawing?

Quite frankly, in the beginning, any good 'gel' pen will do, kind you will find in any local stationary shop. Choose one with fine tip (0.5mm wide or less) if you can find one. Gel pens for writing are often medium tip (0.7 mm) and their lines are often too thick to get good texture. As you progress in your journey and you desire better quality pens for drawing, you can check out my website and videos for more information.

www.pendrawings.me/penpaperchoices

Another great option  is 'fine liners', which you can easily find with fine tip. One very popular brand is 'Pigma Micron', but to reiterate, any good fine point gel pen or marker/fine liner will do in the beginning.

I would suggest not using pencil. Most pencils don't give sufficiently dark lines that you need to create texture with lines alone. Permanence of pen lines also promote good observation and avoid 'draw-erase-draw' cycle that frustrates many beginners. Use of ordinary ball pen is also discouraged as their ink is not dark enough to enable proper texturing.

Most importantly, make sure that you don't get discouraged from trying activities in this workbook because you don't have a 'good quality' pen.

As for paper, in addition to this workbook, any paper that doesn't bleed, like the one you use for normal printing will do. Avoid textured paper as this will interfere with flow of nib. Choose a smooth paper instead. There is again an incredible variety of paper available for drawing and you can find discussion on relative merits of these for pen and ink drawing at the above link.

# Note on Proper Use of Pen for Drawing:

A key aspect of drawing with pen is to let your pen float on the paper with the nib/tip touching and releasing ink.

Never dig into the paper by pressing nib/tip in the paper.

Hold your pen lightly and release the tension in your hand. This will help you get the freedom of pen movement and lightness that contributes to good drawing practice.

A good quality gel pen and marker will provide a nice line with gentle touch on paper. If you find that you need to dig to get the ink out, then change the pen. 'Forcing' ink out of pen is never recommended. It will ruin drawing paper and create hard lines and ruin the drawing experience for you.

In the following pages, different pen strokes are illustrated that can be used to convey different textures. When attempting them, keep your hand supple and most importantly, keep it moving. The stroke shouldn't be done in a slow and deliberate manner, as this makes it rigid and un appealing. At the same time, don't rush through it. Find your speed and rhythm at which the pen line has a natural appeal. This takes time and practice and you will soon find yours.

For other workbooks in this series, please visit www.pendrawings.me/workbooks


Dedicated to all who seek to discover and express their creative side


Version 4,Updated March 2020

Do make use of all the space in this workbook and practice doing all the activities. As with mostly everything else, practice is the key to improving. If you don't like your initial attempt, then don't get discouraged and try again. Enjoy the process of discovering your creative side

**Content:**

**Content, Continued:**

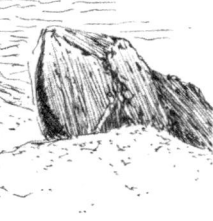

# Templates for Practice:

It goes without saying that practice is key to improvement. I recommend carrying a small pocket sketch book with you and drawing in it when ever you get a chance. A big benefit of pen and ink drawing is that it can be done anywhere as all it takes is a pen and paper.

All the practice exercises in this workbook are kept on odd pages so that they can be easily attempted. That said, unfortunately as the workbook is not spiralbound, you might find it bit cumbersome sometimes. With that in mind, and also to enable additional practice, I am providing practice activities covered in this workbook as a downloadable PDF file at the following location. This will also help those viewing this as an e-book.

## www.pendrawings.me/practice

You can download and print (with free PDF Reader) the practice exercises in this workbook as you need them from the above link. It is often very useful to try the same exercises multiple times with slight variations as suggested here to understand the effect of different choices on the resulting outcome. This will help you develop your own unique drawing style as well. Remember, the aim is not to slavely copy what I have drawn, but to understand the core stroke and its manner of usage and then apply it in your own unique ways. Exercises in this workbook and ones you print and practice will help you in that goal.

## Drawing Stones:

To believably draw a stone, two things need to be accomplished:

**1. Draw the 3d outline.**

**2. Texture and shade it to give it a feel of stone.**

Drawing the outline of a stone is very similar to drawing the outline of a box, except that edges and overall shape must be irregular.
Texturing of stone is done by using specific strokes as discussed later.

First, we learn how to draw simple outline of a stone.

Next, we learn how to texture it and give it a feel of stone.

Drawing a group of stones in different configuration is always a pleasing drawing. This is covered next.

Finally, we learn how to draw simple landscapes with stones.

# How to Draw a Stone Outline:

A stone can be thought of as a box with rough edges and texture. Drawing outline of a stone is very similar to drawing a box.

In a typical view, left side, right side and top of a box are visible. Use following steps to draw these sides. Use rough angular lines to give a feel of stone.

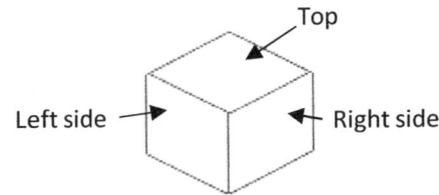

## Drawing Stone Outline:

Start by drawing the top of left and right side

Next, drop lines (height) as shown below

Connect the height lines to draw bottom of left and right side

Draw top by connecting top lines as shown below

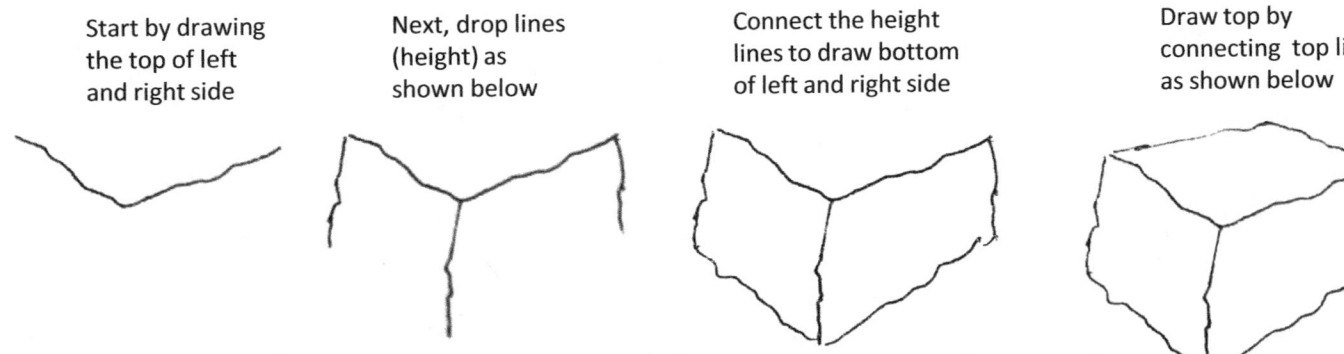

# How to Draw a Stone Outline:

Here are some more examples. By using different sizes and angles for these lines, stones with different feel can be drawn.

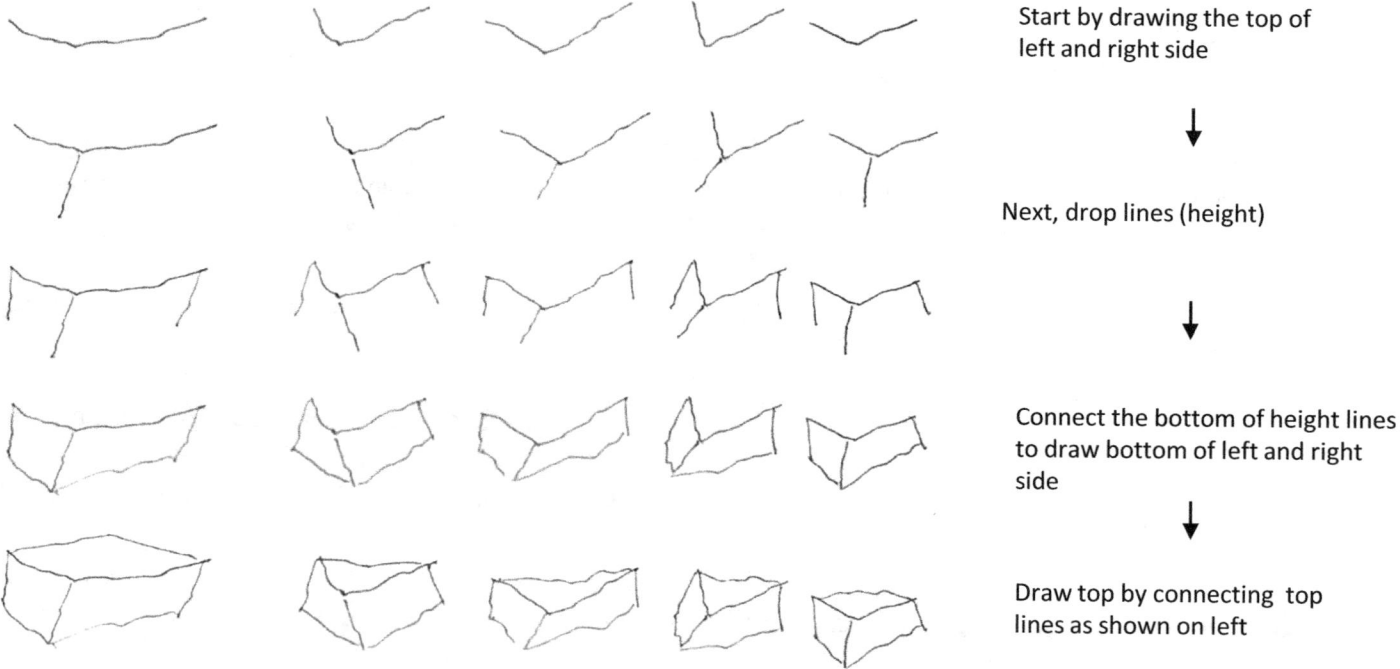

Start by drawing the top of left and right side

↓

Next, drop lines (height)

↓

Connect the bottom of height lines to draw bottom of left and right side

↓

Draw top by connecting top lines as shown on left

# Activity : Practice drawing stone outline below.

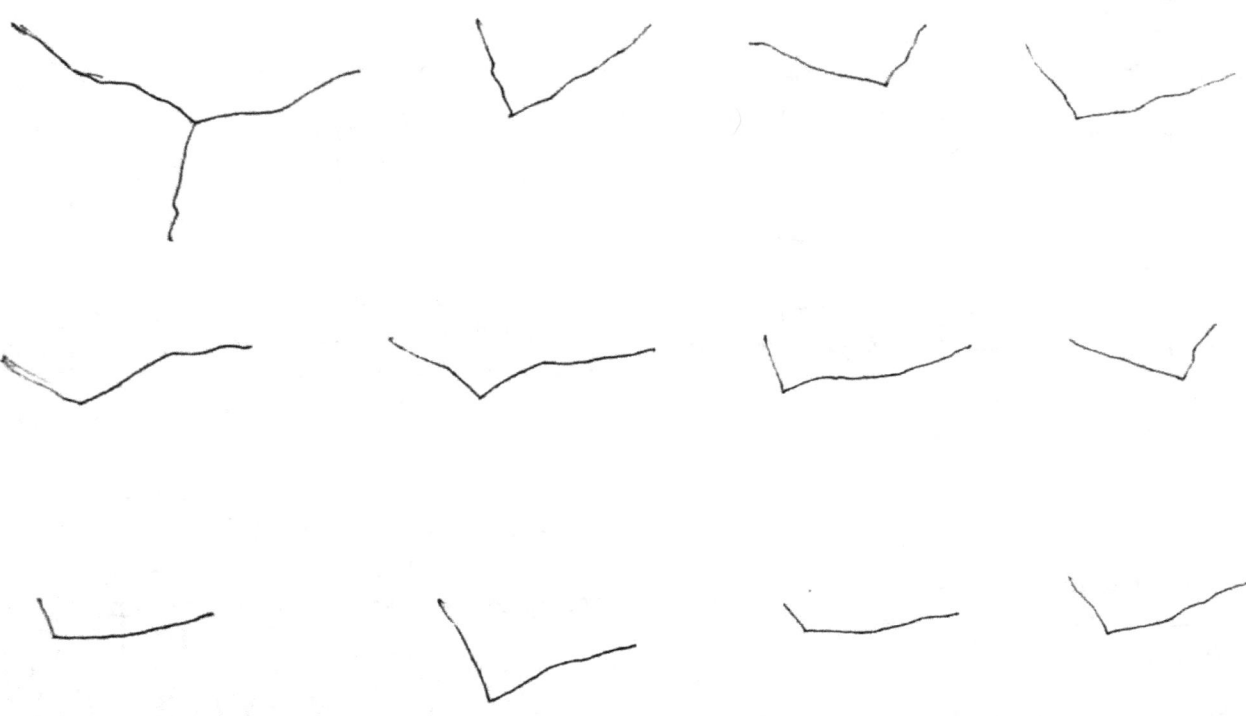

# How to Texture a Stone:

To texture a stone, we need to first give it a 'base' tone and then finish by adding tapered cervices and edge irregularities.

What is a 'base' tone: Stones are usually darker in tone. So, we need to make their sides dark and when drawing with pen, lines are used for this purpose. This process of using lines to give a tone is called 'hatching'.

To darken tone, additional set of hatching lines can be used.

Draw hatching lines to add some dark or tone to the sides

Left side is made darker by using additional set of hatching lines

Second set of hatching lines is used for right side as well

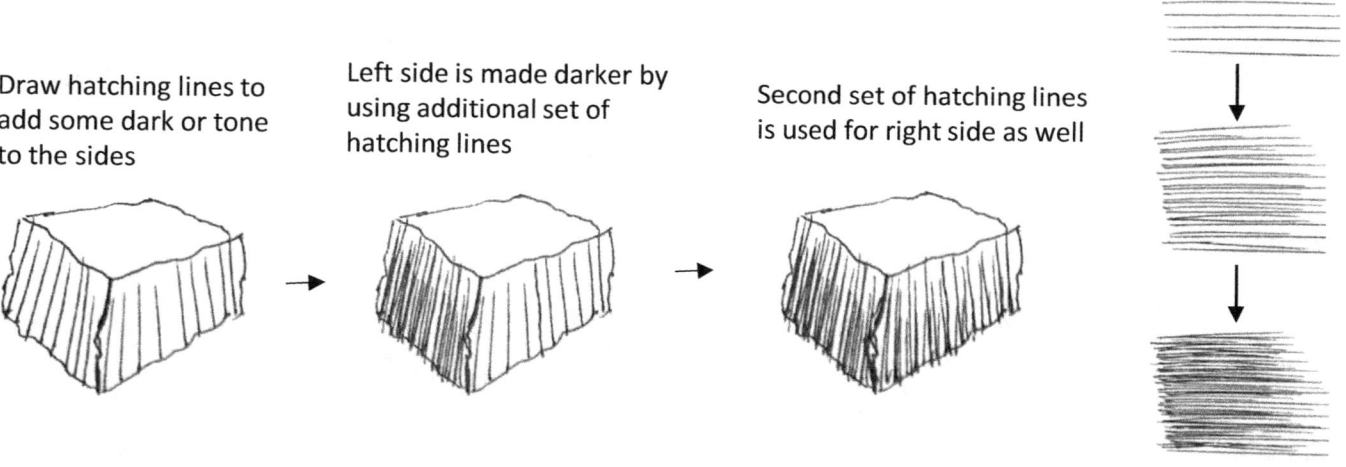

## Shading with Pen:

Shading, or laying down tone, is a fundamental aspect of drawing. With other mediums like pencil or pastels, a broad or chisel tip can be used to lay down consistent tone across wider area. Not so with a pen. Since a pen only has a fine tip, shading with pen consists of laying down multiple lines in an area.  This is called 'hatching'.

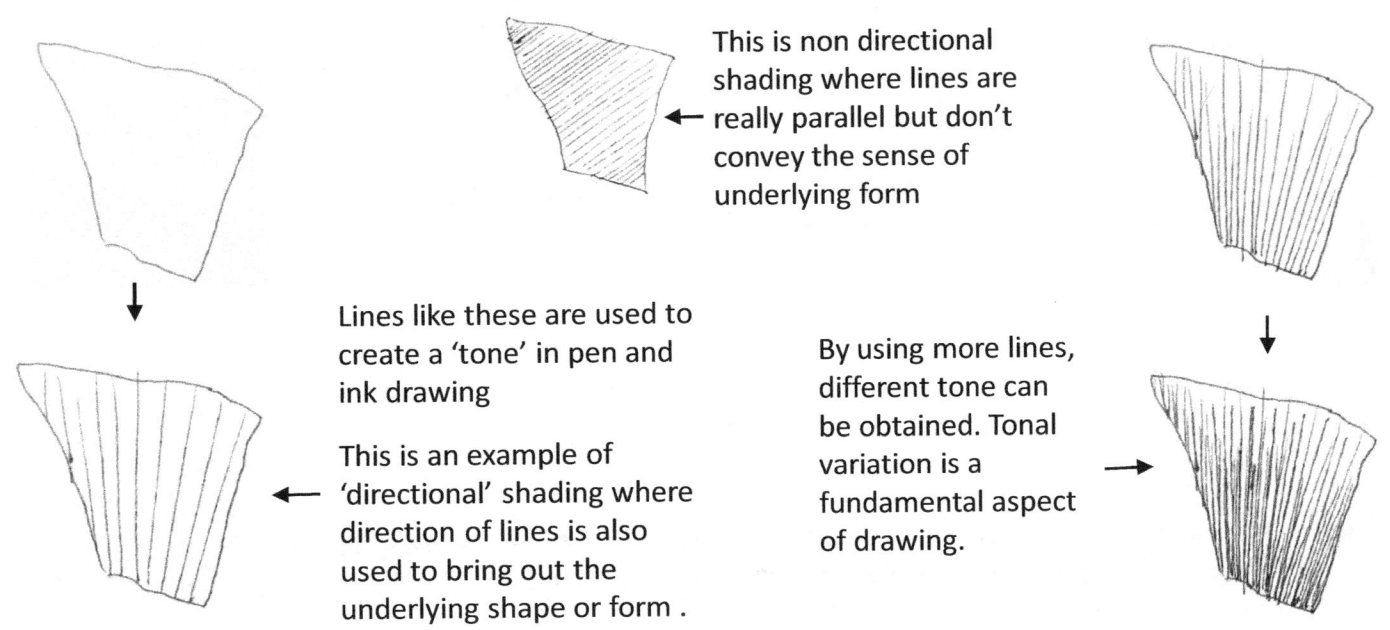

This is non directional shading where lines are really parallel but don't convey the sense of underlying form

Lines like these are used to create a 'tone' in pen and ink drawing

This is an example of 'directional' shading where direction of lines is also used to bring out the underlying shape or form .

By using more lines, different tone can be obtained. Tonal variation is a fundamental aspect of drawing.

# Concept of Tonal Variation

**Light doesn't fall uniformly on any object which has surfaces at different angle to the light source. Surface that is facing the light source is lit brightest while the surface with an angle away from the light source is darkest.**

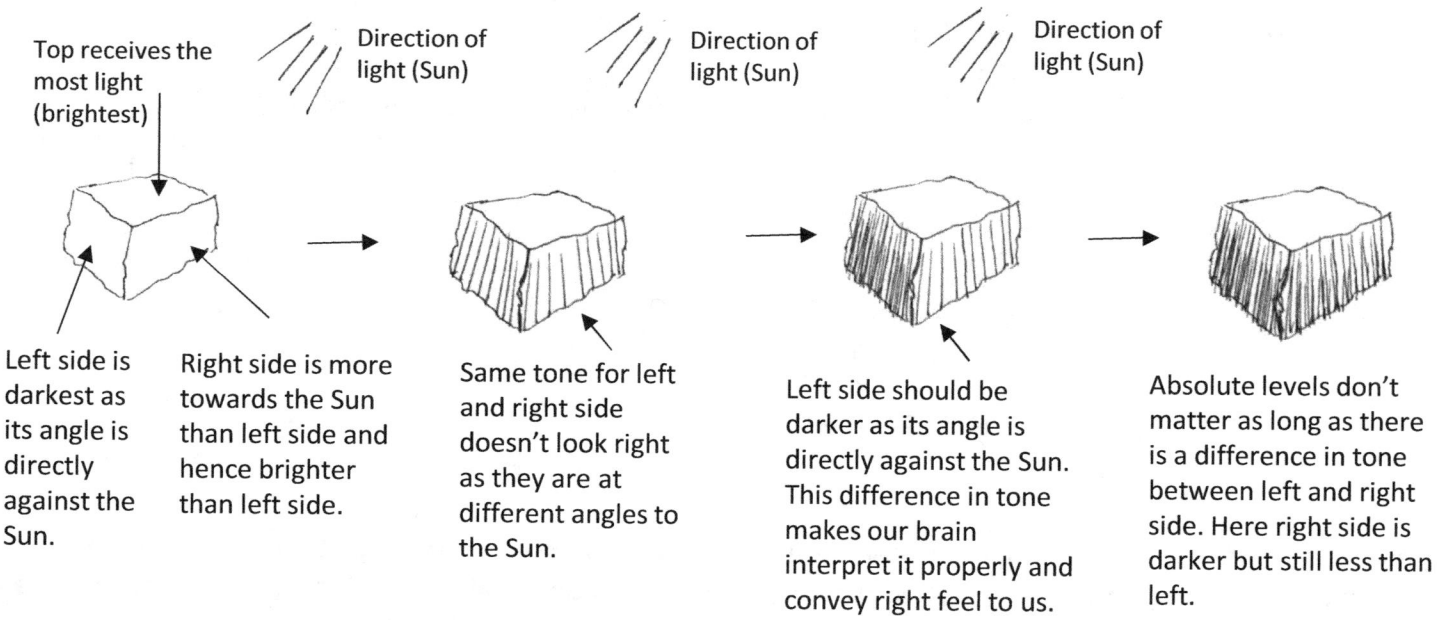

Top receives the most light (brightest)

Direction of light (Sun)

Direction of light (Sun)

Direction of light (Sun)

Left side is darkest as its angle is directly against the Sun.

Right side is more towards the Sun than left side and hence brighter than left side.

Same tone for left and right side doesn't look right as they are at different angles to the Sun.

Left side should be darker as its angle is directly against the Sun. This difference in tone makes our brain interpret it properly and convey right feel to us.

Absolute levels don't matter as long as there is a difference in tone between left and right side. Here right side is darker but still less than left.

# Concept of Surface Definition

In addition to defining tone, in directional hatching, lines are also used to define the orientation and curvature of the surface. The curvature of lines used indicates the curvature of the surface.

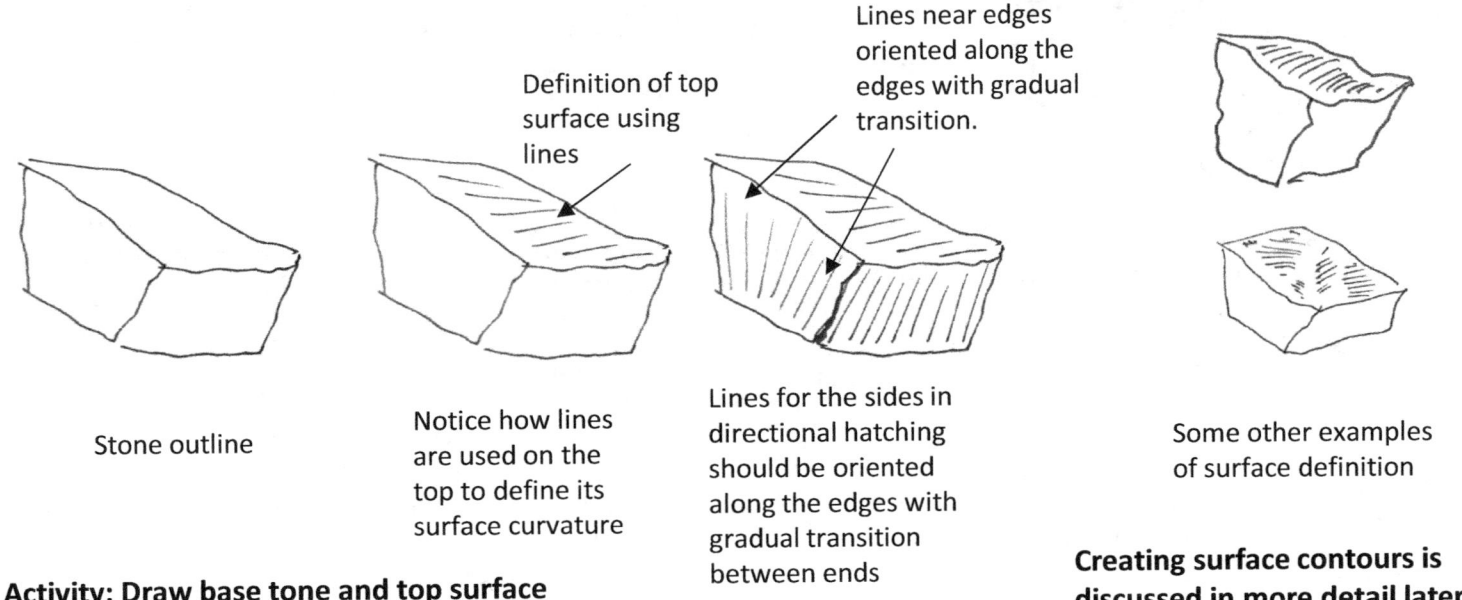

Definition of top surface using lines

Lines near edges oriented along the edges with gradual transition.

Some other examples of surface definition

Stone outline

Notice how lines are used on the top to define its surface curvature

Lines for the sides in directional hatching should be oriented along the edges with gradual transition between ends

**Activity: Draw base tone and top surface definition in outlines drawn earlier.**

**Creating surface contours is discussed in more detail later**

# How to Texture a Stone :

**After 'base' tone is added, to bring out the feel of stone, add tapered cervices and edge irregularities as shown below.**

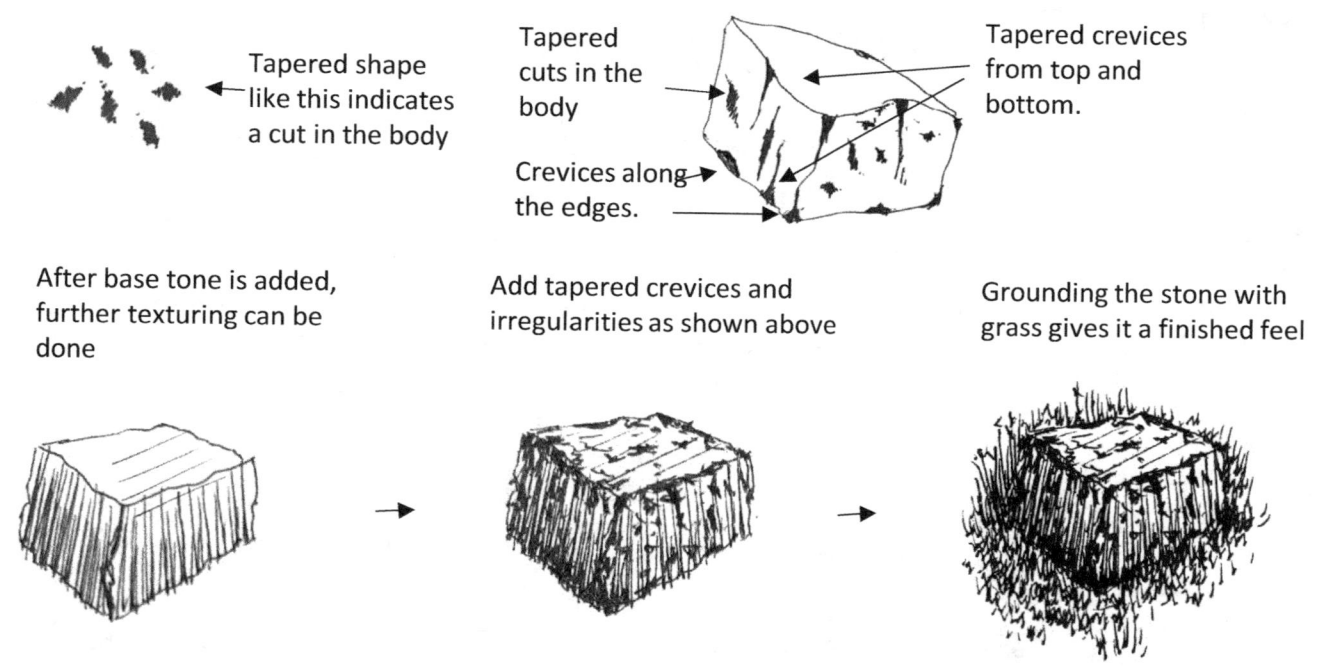

Tapered shape like this indicates a cut in the body

Tapered cuts in the body

Tapered crevices from top and bottom.

Crevices along the edges.

After base tone is added, further texturing can be done

Add tapered crevices and irregularities as shown above

Grounding the stone with grass gives it a finished feel

# Texturing Stone Step by Step:

## Here are some additional example to study.

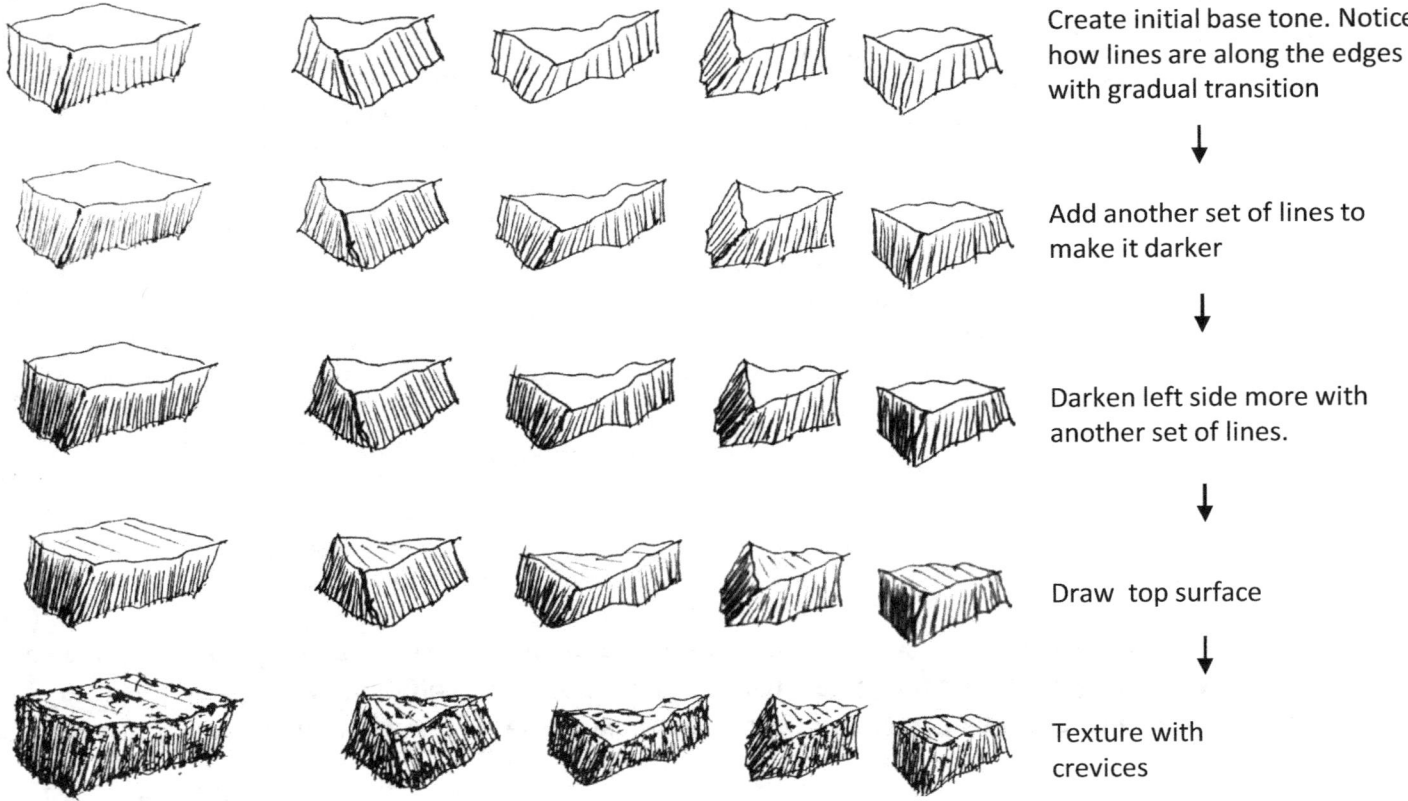

Create initial base tone. Notice how lines are along the edges with gradual transition

↓

Add another set of lines to make it darker

↓

Darken left side more with another set of lines.

↓

Draw top surface

↓

Texture with crevices

## View of Side Plane:

The fundamental thing to keep in mind when drawing stone with 3 sides visible is that the vertical sides should go away from you. In other words, the bottom edges (identified 1 and 2 below) should angle up, or away from the viewer. In addition, the common edge should be larger than other 2 vertically oriented edges (but doesn't have to).

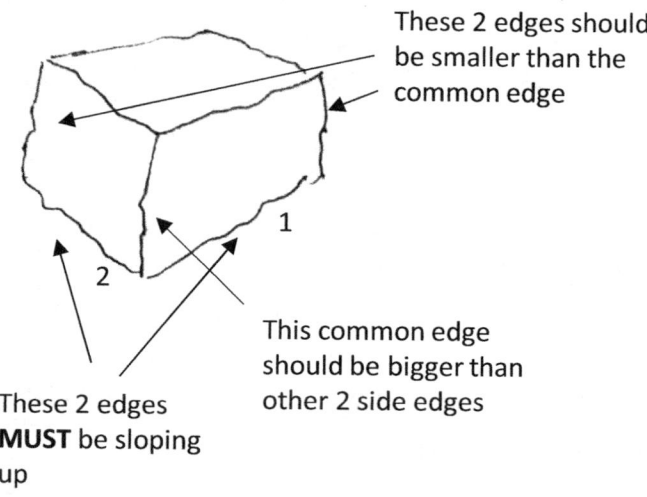

These 2 edges should be smaller than the common edge

This common edge should be bigger than other 2 side edges

These 2 edges **MUST** be sloping up

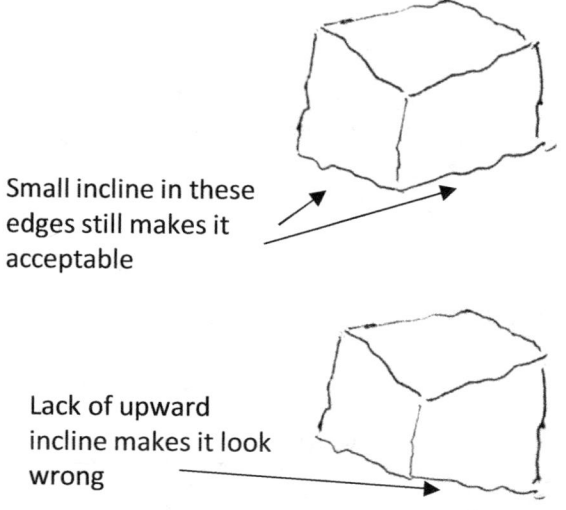

Small incline in these edges still makes it acceptable

Lack of upward incline makes it look wrong

Notice how as the bottom 2 edges lose their upward incline, the shapes looks odd.

# Alternate Steps to Drawing Stones:

Following is yet another way to make stone outline. By laying down vertically oriented edges in the beginning, you can more easily specify the orientation and hence overall shape of stones better.

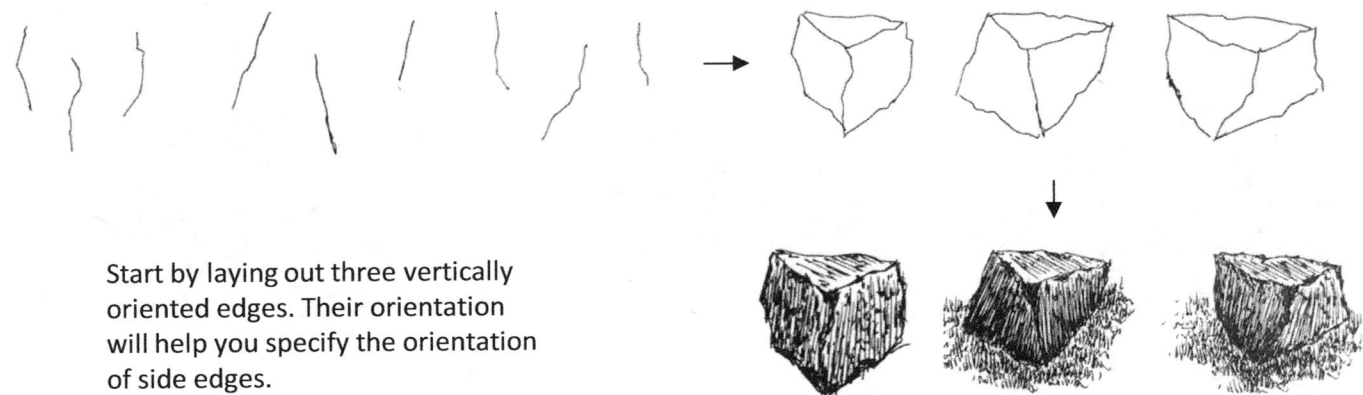

Start by laying out three vertically oriented edges. Their orientation will help you specify the orientation of side edges.

Connect and texture them as before to draw stones.

## More on Texturing:

We saw before that one side of the stone should be lighter than other and top should be lightest. But the level of darkening is a matter of personal preference. In addition, the kind of stroke you use to add tone can also be varied. If you are not comfortable with laying down parallel line, you can use more crevices to texture stone as shown below.

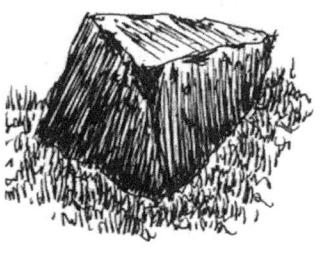 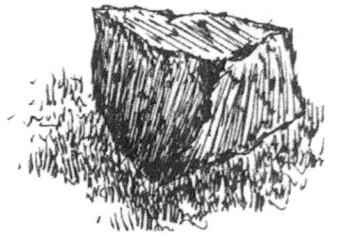 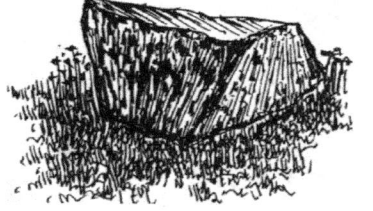

In this stone, I have used more parallel lines to add tone while use of crevices is less. Use of parallel lines gives a 'base' tone that feels natural to stones.

In this stone, I have used less parallel lines and more crevices to add tone to left side. This gives a different feel to the stone.

Here use of parallel lines is minimal and crevices are primarily used for tone. This gives stone a very rough feel.

**Activity : Here are three outlines of same stone. Texture them differently using more or less parallel lines along with tapered crevices as discussed before.**

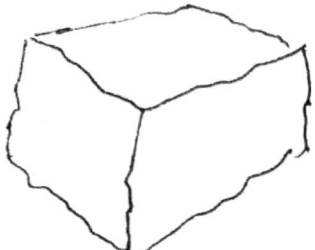
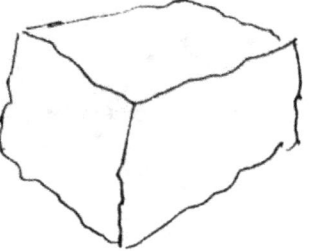
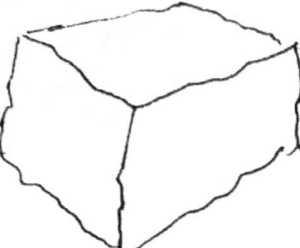

## Alternate Texturing of Stones:

Instead of parallel lines (hatching), dots and ticks can also be used to texture stone. This gives a very different feel to the stone. Dots and ticks adds more feel of roughness to the stone.

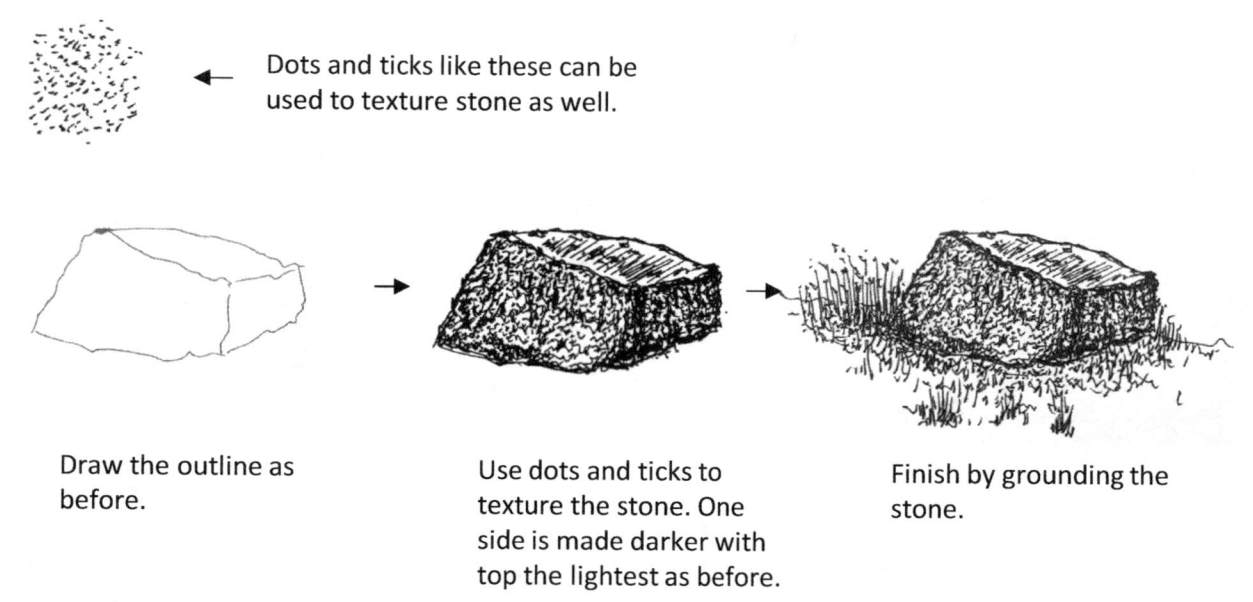

Dots and ticks like these can be used to texture stone as well.

Draw the outline as before.

Use dots and ticks to texture the stone. One side is made darker with top the lightest as before.

Finish by grounding the stone.

## Alternate Texturing of Stones, Another Example:

Dots and ticks let you have fine control over laying down tone. If you are not comfortable doing hatching, then this alternate approach can be used. Combine this with other techniques discussed earlier to give interesting feel to the stone.

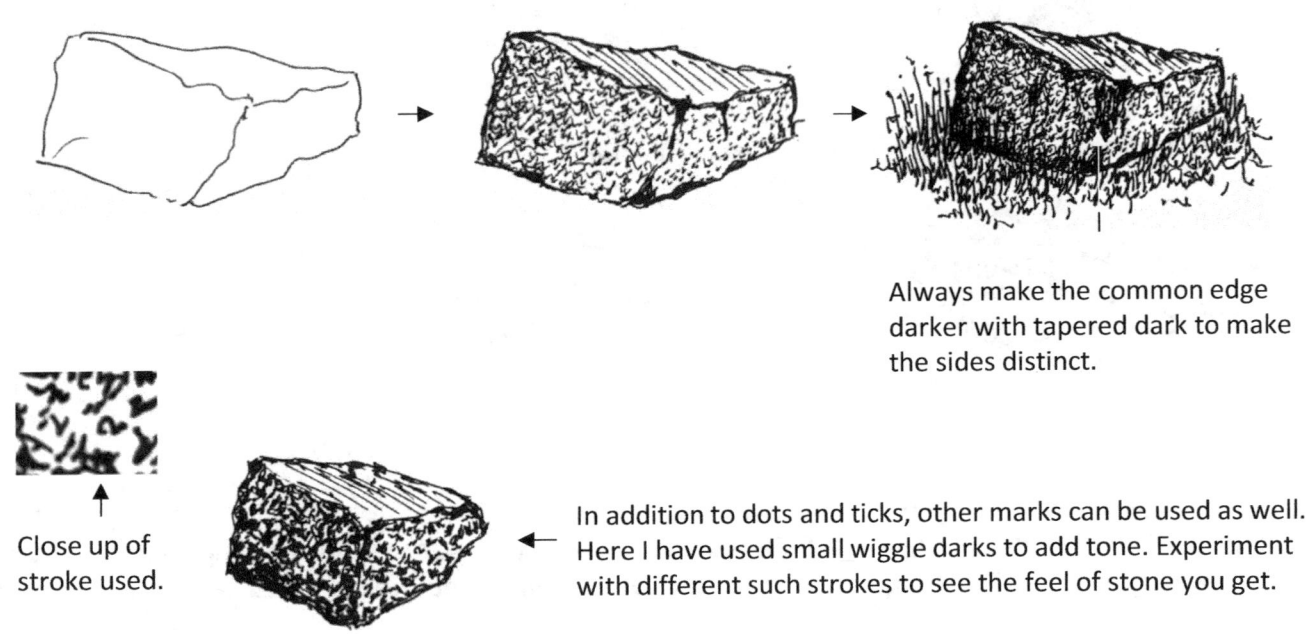

Always make the common edge darker with tapered dark to make the sides distinct.

Close up of stroke used.

In addition to dots and ticks, other marks can be used as well. Here I have used small wiggle darks to add tone. Experiment with different such strokes to see the feel of stone you get.

## More on Texturing of Stones:

**Hatching and dots and ticks can be combined as well to texture stones. Hatching gives a smooth base tone where as dots and ticks gives a rougher tone. Relative intensity of their use will determine the feel of the stone. Experiment with different combination of techniques to see the feel you get in your stone drawing.**

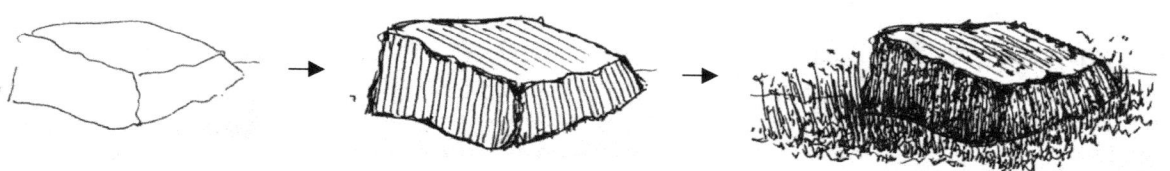

Here I used hatching to give first layer of tone but used dots and ticks to give additional tone.

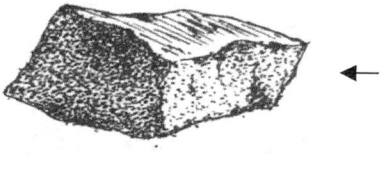

Using very fine dots only also gives different feel compared to use of bigger dots and ticks. Tone can also be finely controlled with use of fine dots only.

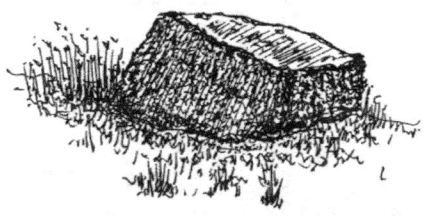

Yet another example.

**Activity : Texture the following stones using dots and ticks. Vary their size and combine with hatching to see the effect on the outcome.**

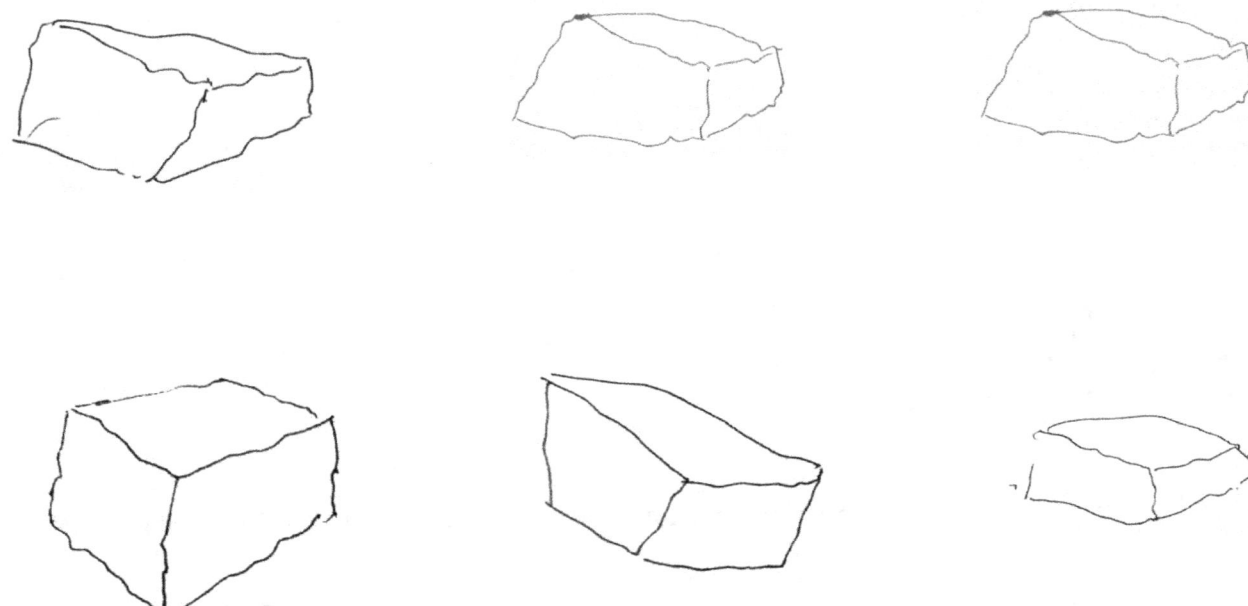

## Adding Edge Cuts:

'Edge Cuts' are a great way to indicate roughness in a stone. They essentially indicate a cut in the edges of the stone and can be drawn as following.

### Drawing Edge cut in the Outside Top Edge

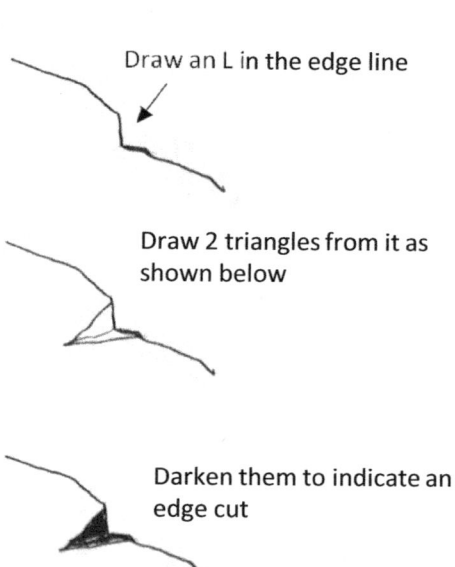

Draw an L in the edge line

Draw 2 triangles from it as shown below

Darken them to indicate an edge cut

### Drawing Edge cut in edge connecting top and sides

Draw 2 triangles as shown

Darken them as shown to indicate an edge cut

### Edge Cuts vs. Crevices

Edge cuts →    Tapered Crevices

Edge cuts and tapered cervices gives different feel and when used together gives a feeling of roughness.

# Drawing Stones with Edge Cuts:

**Add edge cuts as discussed previously and also shown below. Rest of the steps are as discussed before.**

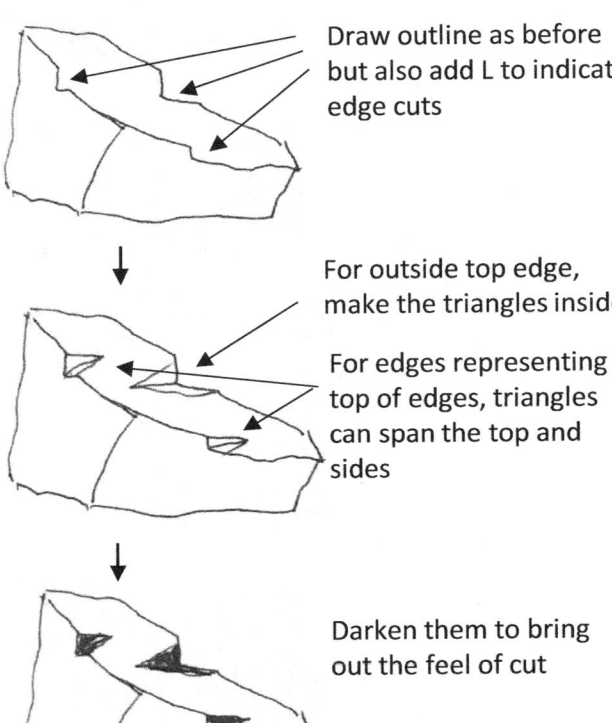

Draw outline as before but also add L to indicate edge cuts

For outside top edge, make the triangles inside

For edges representing top of edges, triangles can span the top and sides

Darken them to bring out the feel of cut

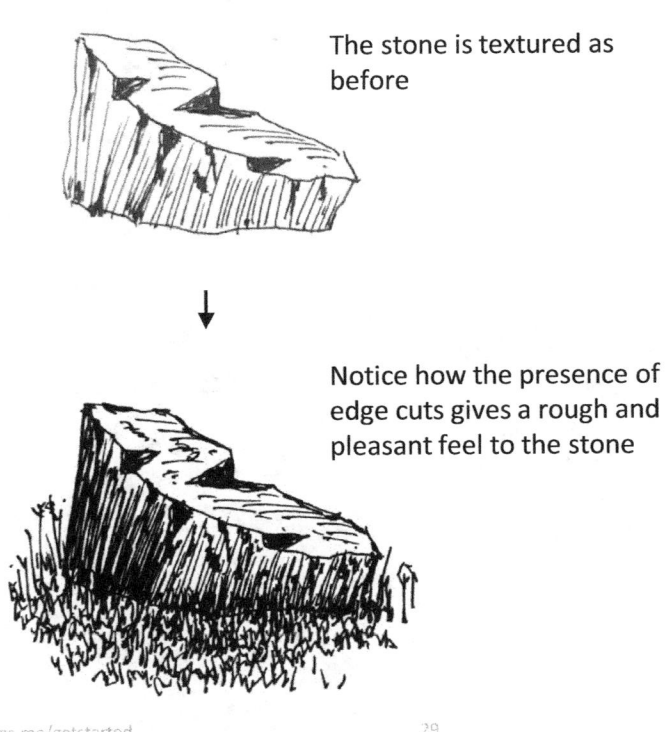

The stone is textured as before

Notice how the presence of edge cuts gives a rough and pleasant feel to the stone

# Stones with Edge Cuts, Additional Examples:

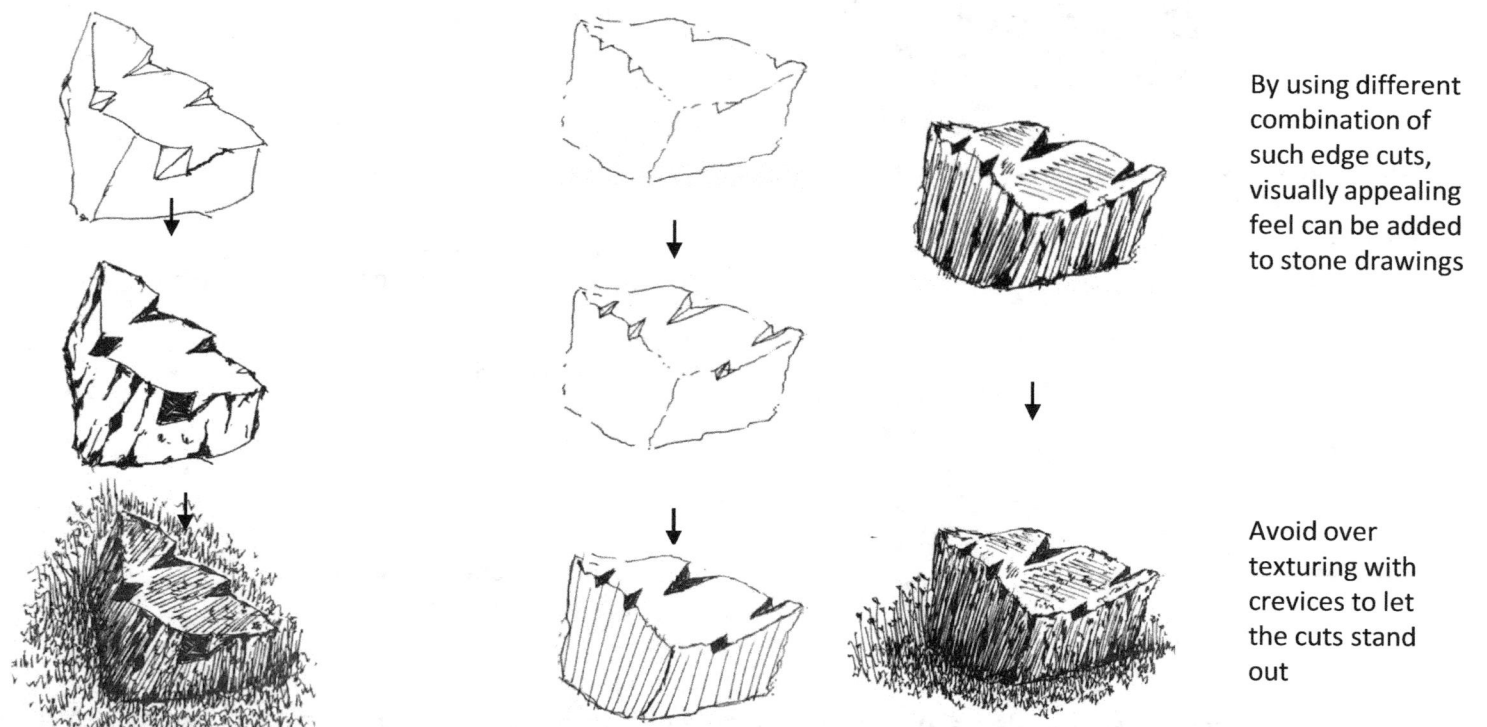

By using different combination of such edge cuts, visually appealing feel can be added to stone drawings

Avoid over texturing with crevices to let the cuts stand out

**Activity : Practice drawing edge cuts below. Draw stones incorporating edge cuts.**

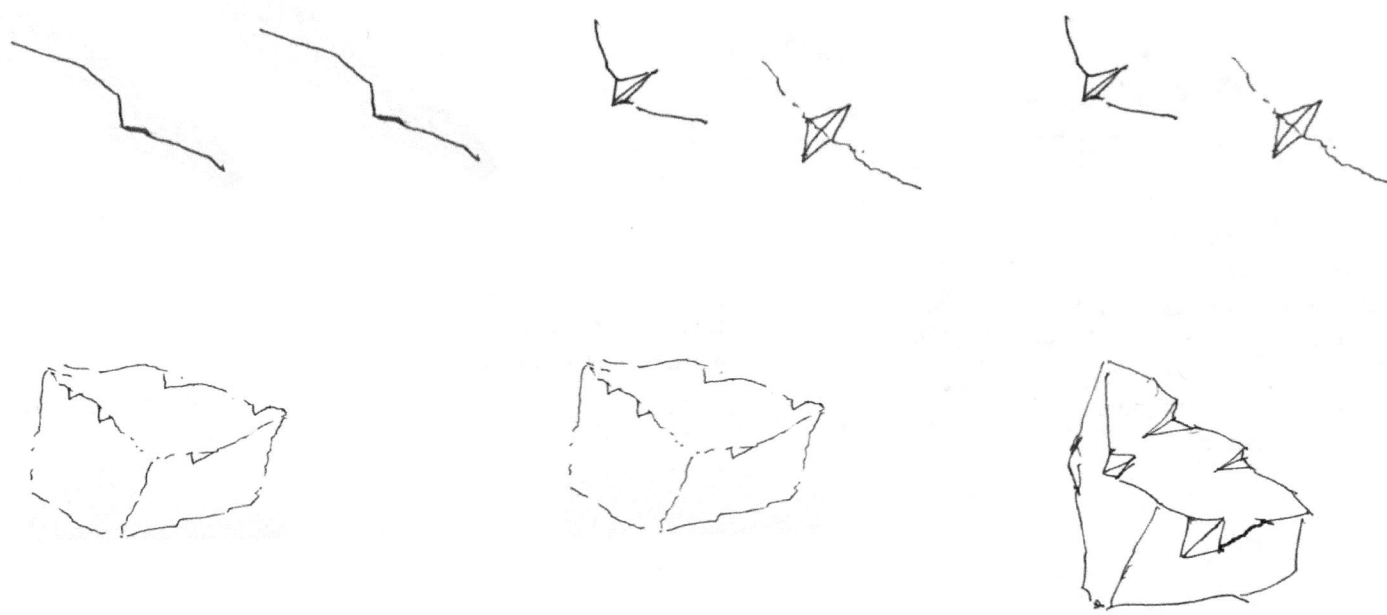

## Using More Interesting Outlines:

In earlier examples, the lines for outline were simple. Next step up is to use more 'dramatic' or angular lines which gives more interest to the drawing.

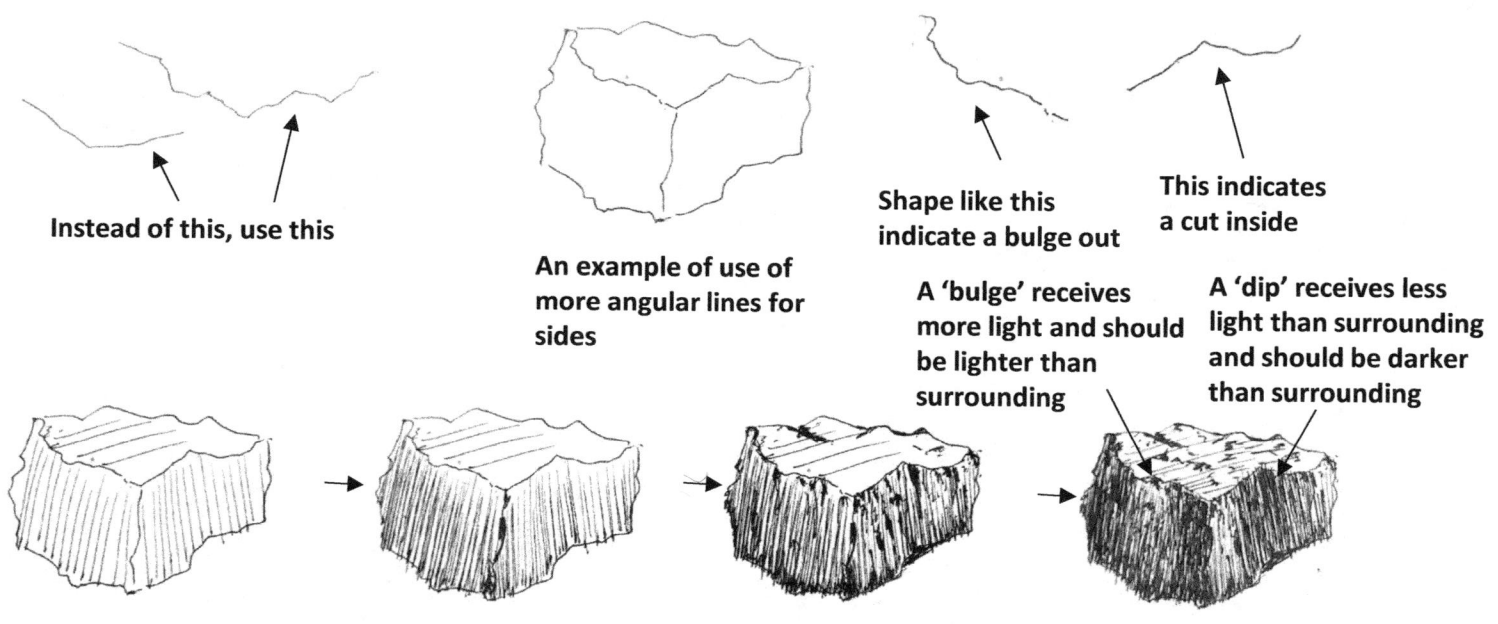

Instead of this, use this

An example of use of more angular lines for sides

Shape like this indicate a bulge out

This indicates a cut inside

A 'bulge' receives more light and should be lighter than surrounding

A 'dip' receives less light than surrounding and should be darker than surrounding

Draw the lines for base tone along the contour of top and bottom. Darken the 'dip' more and leave 'bulge' lighter compared to surrounding.

**Activity : Finish the following stone outlines and texture them. Draw some of your own.**

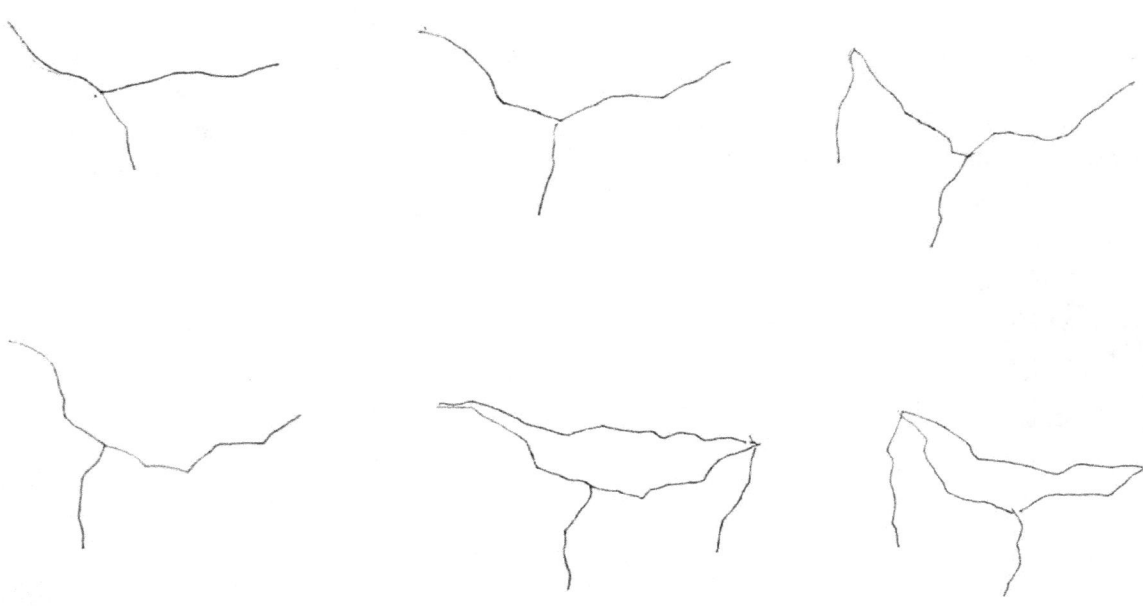

## Using More Interesting Outlines, Continued:

**Use more interesting outlines with multiple bulges and cuts to give more visual interest to the stone. Keep in mind that you need to be able to properly texture the undulating surface with right tone. So use the level of detail consistent with the size of your drawing.**

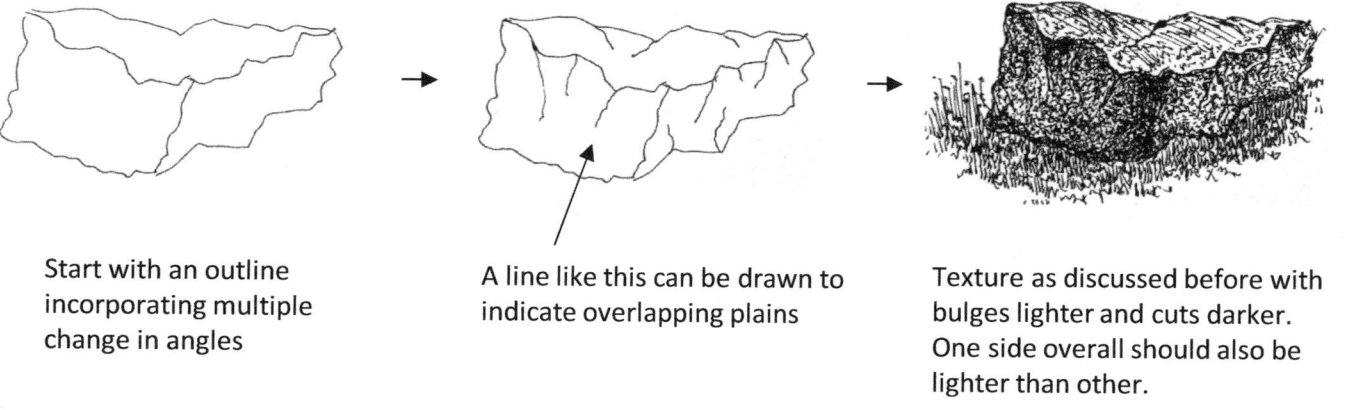

Start with an outline incorporating multiple change in angles

A line like this can be drawn to indicate overlapping plains

Texture as discussed before with bulges lighter and cuts darker. One side overall should also be lighter than other.

## Using More Interesting Outlines, Another Example:

Following is yet another example of use of more interesting outlines. Notice that I have darkened the overlapping plains below to bring them out further.

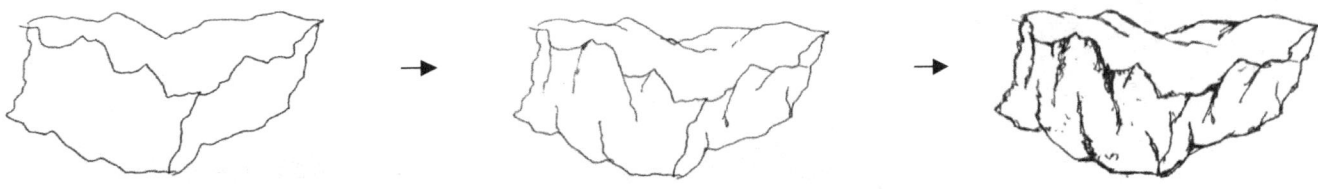

There is no limit to how such interesting outlines can be used to create stones with great visual appeal. Plain lines can be darkened to bring them out even further..

Parallel lines are used to texture this stone. Contrast the feel of this stone with the stone on previous page which is textured with dots and ticks.

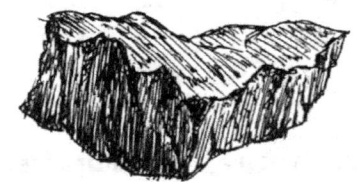

## Adding Plain Lines in the Body:

So far we have drawn the plain lines from the edges. A plain line can also be drawn in the body itself and this can be used to indicate a cut in the body. Following is an example.

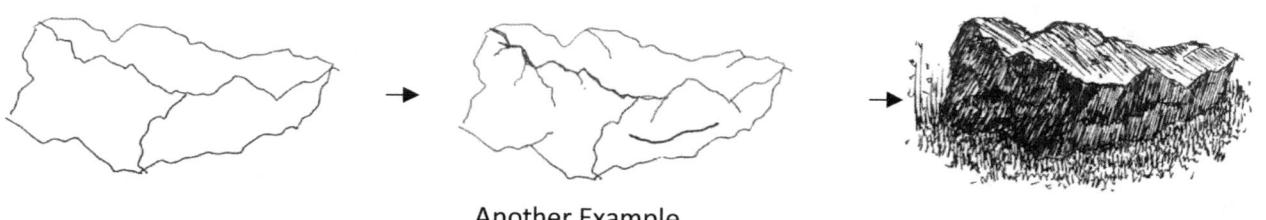

Plain lines in the body.

Start by drawing outline as before. Next add plain lines in the body. Texture as before but also make the plain lines darker in a tapered manner.

Another Example.

**Activity : Texture the following stone outlines. Draw one of your own.**

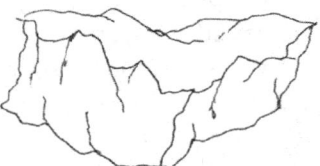

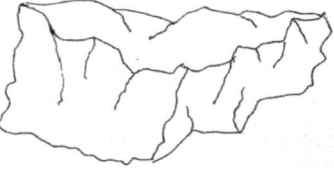

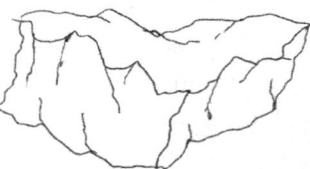

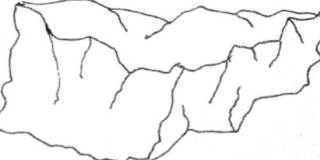

# Drawing Multi Sided Stones :

**So far we looked at stones with a left and a right side. But stones with more sides are visually more pleasing and can be drawn in same manner as shown below.**

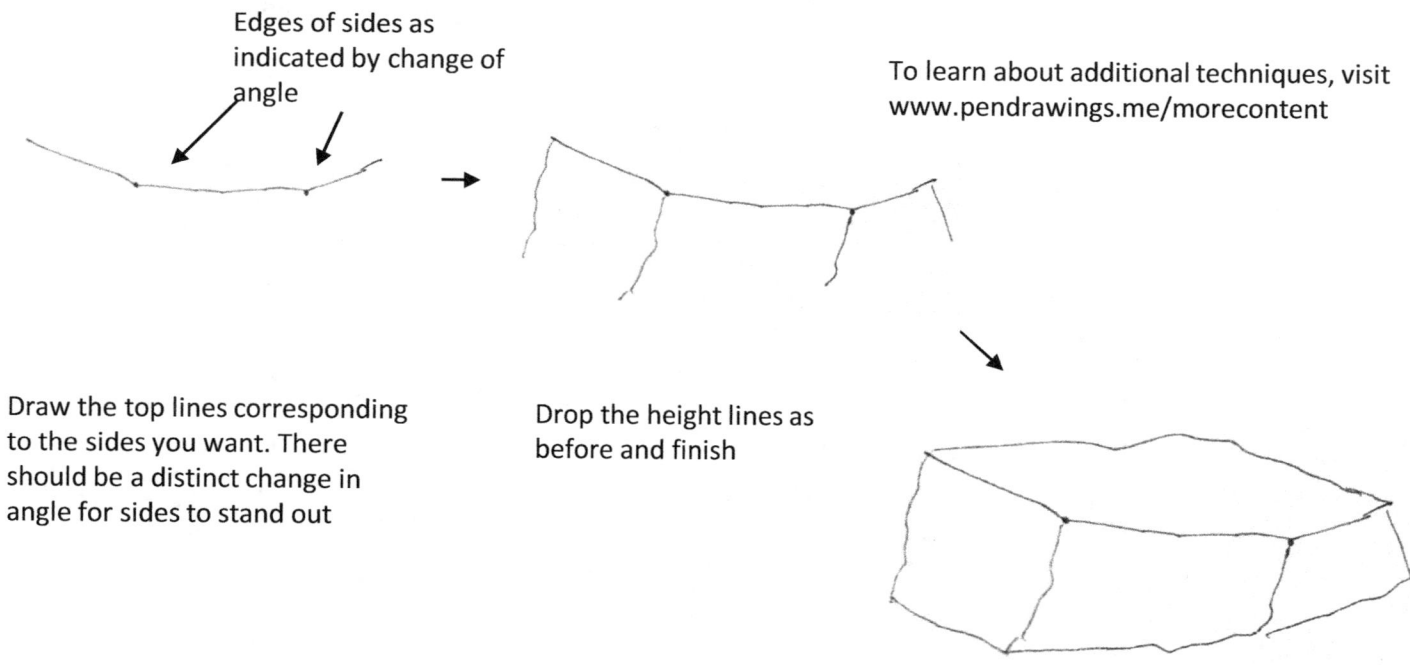

Edges of sides as indicated by change of angle

To learn about additional techniques, visit www.pendrawings.me/morecontent

Draw the top lines corresponding to the sides you want. There should be a distinct change in angle for sides to stand out

Drop the height lines as before and finish

## Texturing Multi Sided Stones :

Different sides in a multisided stone should be darkened in a consistent manner with sides against the light source darker than sides more towards the light source.

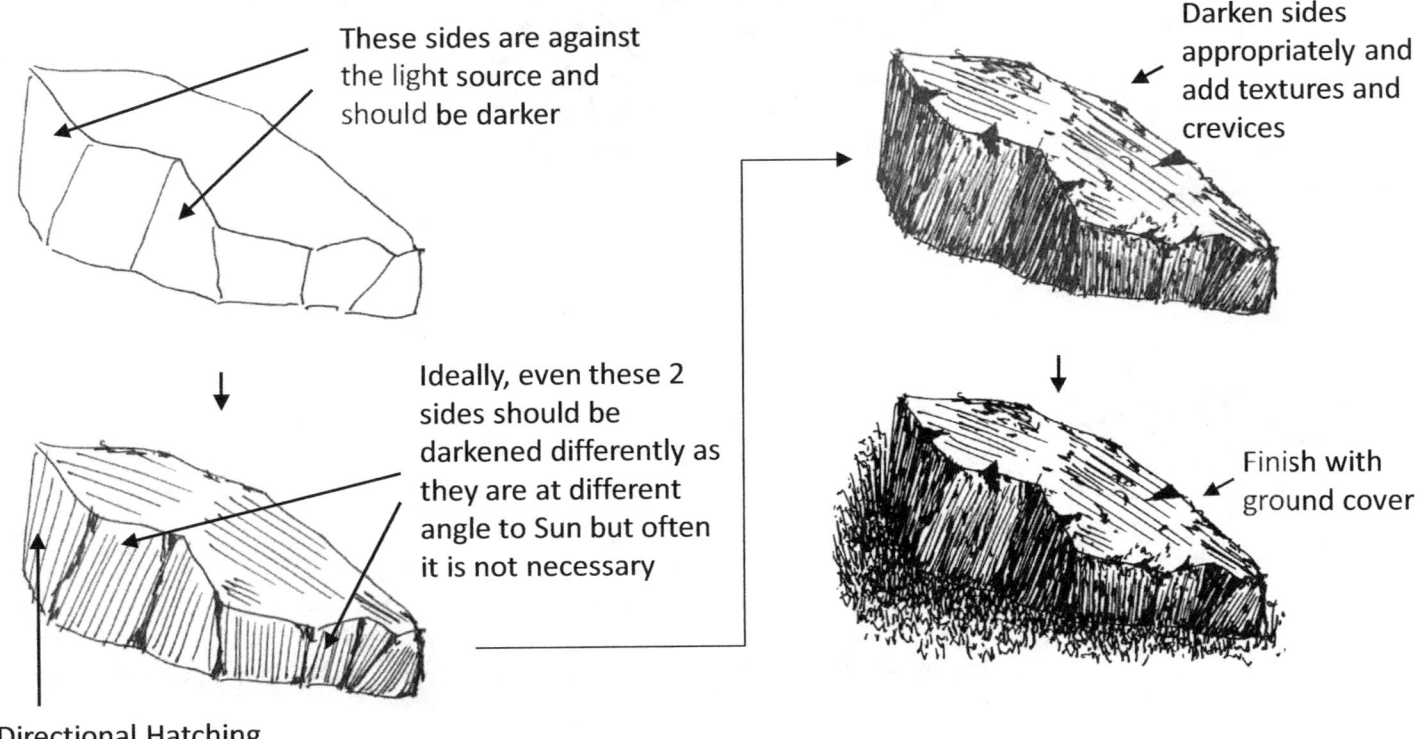

These sides are against the light source and should be darker

Ideally, even these 2 sides should be darkened differently as they are at different angle to Sun but often it is not necessary

Directional Hatching

Darken sides appropriately and add textures and crevices

Finish with ground cover

# Texturing Multi Sided Stones :

**Here is another example. Again, sides against the light source are made darker.**

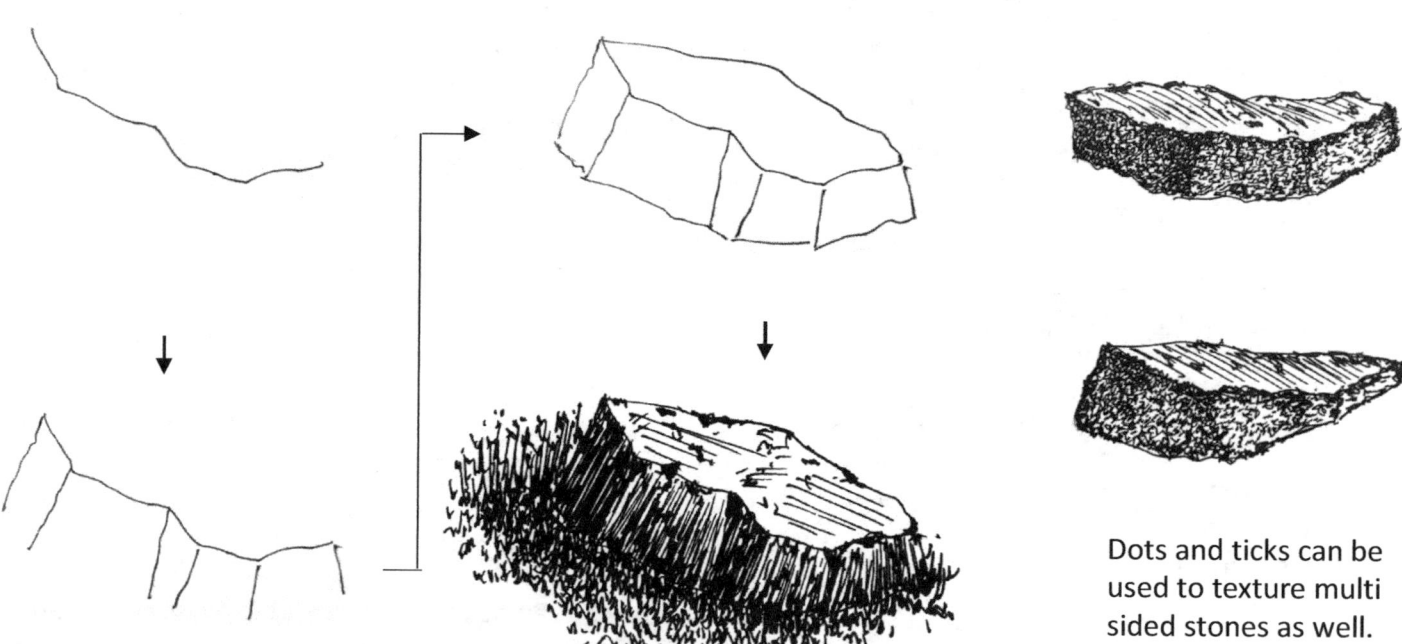

Dots and ticks can be used to texture multi sided stones as well.

## Drawing Multi Sided Stone, Alternate Approach :

In an alternate approach, you can draw the top and bottom first and then connect the two with height lines. This approach is sometimes easier in getting a nice feel for stones. Often, when drawing height lines first, you become very conscious of need to have different sides etc. and that often results in unappealing design. This approach of drawing the bottom independently first and then connecting with height lines gives visually appealing stones.

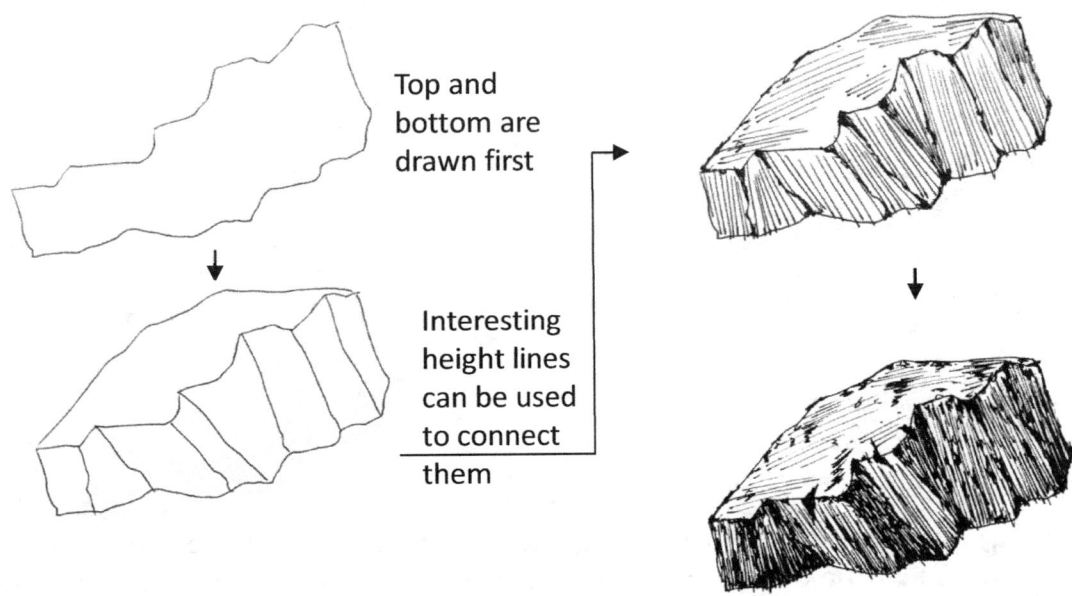

Top and bottom are drawn first

Interesting height lines can be used to connect them

## Curved Top vs Multi Sides :

When the top is curved but bottom of a side is straight, it gives us a side with interesting shape of top as we discussed before. When the bottom is curved/angled as well, it results in multi sided stone. This understanding is helpful in drawing right top and bottom surfaces to get the right feel of stone.

Another Example

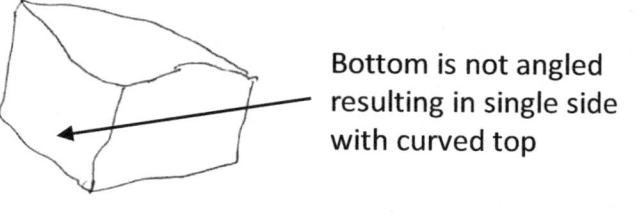

Bottom is not angled resulting in single side with curved top

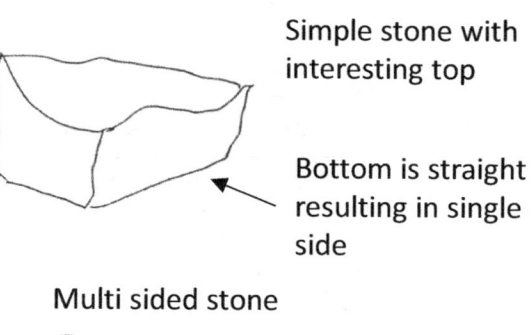

Simple stone with interesting top

Bottom is straight resulting in single side

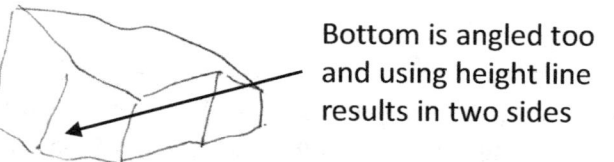

Bottom is angled too and using height line results in two sides

Multi sided stone

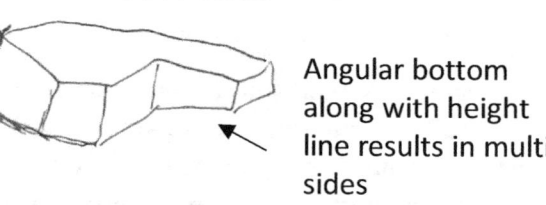

Angular bottom along with height line results in multi sides

**Activity : Finish the following stone outlines with multiple sides and texture them. Draw some of your own.**

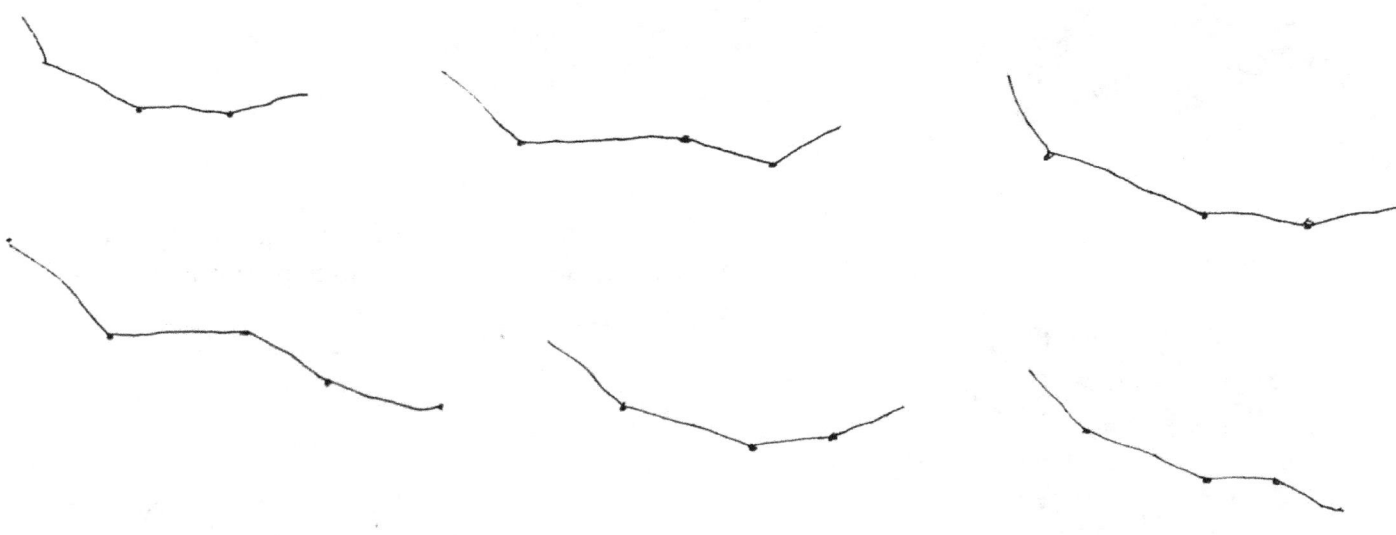

## Using Interesting Outlines for Multi Sides :

**We have used mostly simple edges in previous examples to illustrate the concept of multi sides. Interesting outlines with bulges and cuts as we saw before can be used for multi sides as well to add more visual appeal.**

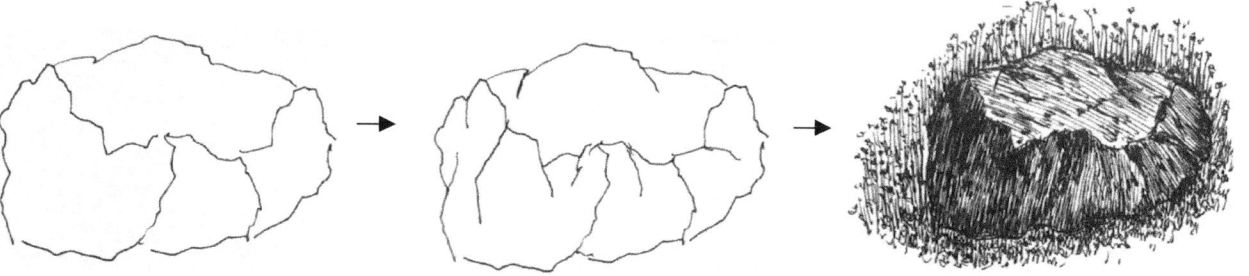

Use of interesting outlines for multi sides. Note that with many more small plains from the outline, the sides start to lose their distinctiveness.

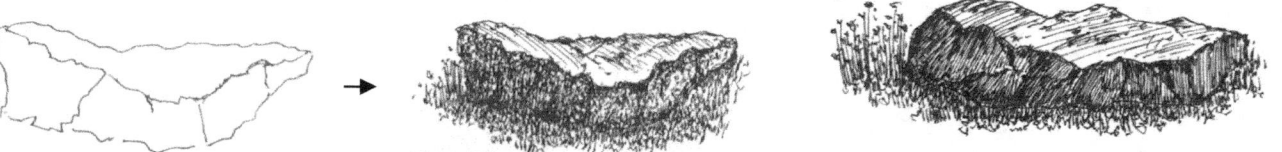

More examples. In a drawing with many stones, use a mix of interesting plain outlines to add variety. Use of variety in terms of shapes, outlines and size always increases the visual appeal.

**Activity : Finish the following stones with interesting outlines. Draw some of your own.**

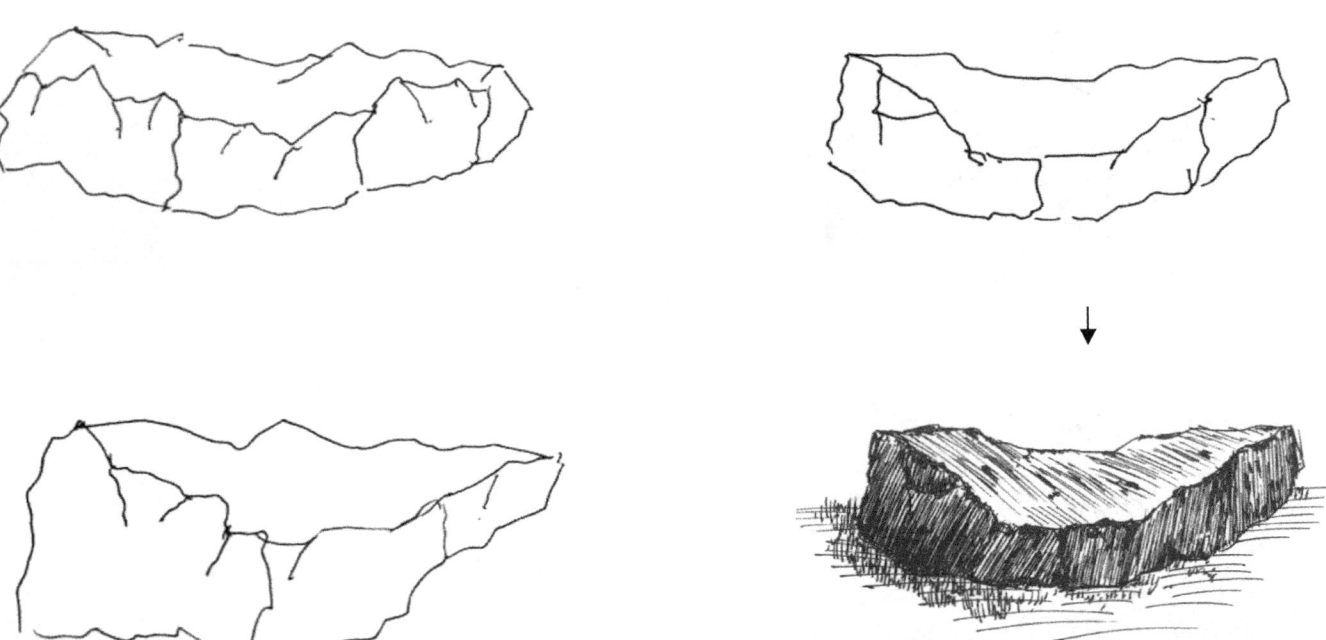

## Drawing Multi Level Stones:

**Layers of side faces can be drawn on a stone as shown below. The key is to draw the edges and then connect them to create additional plains on top.**

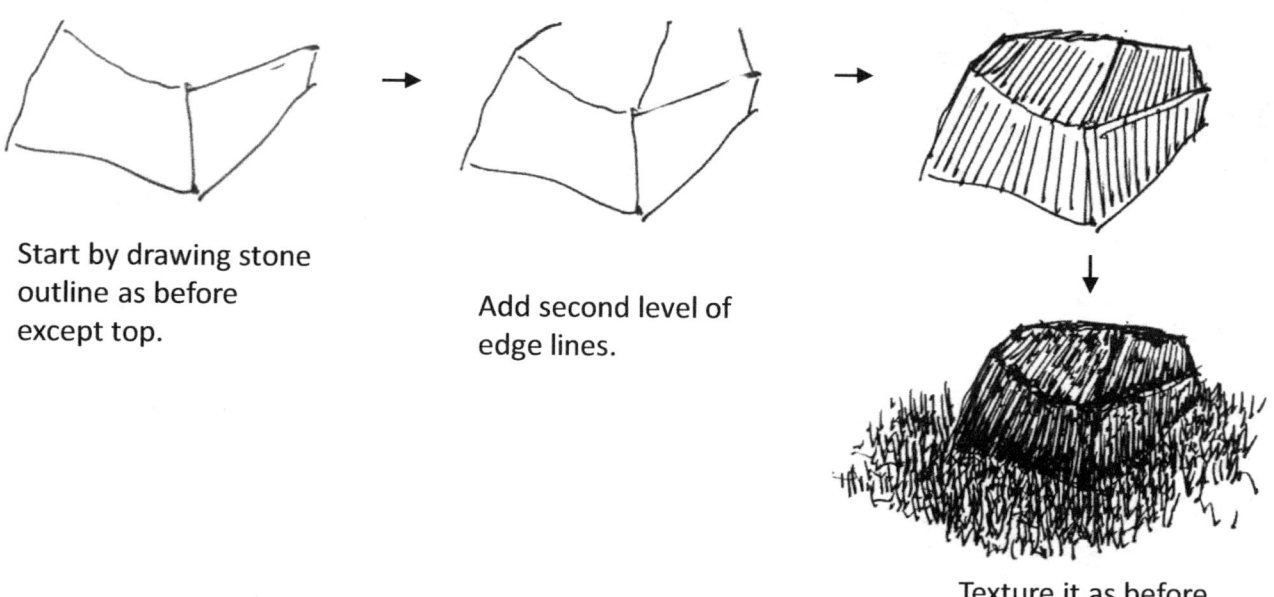

Start by drawing stone outline as before except top.

Add second level of edge lines.

Texture it as before

# Drawing Multi Level Stones, Additional Examples:

Following are some more examples. By changing the angle and size of edges, limitless variations on this can be drawn.

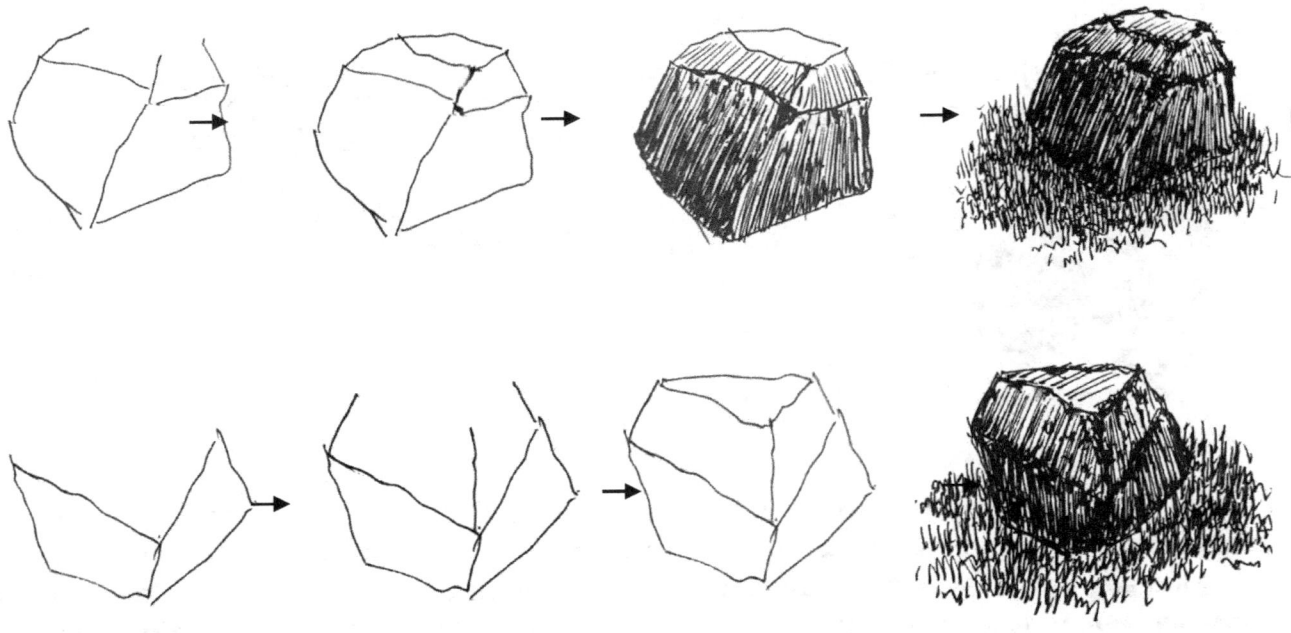

## Level of Texturing in Drawing Multi Level Stones:

Before we saw how one side of a stone should be lighter than other. With multi level stones we have additional surfaces and question becomes as to what should be the level of tone for these surfaces. The key is to assume a light source and then try to give tones to the surfaces based on how much light they would receive from the angle of assumed light source. This is similar to what we did with multi sided stones.

This side is more towards the light and hence would have lighter tone.

Direction of light (Sun)

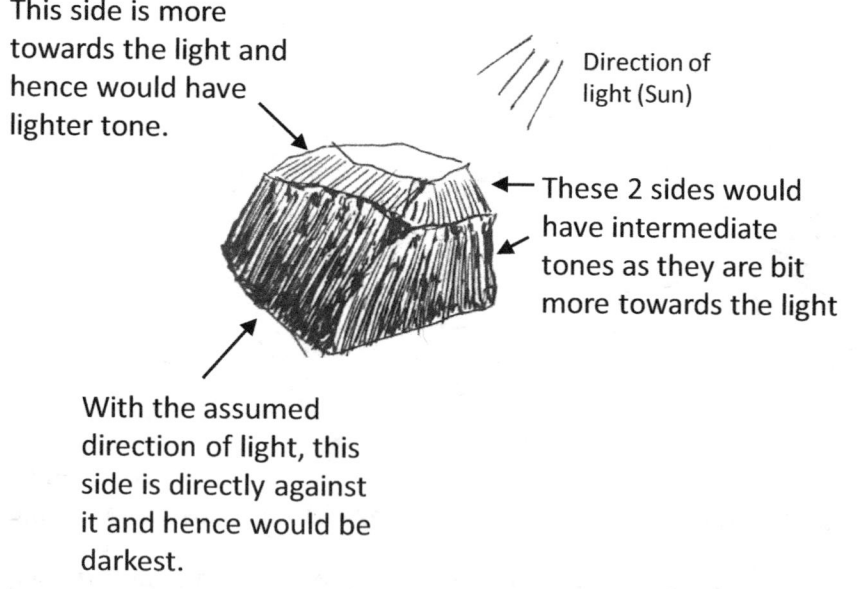

These 2 sides would have intermediate tones as they are bit more towards the light

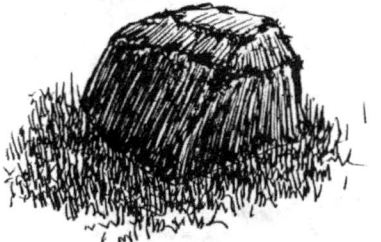

With the assumed direction of light, this side is directly against it and hence would be darkest.

Make sure the tone on a surface is consistent with the amount of light it will receive from assumed direction of light source.

## Activity:

Finish and texture the following stones. Try drawing different top level sides on same bottom to understand how versatile this technique is.

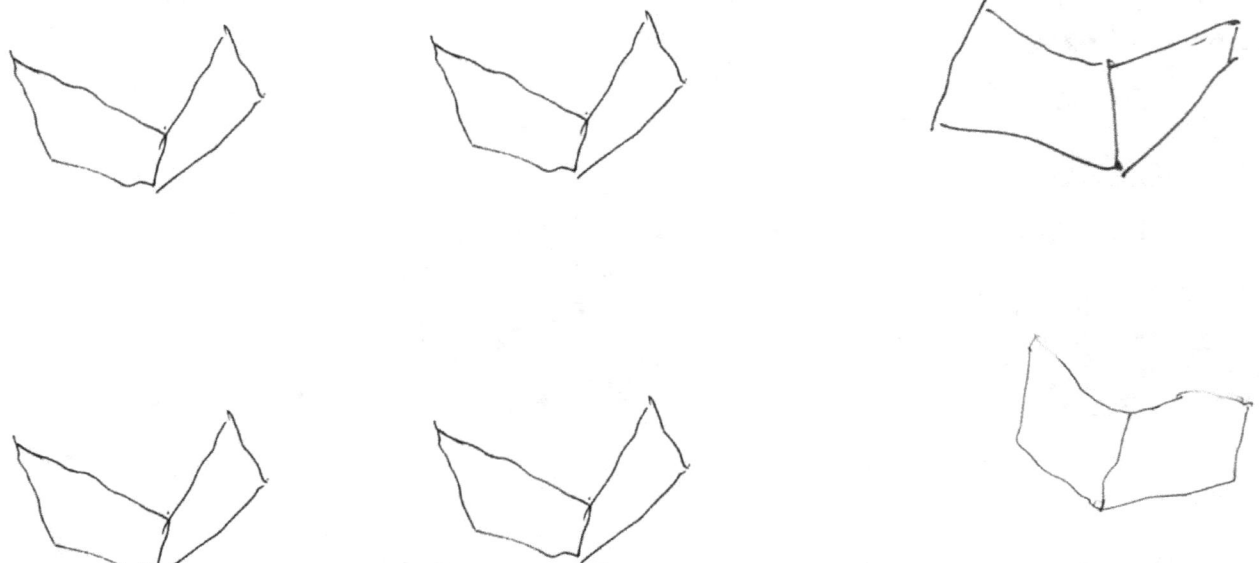

## Using Interesting Outlines for Multi Levels :

Just as with multi sides, more interesting outlines can be used to create more visual interest. Below are few examples.

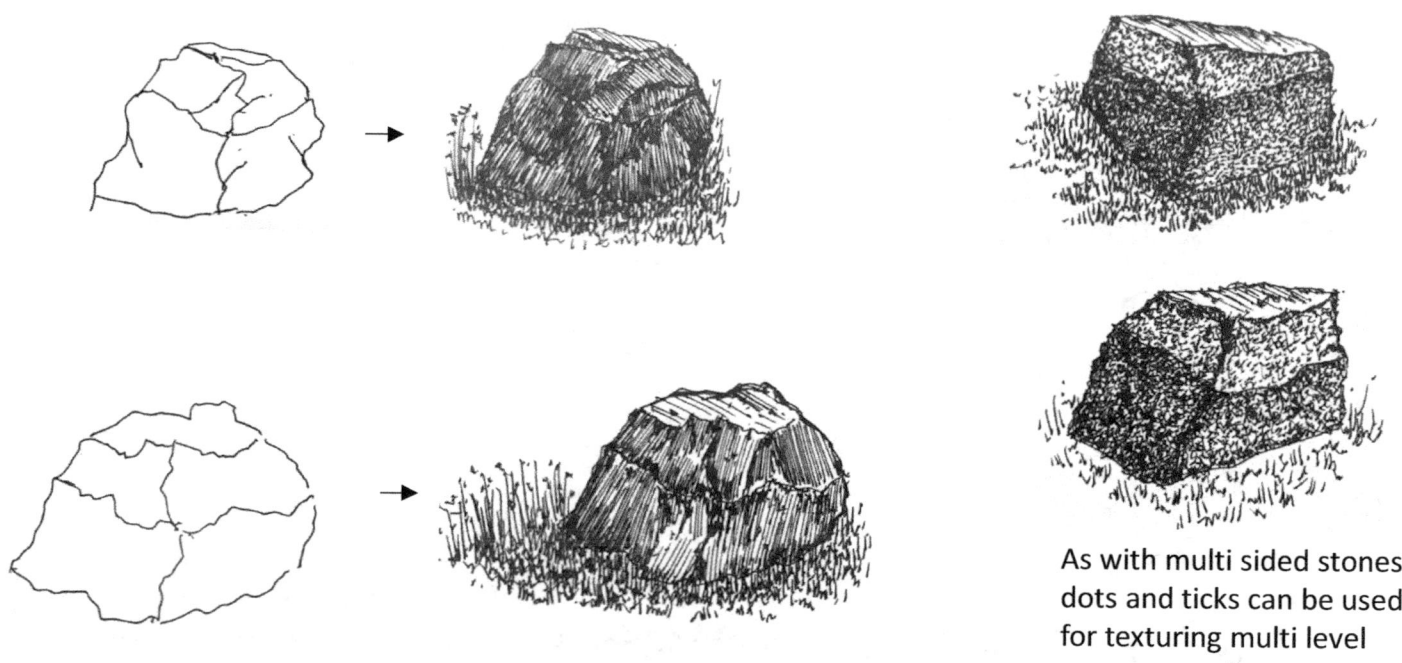

As with multi sided stones, dots and ticks can be used for texturing multi level stones as well.

**Activity : Finish the following stones with interesting outlines. Draw some of your own.**

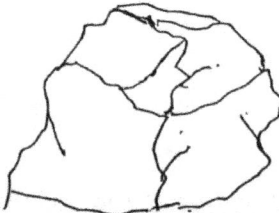

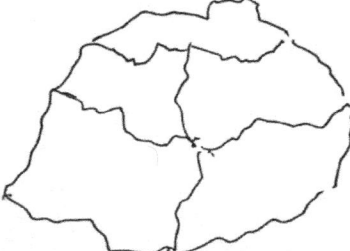

## Combining Multi Sided and Multi Level Stones:

**Multi Sided and multi-level techniques can be combined to draw stones with multiple sides and levels. Again by changing the number of sides and angle of edges, limitless variations on this can be drawn.**

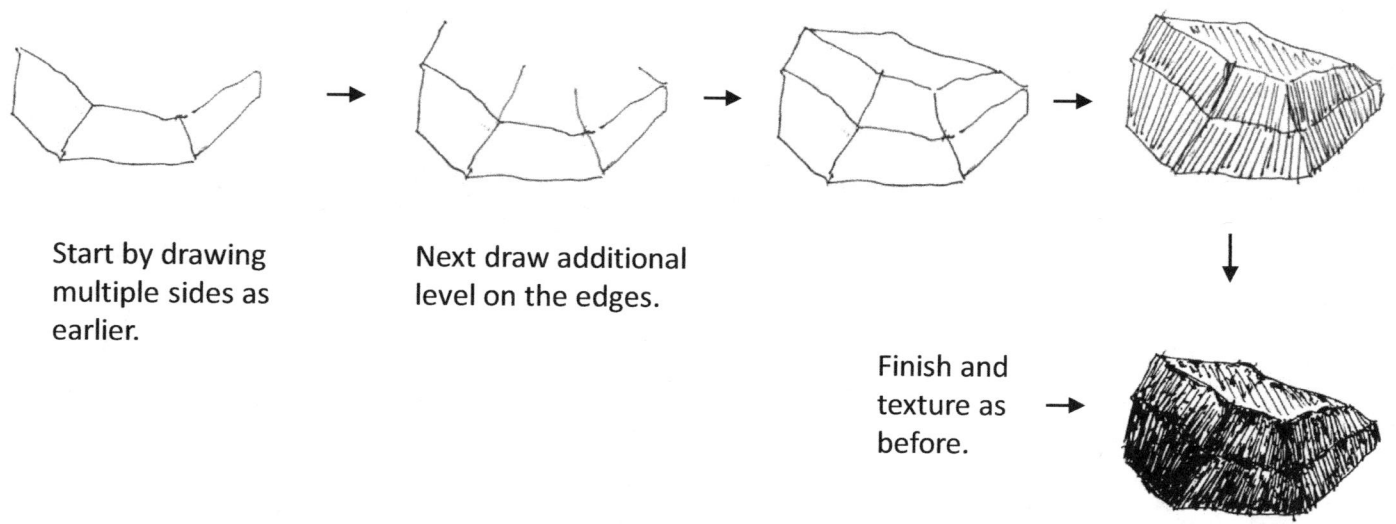

Start by drawing
multiple sides as
earlier.

Next draw additional
level on the edges.

Finish and
texture as
before.

# Combining Multi Sided and Multi Level Stones, Additional Examples:

Right level of tone for different sides becomes more challenging as additional sides are added. Key is to be consistent with the level of tone on a side to be in line with the amount of light it would receive from an assumed light source.

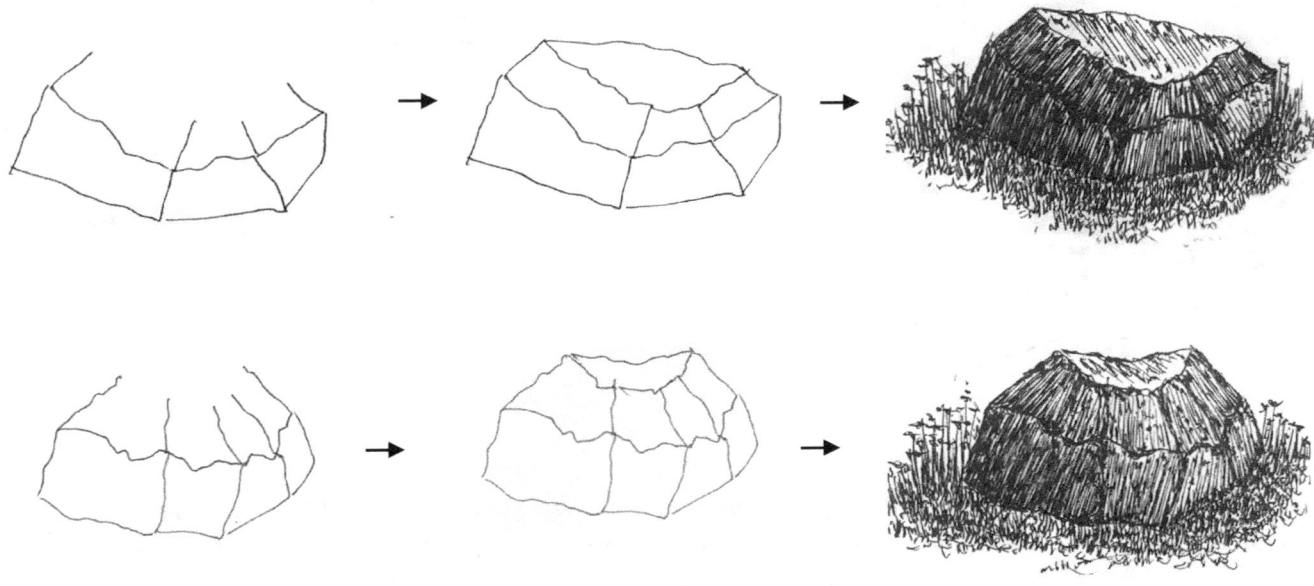

# Combining Multi Sided and Multi Level Stones, Additional Examples:

There is no limit to the complexity of stones that can be drawn by using more sides and levels. But keep in mind that complexity of stones that can be drawn also depends on its size. To add more sides and levels, draw stones at bigger size as the sides need to be textured appropriately with right tone.

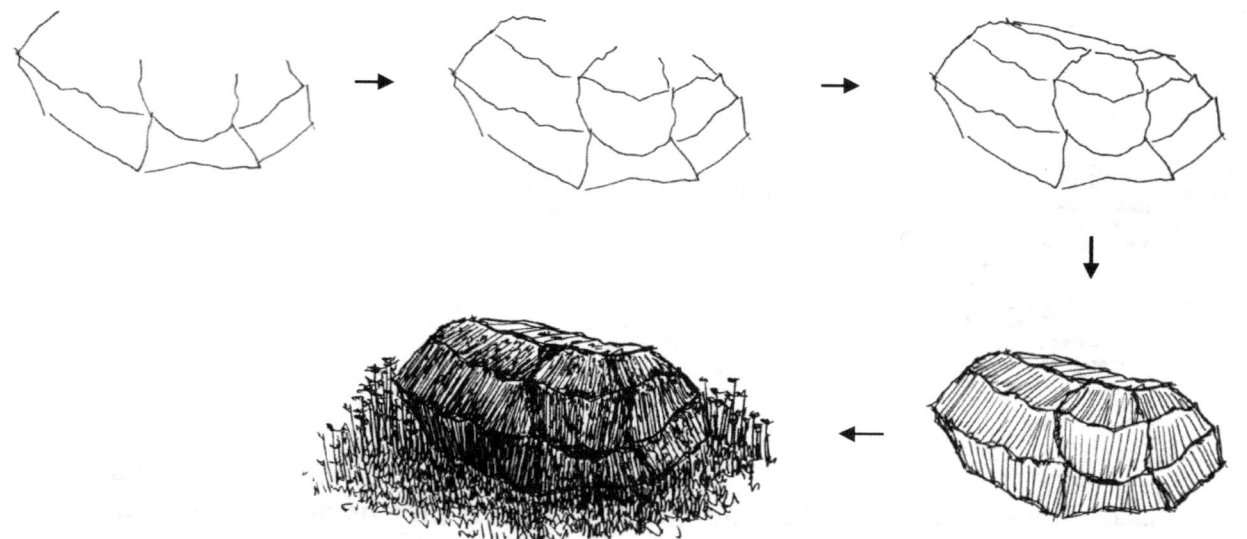

**Activity : Finish the following stones. Draw some of your own.**

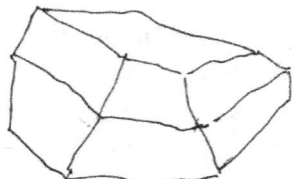
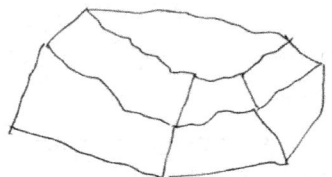
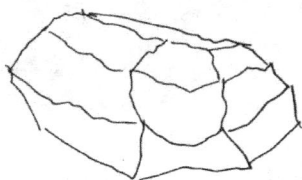

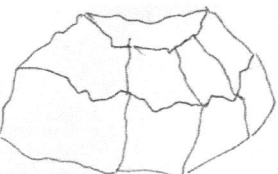
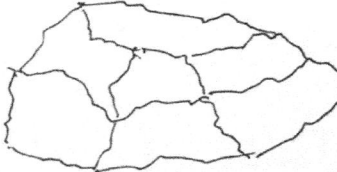

# Following are some more examples:

**Notice how the angle of bottom edge sets the overall shape of the stone. Bottom edges that angles back gives more dimensionality where as flatter bottom edges need more tonal changes to bring out their form.**

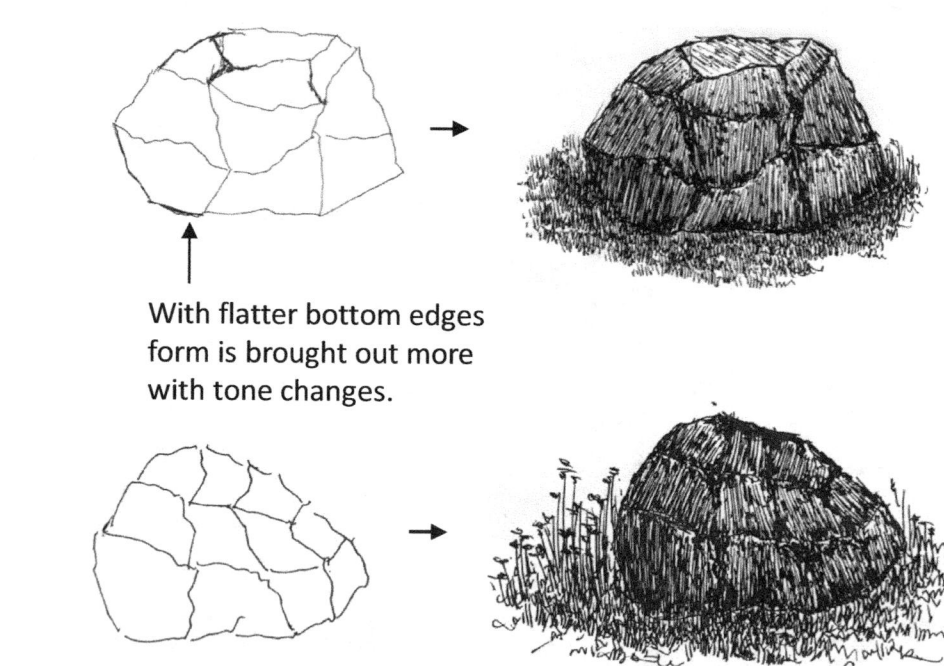

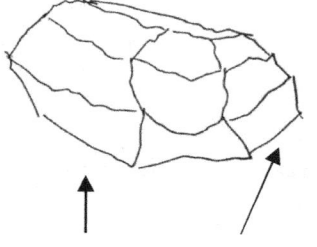

When bottom edges are angled sharply back, it creates depth/dimensionality in the drawing.

With flatter bottom edges form is brought out more with tone changes.

## Using Interesting Outlines:

Just as with multi sides and multi level stones, more interesting outlines can be used with stones combining them to create stones with more appeal. Below is an example.

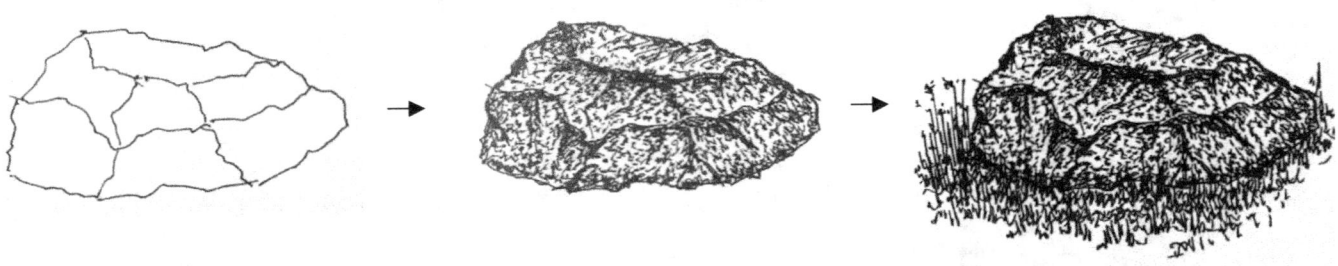

**Activity: Texture the following stone. Draw one of your own.**

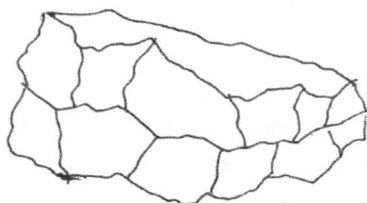

## Stones with Different Plains on Sides:

So far we have focused on drawing multiple sides and level with clear structure around it. This of course is not a requirement and next step is to understand how multiple 'plains' can be created on the sides of the stone. The process is as shown below.

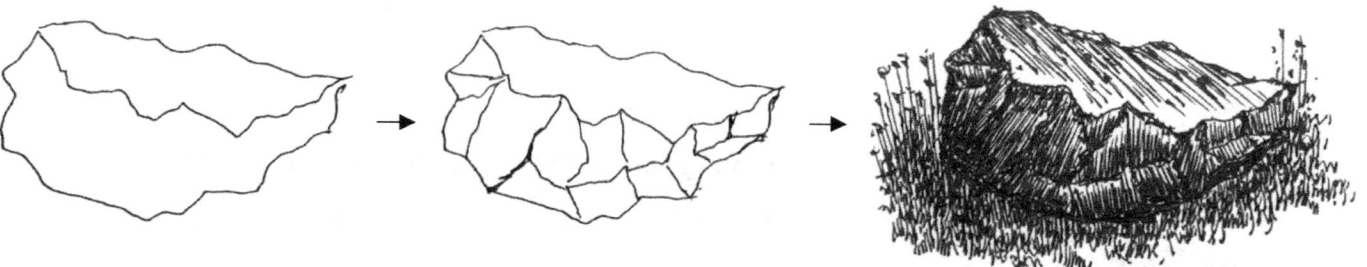

Start by drawing an outline as shown. Next, instead of defining plains as sides and levels, they can be defined to span levels and in any orientation. This gives a different feel to the stones.

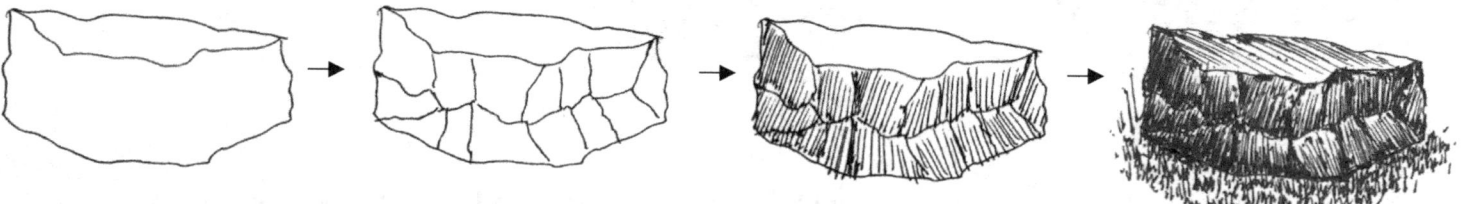

In the same outline, different choices can lead to different plains for stones. In the example above, more typical sides and level choices for plains is made.

## Stones with Different Plains on Sides, Additional Examples:

Here are some more examples. Again keep in mind that as plain get smaller, they are difficult to texture with right tone. The volume and size of plains should be based on the overall size of the drawing.

**Some more examples**

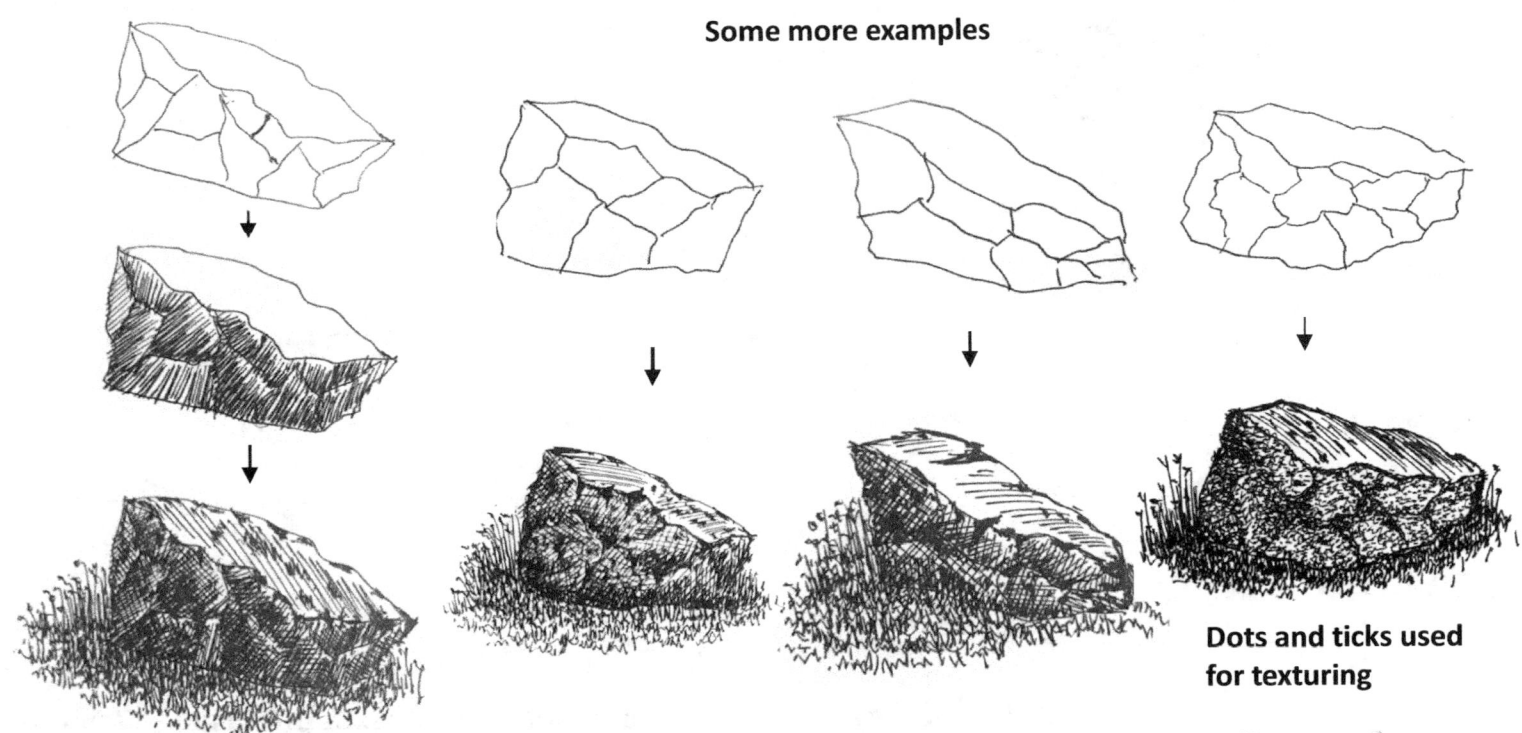

Dots and ticks used for texturing

**Activity : Finish and texture the following stones. Draw some of your own.**

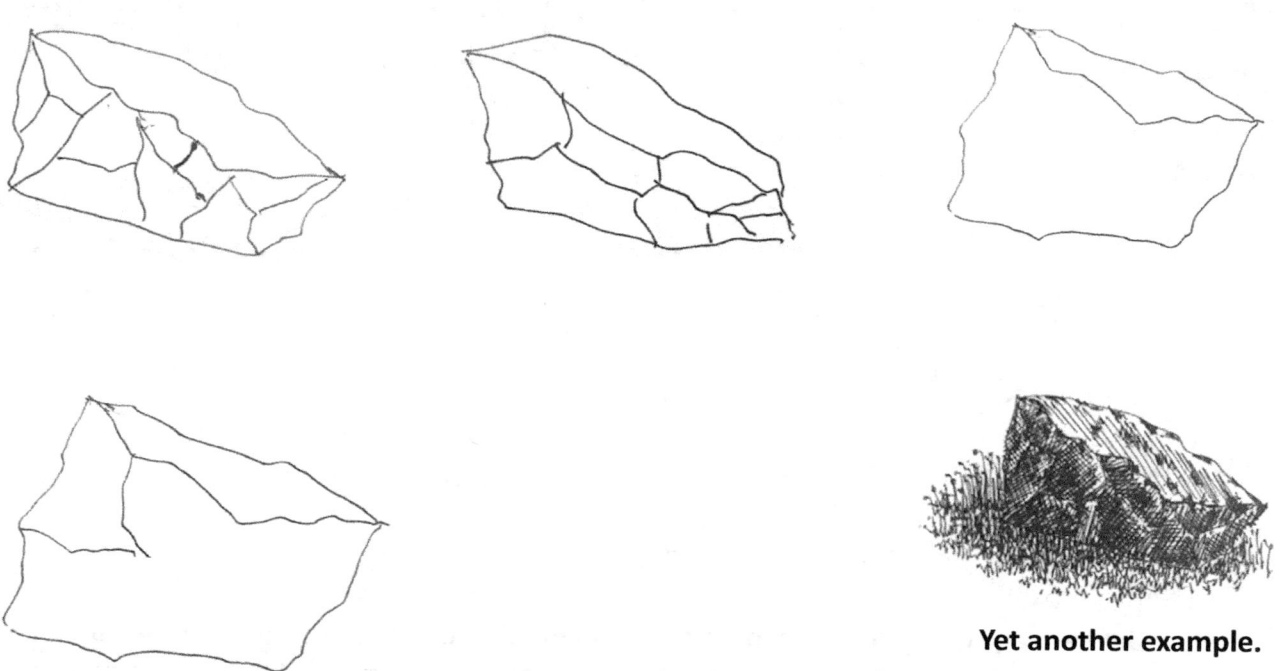

**Yet another example.**

## Creating Stones with Plains:

We started with a simple stone with 2 visible sides. Next we extended it by adding more sides. Multiple levels were next added and this was last extended to created ad hoc plains representing the side. In all this, the top was still mostly drawn as flattened plain. We now extend by drawing stones where the top consists of multiple plains as well.

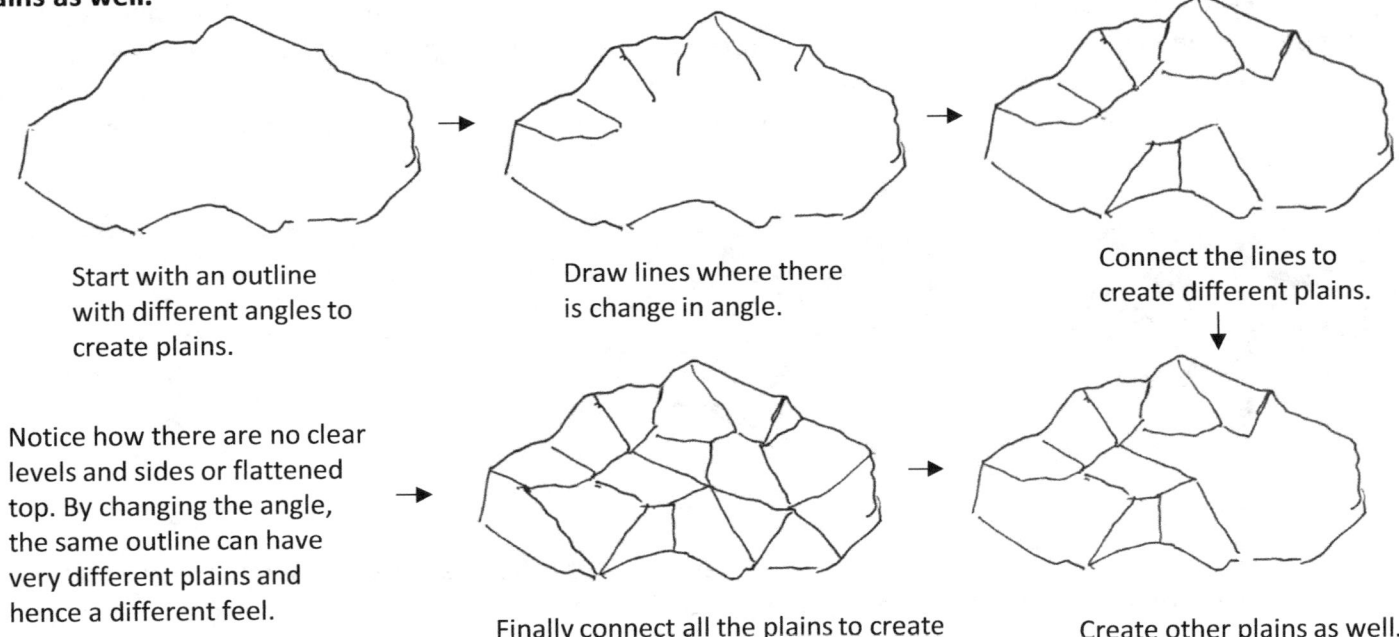

Start with an outline with different angles to create plains.

Draw lines where there is change in angle.

Connect the lines to create different plains.

Notice how there are no clear levels and sides or flattened top. By changing the angle, the same outline can have very different plains and hence a different feel.

Finally connect all the plains to create additional plains in the middle..

Create other plains as well.

## Texturing Multiple Plains:

**Different angled plains need to have the appropriate amount of tone based on the intensity of light they would receive from an assumed light source. This is similar to what we have seen before for multi sided and multi level stones. More plains just makes it more challenging.**

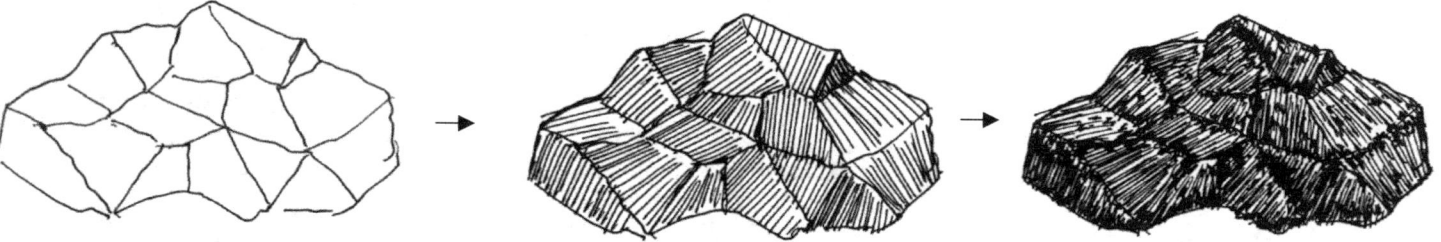

Start by using hatching to give it a base tone. Notice how the orientation of lines brings out the orientation of plain. Also the lines are oriented along the edges of individual plains with gradual transition between as discussed before.

Use additional lines to give proper tone. Irregularly darken the plain edges and add tapered cervices to give a rough feel.

## Texturing Multiple Plains, Another Example:

As you can imagine, very different type of stones can be draw with this technique. By changing the size, shape of plains and their relative orientation, stones with limitless feel can be drawn. Try one now.

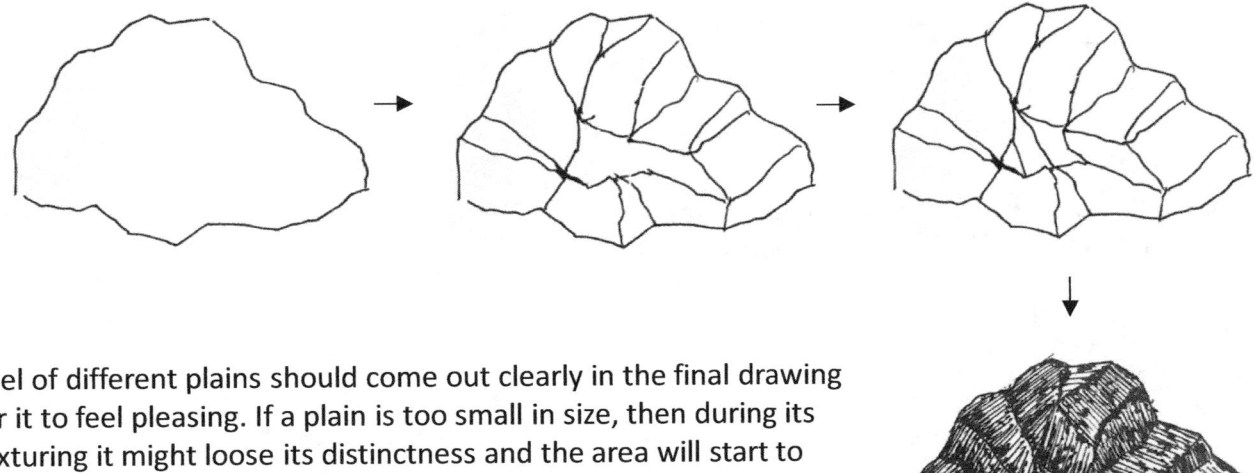

Feel of different plains should come out clearly in the final drawing for it to feel pleasing. If a plain is too small in size, then during its texturing it might loose its distinctness and the area will start to look like a dark mess. For this reason, choose the size of drawing in relation to details and the minimum size of plain you want to add. In this drawing, any size of plain lower than the one in middle would not look good.

## Avoid Such Plains:

It is important to have adjacent plains that have a distinct change in angle in relation to each other which is perceptible by our eyes. Below you can see 2 plain that directly face viewers and hence their relative change of angle is not perceptible and looks odd.

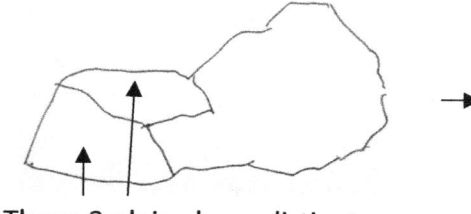 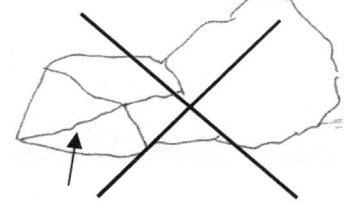

These 2 plains have distinct change of angles relative to each other and looks plausible.

Now I added this line to divide this plain in 2. But this line directly faces viewer and doesn't indicate change in angle between 2 new plains and hence looks odd.

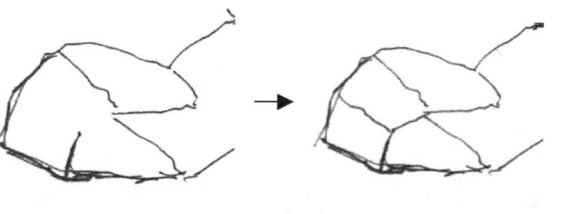

This is more plausible way of adding more plains. Every plain now has perceptible angular difference with each other and hence feels plausible.

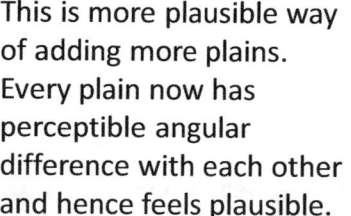

**Activity : Create multi plains in the first drawings below. Texture them as discussed earlier.**

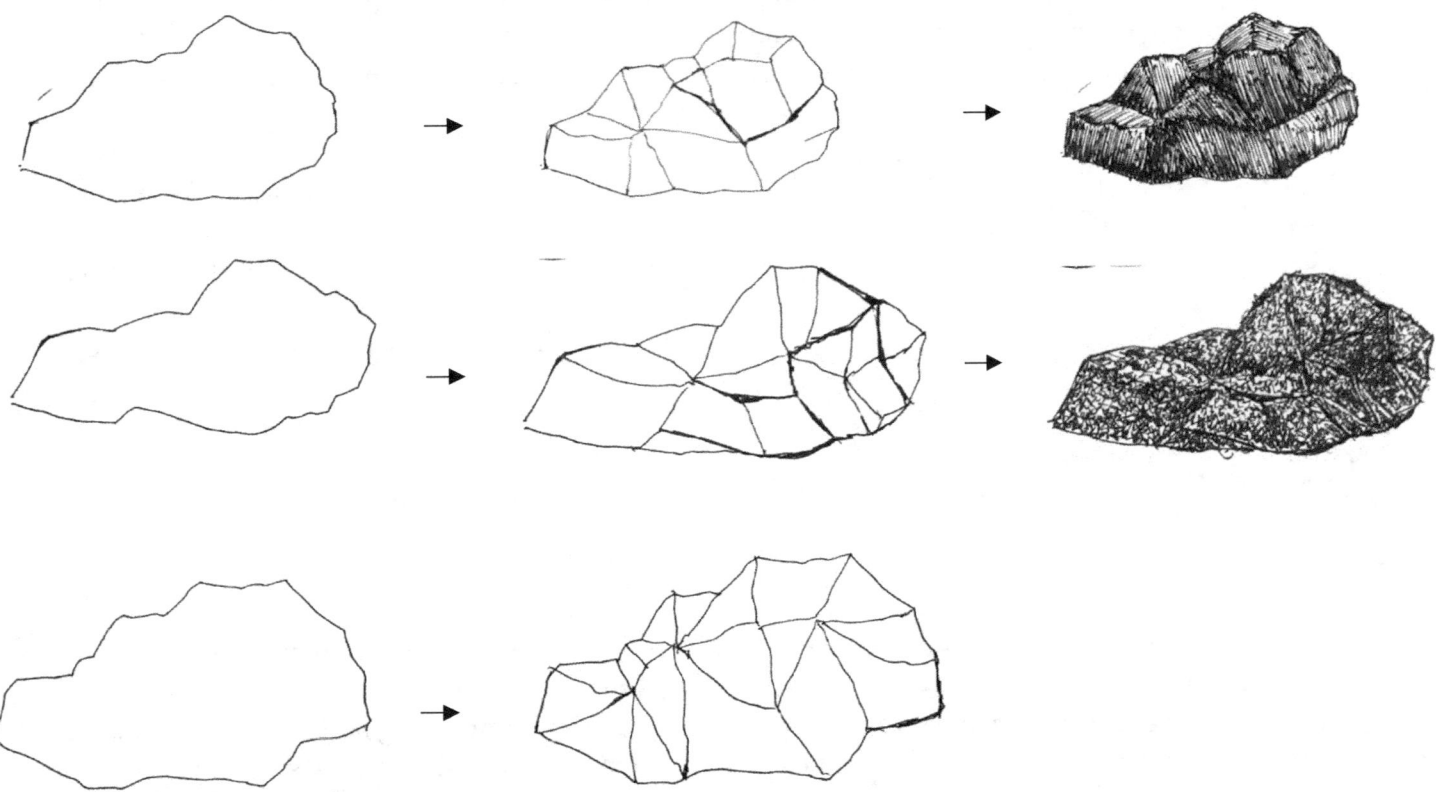

## It is All About Plains:

A 'Plain' is the foundation element of a stone. A surface at a particular orientation is essentially referred to as a 'plain'. A stone is simply different plains connected together to create an 'enclosed space'. Nature of plains (size, shape, orientation) used to create a stone defines the final appearance of stone. It is important to understand this concept so that you can visualize and drawn any stone from your imagination.

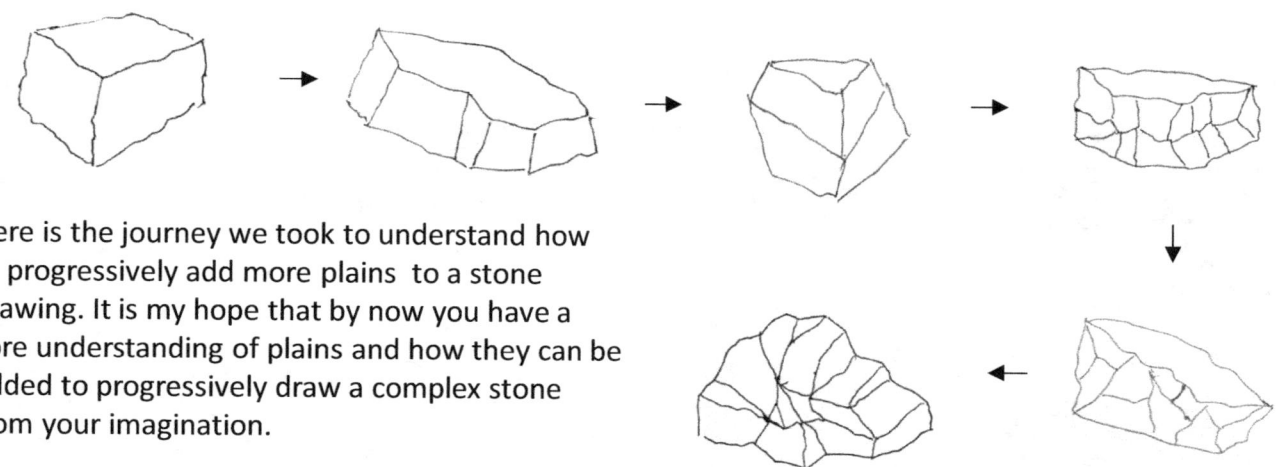

Here is the journey we took to understand how to progressively add more plains to a stone drawing. It is my hope that by now you have a core understanding of plains and how they can be added to progressively draw a complex stone from your imagination.

A complex stones with more plains isn't necessarily best for all drawings. The complexity of stones to draw will be based on the size of the drawing and if they are the focal points. Presence of other elements will also affect the stones that will be suitable for a drawing .

## Drawing Rounded Stones with Flat Top:

**Next we look at stones with more of rounded forms. Stones with rounded edges and flat faces are very easy to draw and add visual interest in any setting. They are very easy to draw as shown below.**

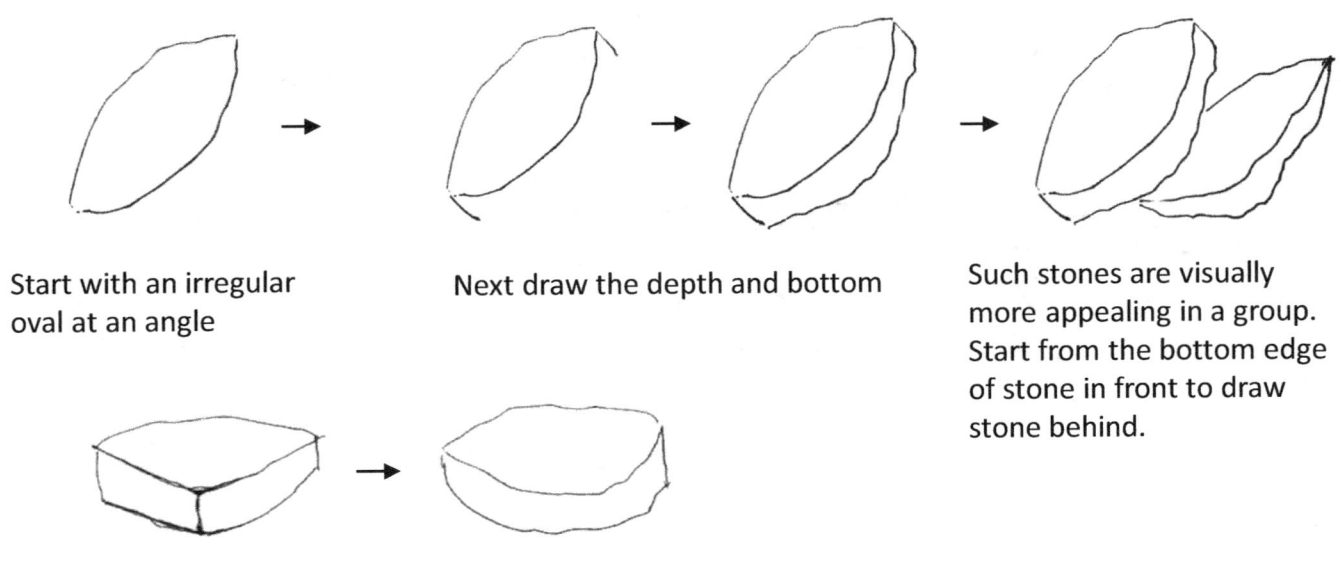

Start with an irregular oval at an angle

Next draw the depth and bottom

Such stones are visually more appealing in a group. Start from the bottom edge of stone in front to draw stone behind.

When the top and bottom are given curved forms, sides go away and rounded form results.

# Drawing Flat Top Rounded Stones:

**Always start with the stone in front and then add stones behind. Use different sizes and angles to add visual interest.**

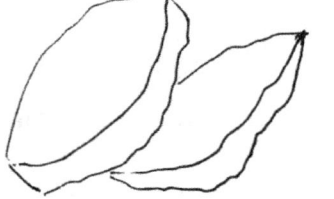

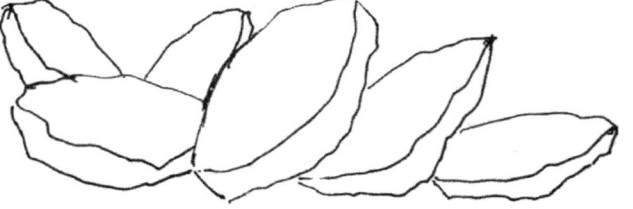

Always draw the stones in front first and then behind.

By drawing such stones in different sizes and angles, a pleasing view can be easily drawn.

# Texturing Flat Top Rounded Stones:

**To texture these stones, make the sides dark and define surface contours of top surface.**

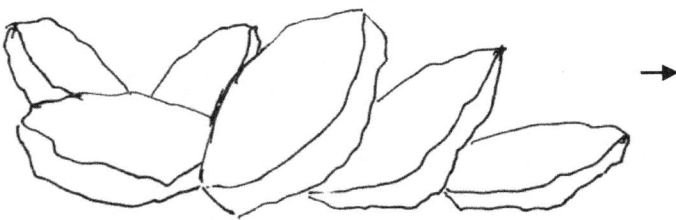

Outline of a group of
angled stones

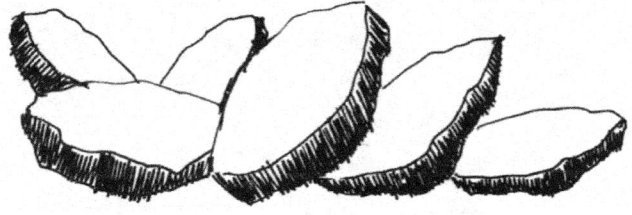

First darken the sides using parallel lines.

## Texturing Flat Top Rounded Stones, Continued:

**Use parallel lines to define surface contour for the top as discussed earlier.**

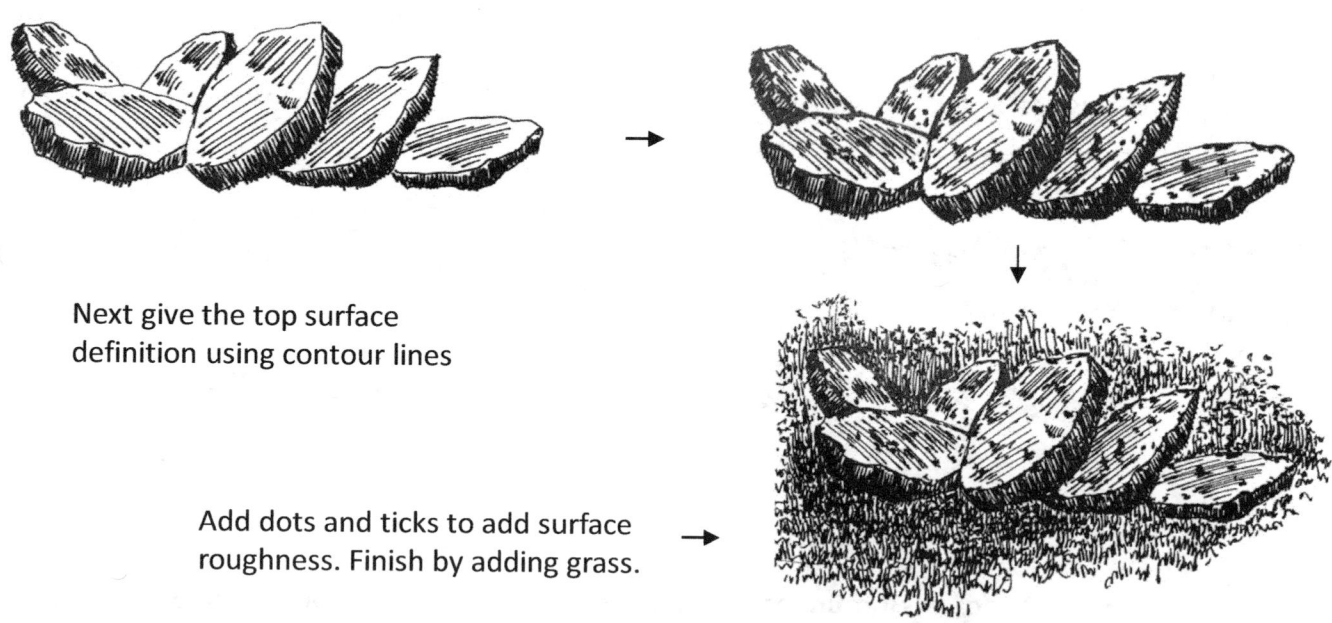

Next give the top surface
definition using contour lines

Add dots and ticks to add surface
roughness. Finish by adding grass.

## Texturing Flat Top Rounded Stones, Another Example:

Following is another example of drawing angled flat face stones. By using different shapes and sized, limitless variations on this can be drawn.

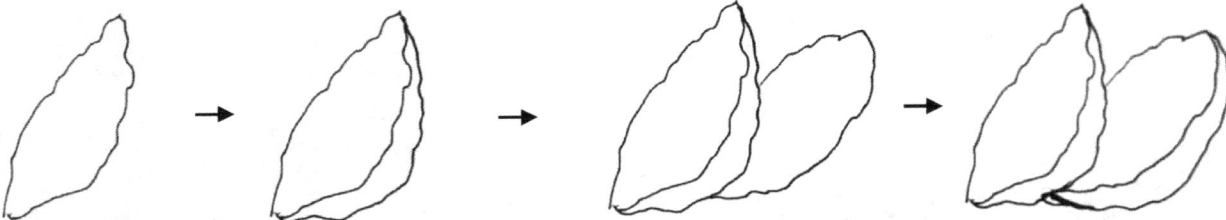

The bottom meets the top at the end in gradual transition. This takes away the depth at the edges of stone.

## Texturing Angled Stones, Another Example, Continued:

**Add additional stones in the back and texture them as before.**

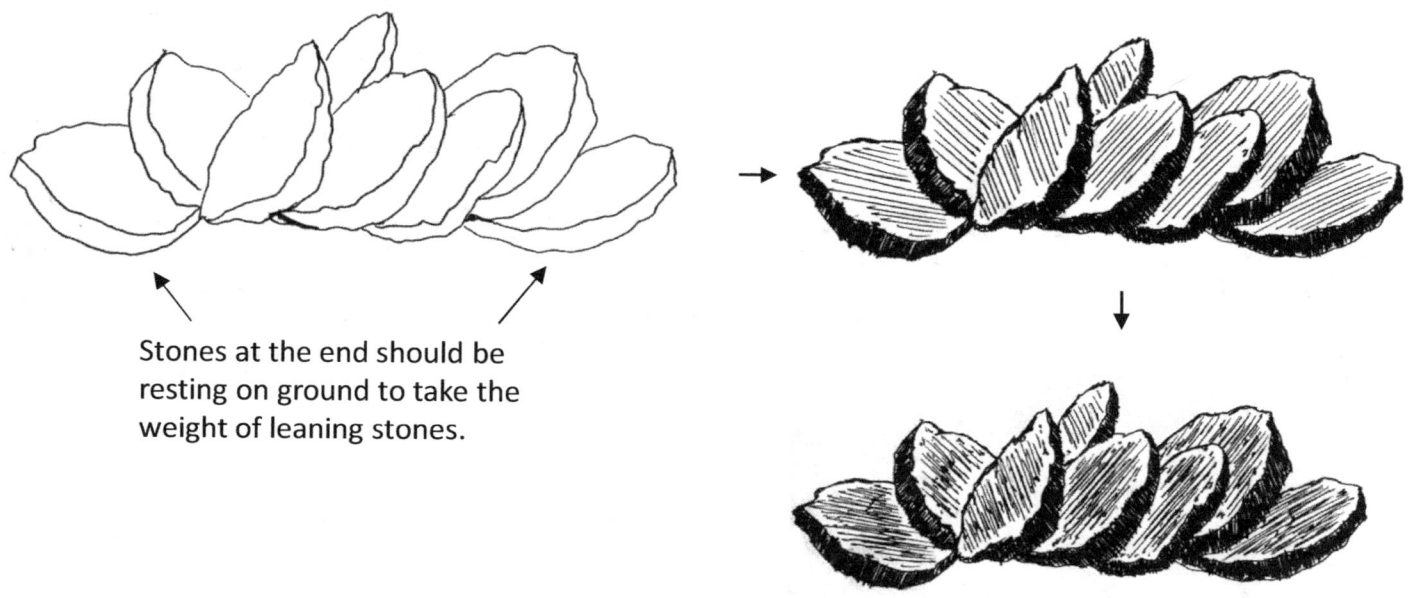

Stones at the end should be resting on ground to take the weight of leaning stones.

Use of less dots and ticks gives a bit smoother appearance to the top.

## Activity: Finish and Texture following Flat Top Rounded Stones:

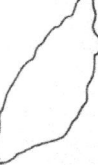 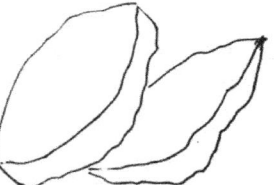 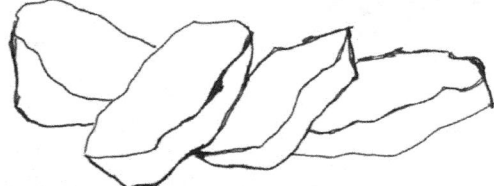

## Drawing Rounded Stones with No Edges:

**Next step is to draw rounded stones that don't have edges but instead an overall rounded form. They can be drawn as shown below.**

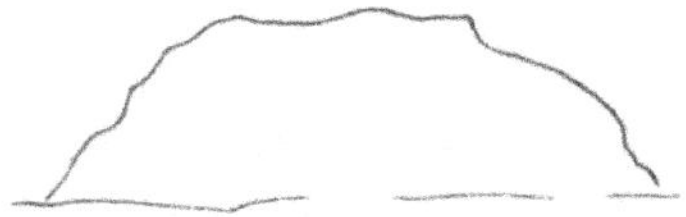

Create a rounded outline.
Don't make it perfectly
rounded and smooth

↓

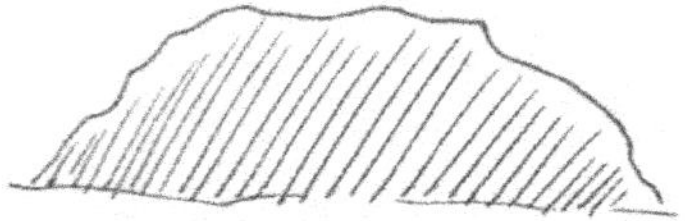

Add a base tone with
angular parallel lines

↓

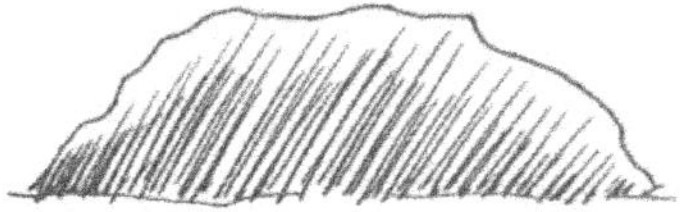

Add another set of lines in
bottom 2/3 to get middle tone

↓

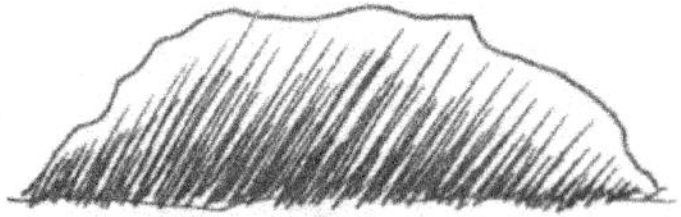

Add another set of lines in
bottom 1/3 to get dark tone

↓

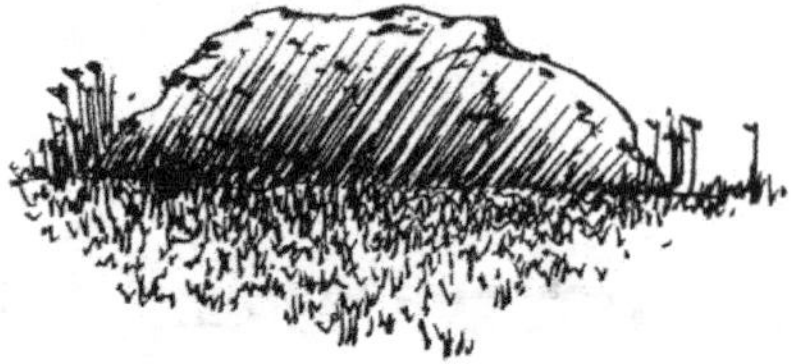

Finish with cervices
and edge irregularities

**Importance of Tonal Variation**

In angular stone,
different sides have
different tones

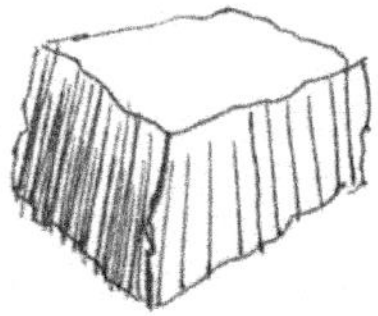

In a rounded stone,
top is lightest as it
receives most light,
while bottom is
darkest

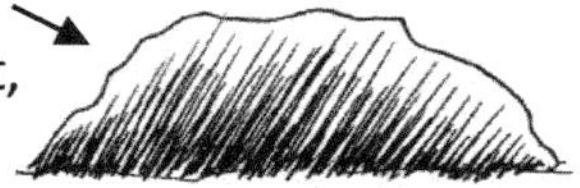

**Such tonal variations are required to bring
out the form. Otherwise, the object
appears flat.**

# Drawing Rounded Stones with No Edges, Additional Examples:

Following are some additional examples. Notice that if the tone change is gradual then the stone has more of a rounded form as in top stone below. If the tone suddenly transitions from dark to light as in bottom stone below, then the transitions line implicitly creates a plain and the stone doesn't have as much of a rounded appeal.

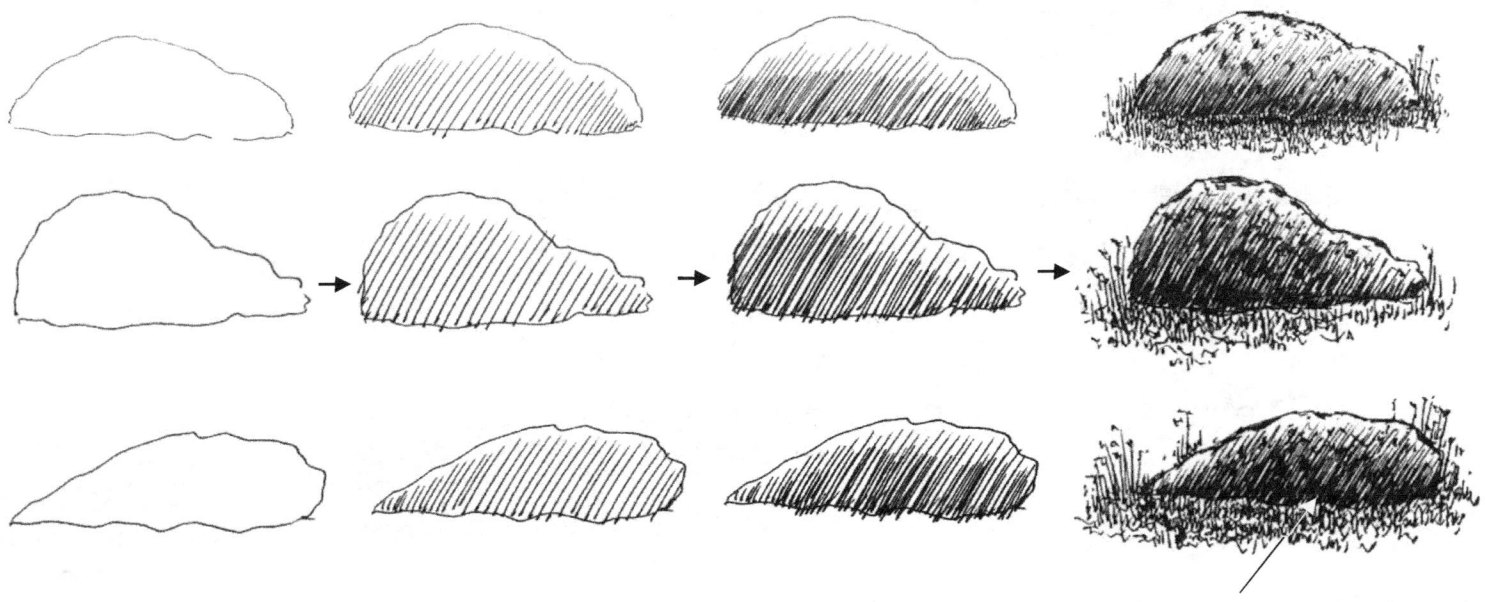

Stone has a dark underside due to sudden tonal change.

# Drawing Rounded Stones with No Edges, Additional Examples:

Dots and ticks are very suitable for texturing such stones as the examples below illustrate. Again, a smooth tonal transition will indicate a well overall rounded form where as abrupt transition will indicate a rougher plain at the bottom.

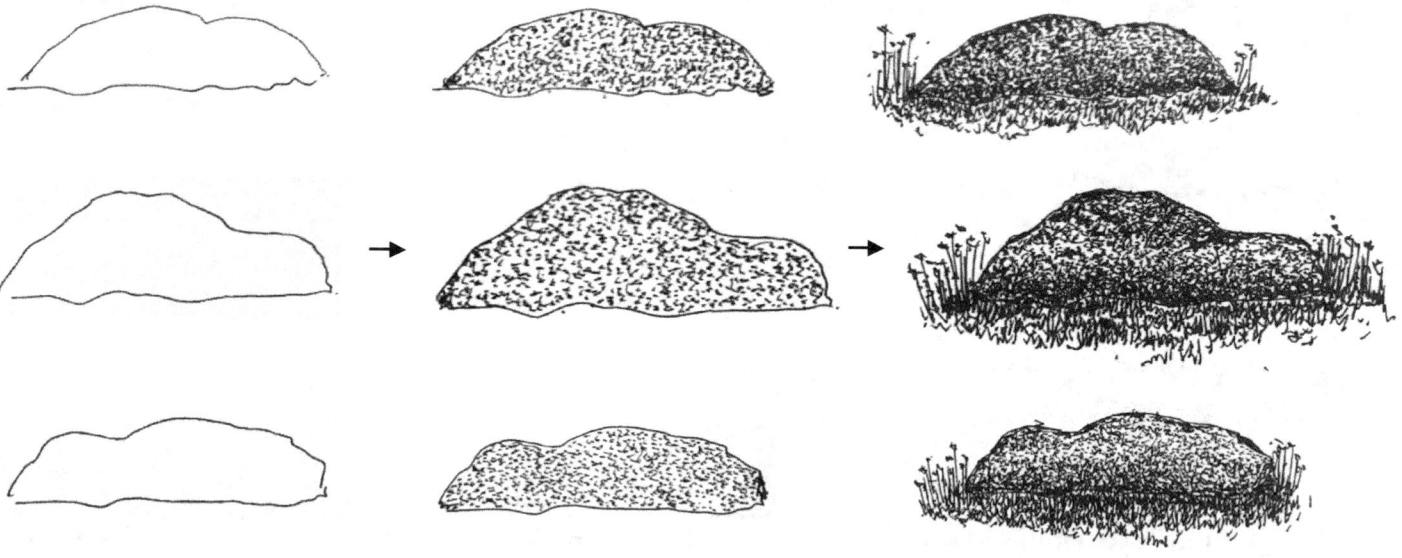

**Activity : Finish the following rounded stones per earlier instructions. Draw some of your own.**

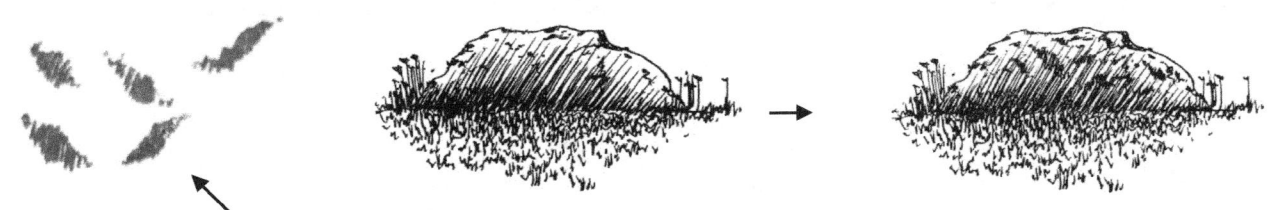

Tapered shapes like these can also be added to indicate a 'cut' in the body giving stone more rough appearance.

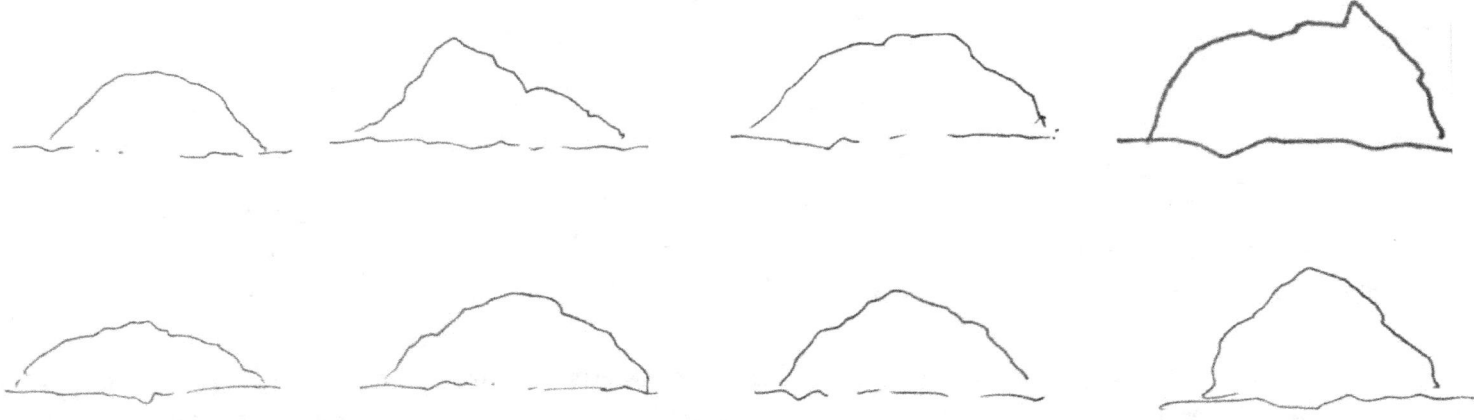

## Understanding the Transition of Sides:

**It is very important to understand how different types of stones we have looked at so far evolve from each other. This will help you be able to 'design' any shape of stones with appropriate sides and edges.**

Sides result when top and bottom have distinct change in angles connected by height lines.

As the change in angle disappears with smooth line, distinct sides disappear.

If the vertical height/edge line is removed and top made more rounded, then rounded stone result.

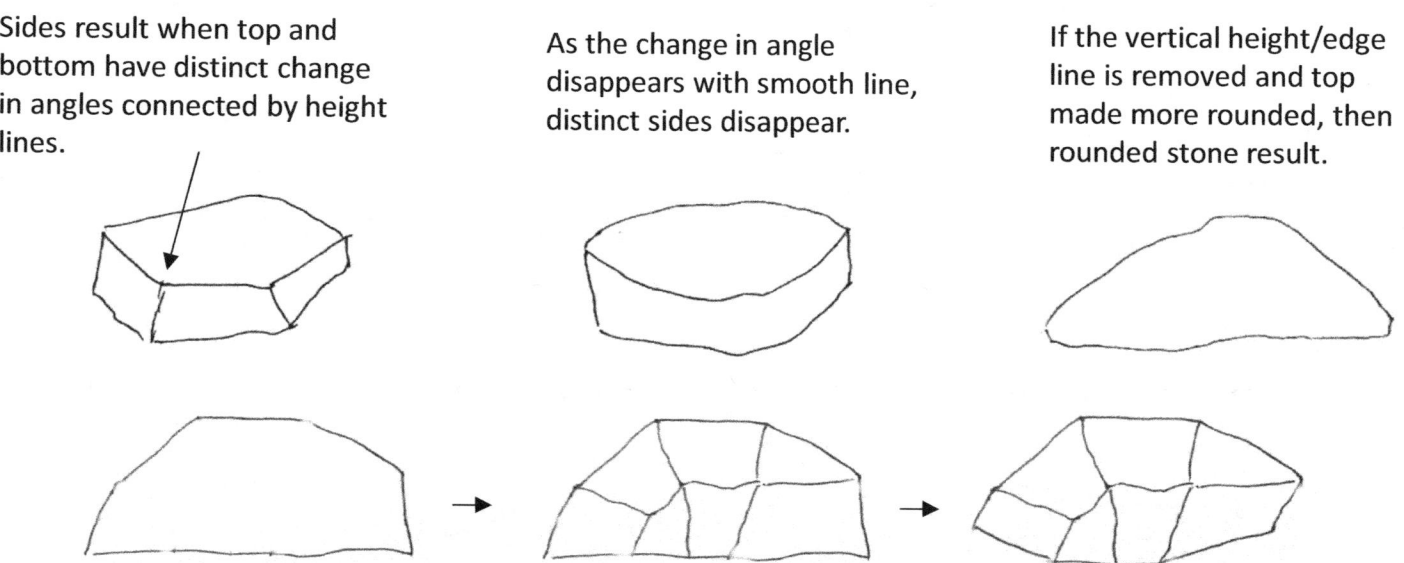

If the top and bottom of rounded stone is made angular then lines can be used at transition point to define plains resulting in stones with sides .

## Adding Cuts to Rounded Stones:

**Cuts can be added to rounded stones we drew earlier to give them a different feel. These cuts are textured dark and contrast between this dark and white of remaining stone makes them visually enticing.**

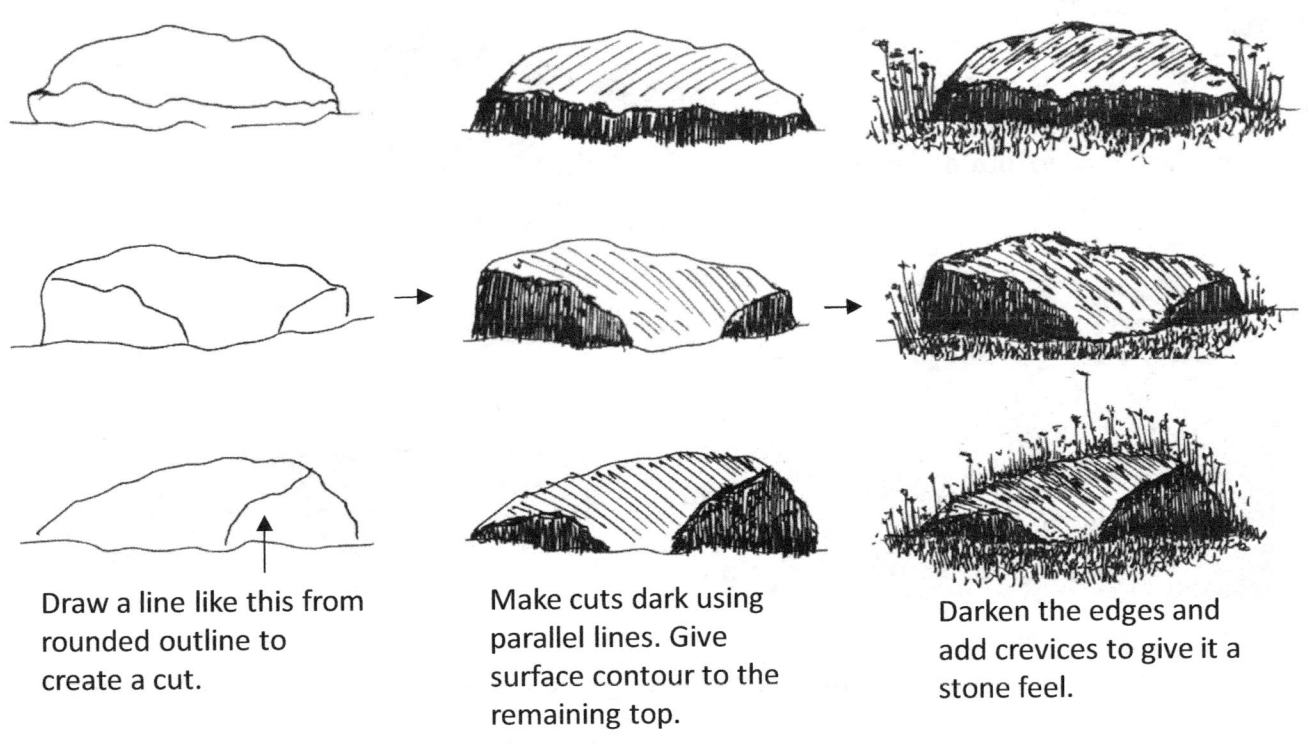

Draw a line like this from rounded outline to create a cut.

Make cuts dark using parallel lines. Give surface contour to the remaining top.

Darken the edges and add crevices to give it a stone feel.

## Adding Cuts to Rounded Stones, More Examples:

**Following are some more examples. There is no limit to the type of stone you can draw in this manner.**

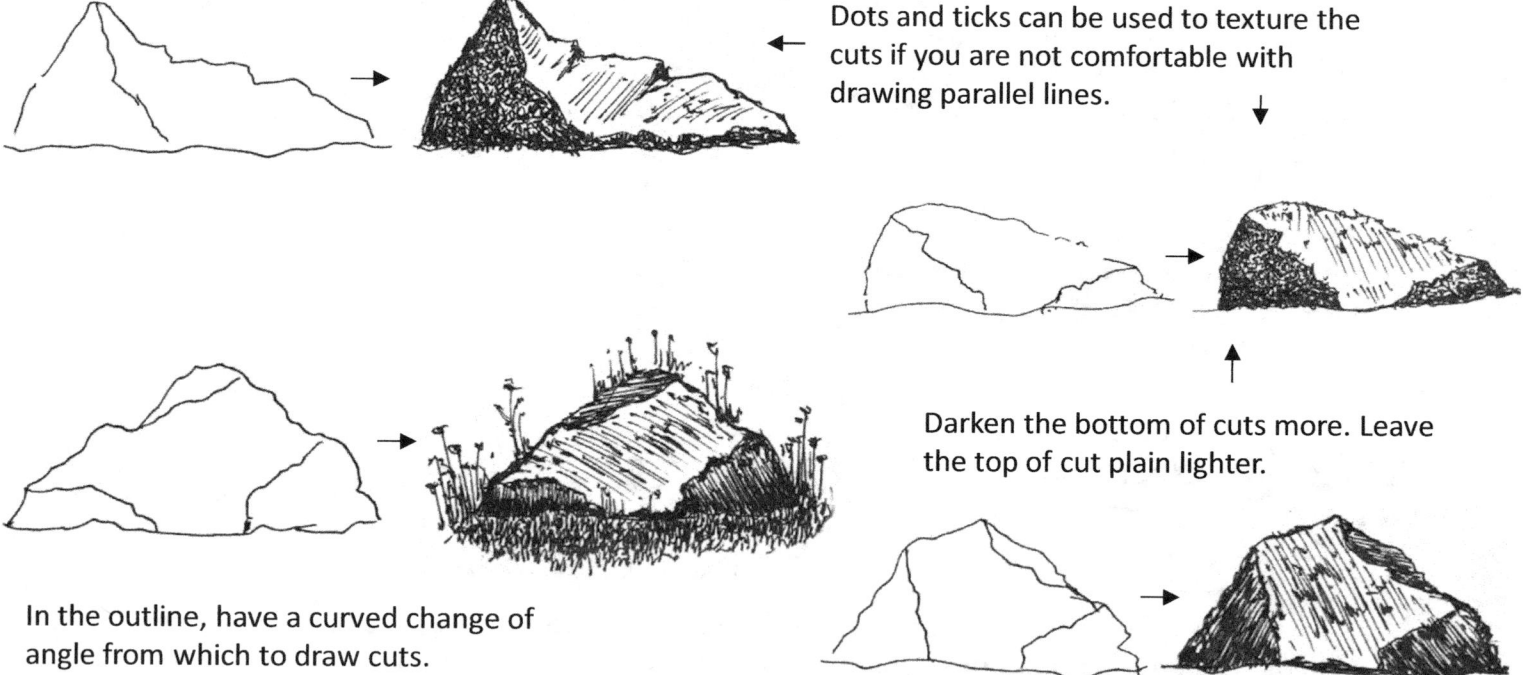

Dots and ticks can be used to texture the cuts if you are not comfortable with drawing parallel lines.

Darken the bottom of cuts more. Leave the top of cut plain lighter.

In the outline, have a curved change of angle from which to draw cuts.

**Activity : Finish the following rounded stones with cuts per earlier instructions. Draw some of your own.**

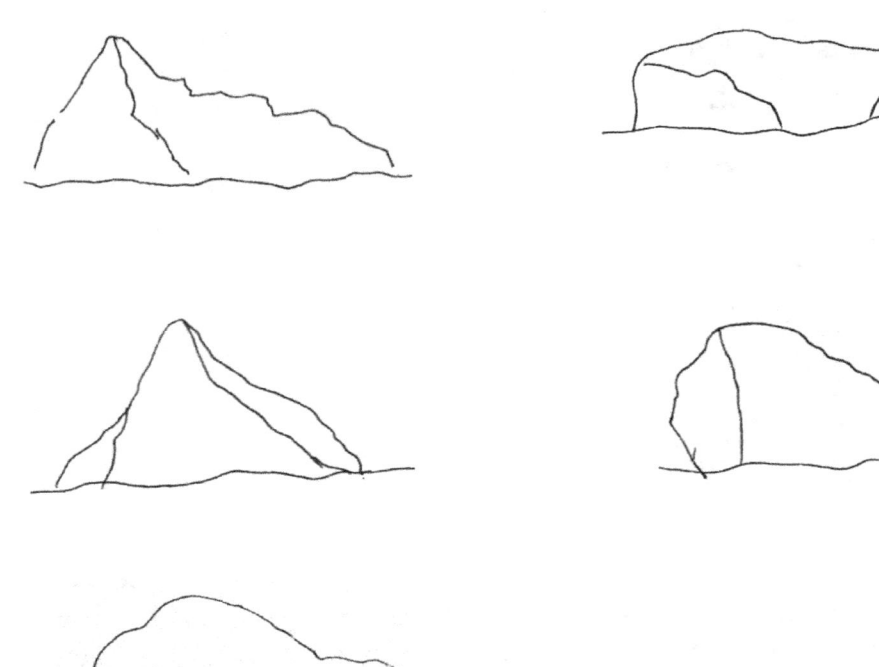
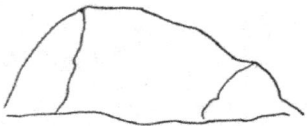

## Drawing Large Stone:

Technique discussed previously is ideal for drawing large stones. Though large stones can be drawn with any of the techniques presented so far, rounded form with cuts gives most pleasing feel as the size of stone increases. Also experiment drawing large stones with other techniques.

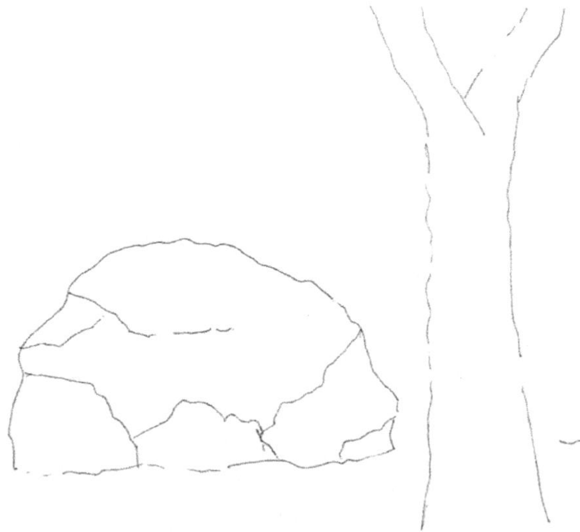

Outline (reduced in size).

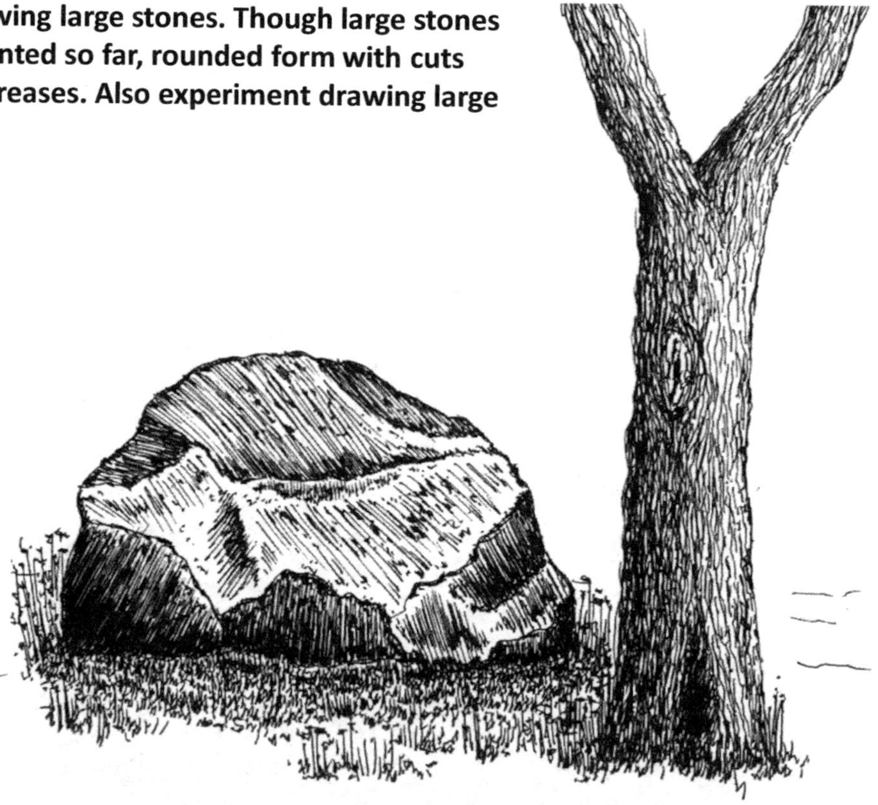

## Drawing Stones With Surface Contours:

Line is used for many different purposes in pen and ink drawing. We saw earlier how it is used to give tone and also bring out the form using directional hatching. Another fundamental use of line is to give a surface definition, i.e. to define the curvature/contour of a surface. This is done using tapered lines as shown below.

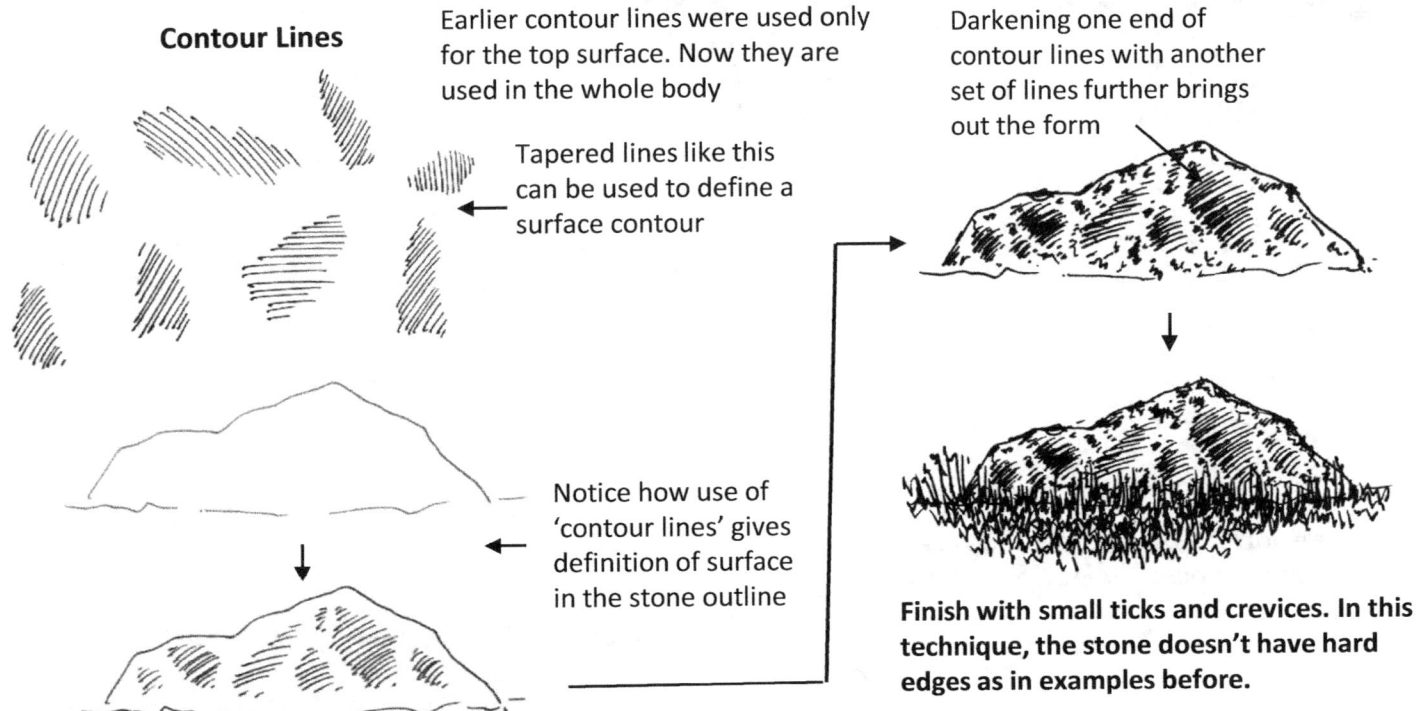

**Contour Lines**

Earlier contour lines were used only for the top surface. Now they are used in the whole body

Tapered lines like this can be used to define a surface contour

Darkening one end of contour lines with another set of lines further brings out the form

Notice how use of 'contour lines' gives definition of surface in the stone outline

**Finish with small ticks and crevices. In this technique, the stone doesn't have hard edges as in examples before.**

# Drawing Stones With Surface Contours:

**Here are some additional examples of this technique.**

By using different orientation and size for surface contours, different feel for stone can be obtained in the same outline.

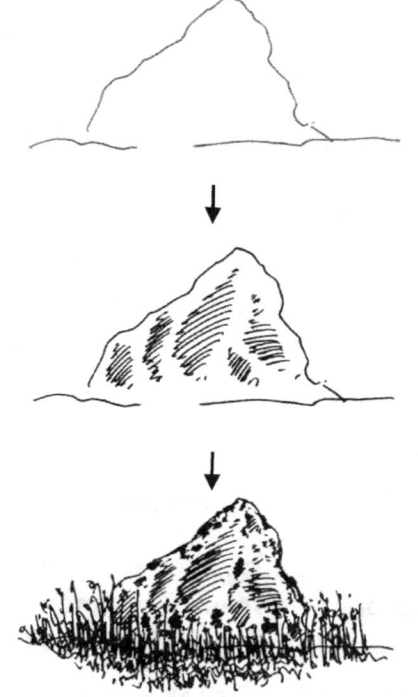

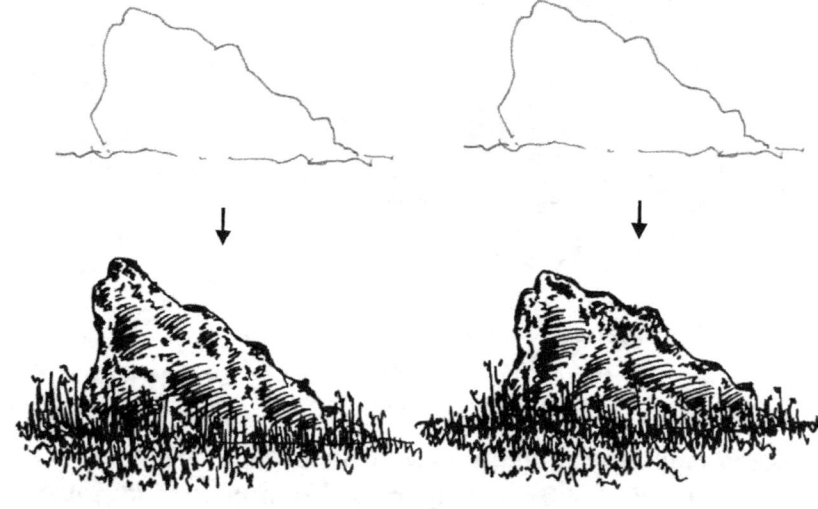

## Activity: Drawing Stones With Surface Contours:

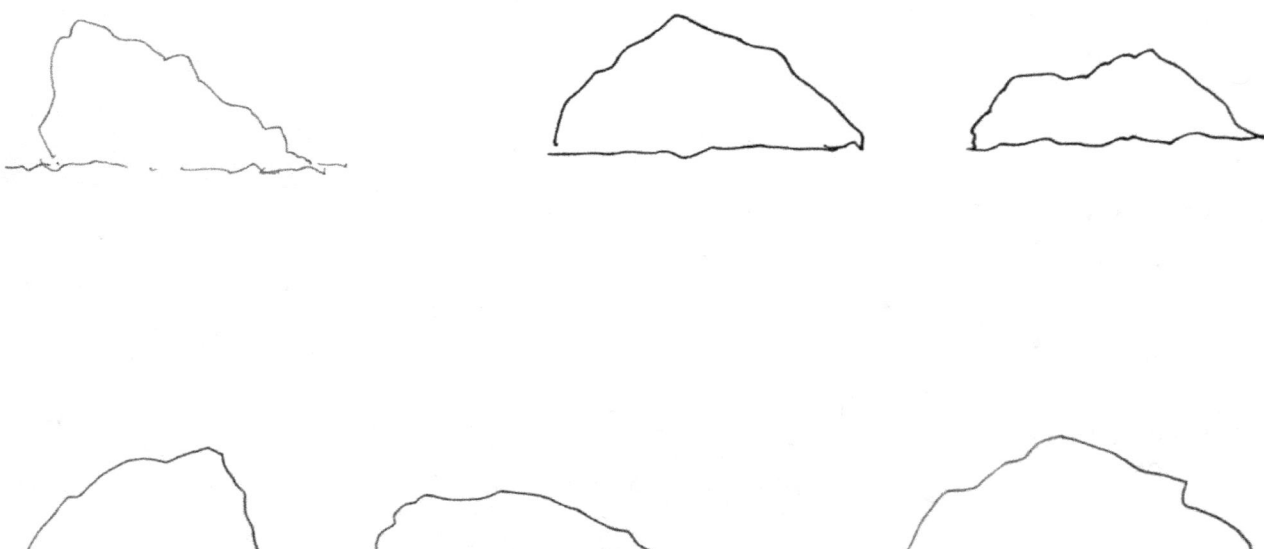

## Drawing Stones with Vertical Edges:

**In the rounded form of stones, vertical edges can be** introduced **as shown below. This gives a very different zagged feel to the resulting stone.**

Draw an outline like this with vertical sections

From the vertical section drop two lines that meet to define a vertical plane

Darken the vertical edges to define them

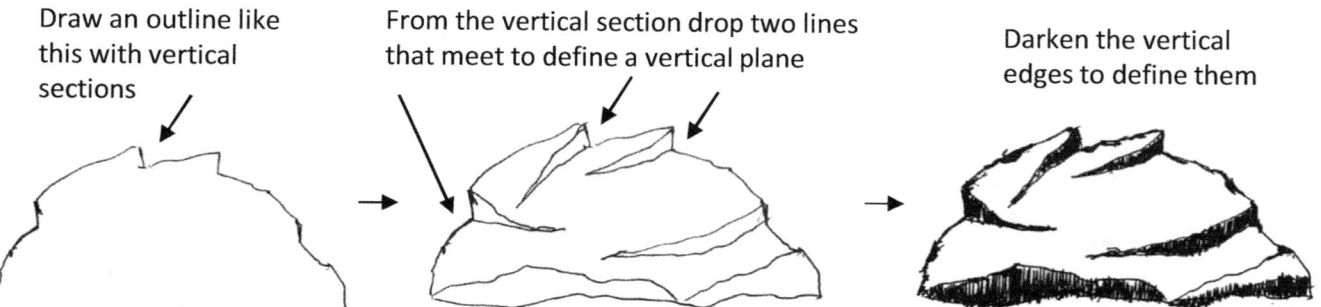

# Drawing Stones with Vertical Edges, Continued:

**Make sure the edges and overall shape is irregular and interesting. Make edges different sizes at different angles to add visual interest.**

Draw surface contours with parallel lines

Add ticks and tapered darks to add surface roughness

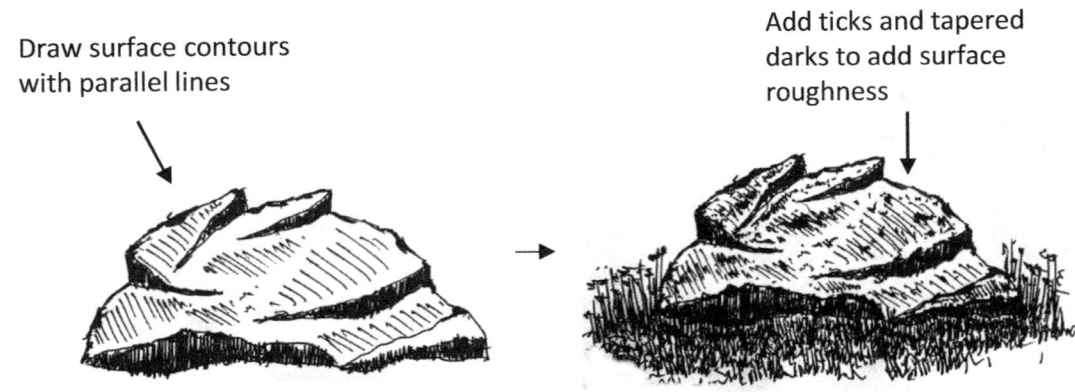

## Drawing Stones with Vertical Edges, Additional Example:

This is a very versatile technique and by using different shapes and sizes, stones with very different feel can be drawn. Following is another example.

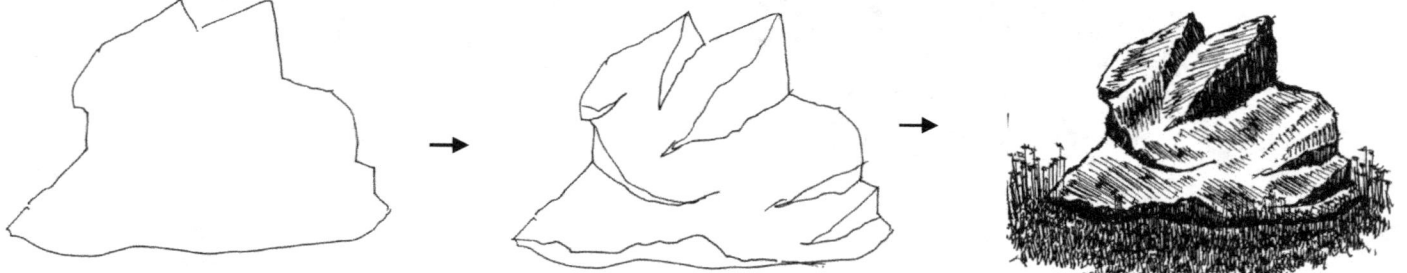

## Drawing Stones with Vertical Edges, Alternate Approach:

In this alternate approach, start by drawing the vertical edges first. Then connect the edges to define the shape of stone and finish as before.

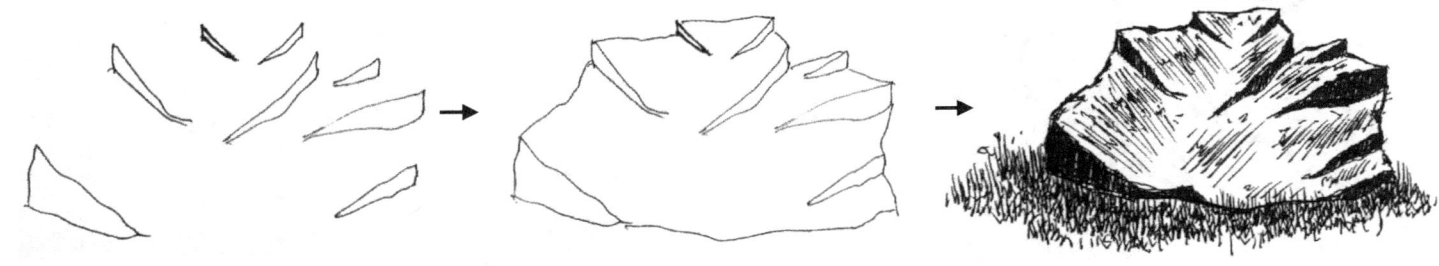

**Start by drawing the vertical edges in the manner shown above**

**Connect the top and bottom of successive edges to define the outline**

**Finish as before**

# Drawing Stones with Vertical Edges, Alternate Approach, Another Example:

Benefit of this approach is that by focusing on the vertical edges and their layout in the beginning, you can easily create any desired shape. Limitless variations are possible. Try one now.

Connect the top and bottom
of successive edges

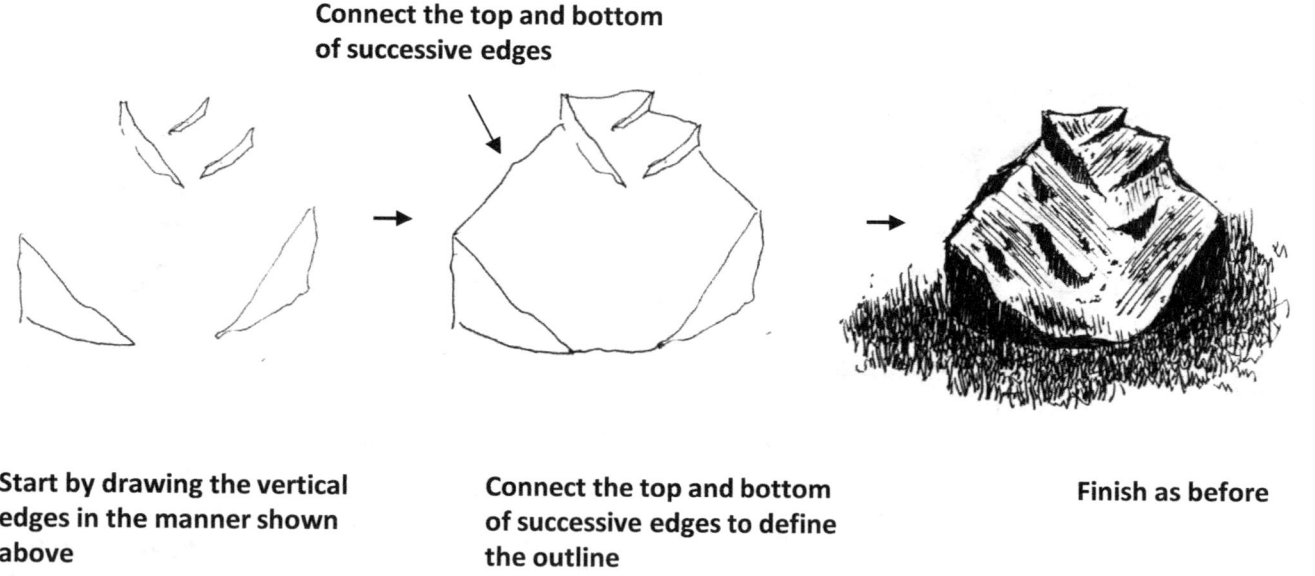

Start by drawing the vertical edges in the manner shown above

Connect the top and bottom of successive edges to define the outline

Finish as before

# Drawing Stones with Vertical Edges,  Yet Another Approach:

Here is yet another approach where the vertical edges are drawn later. I am showing these different approaches as practicing them will get you fully familiar with how to create different plains. Once you are proficient, you will be able to draw one on the fly.

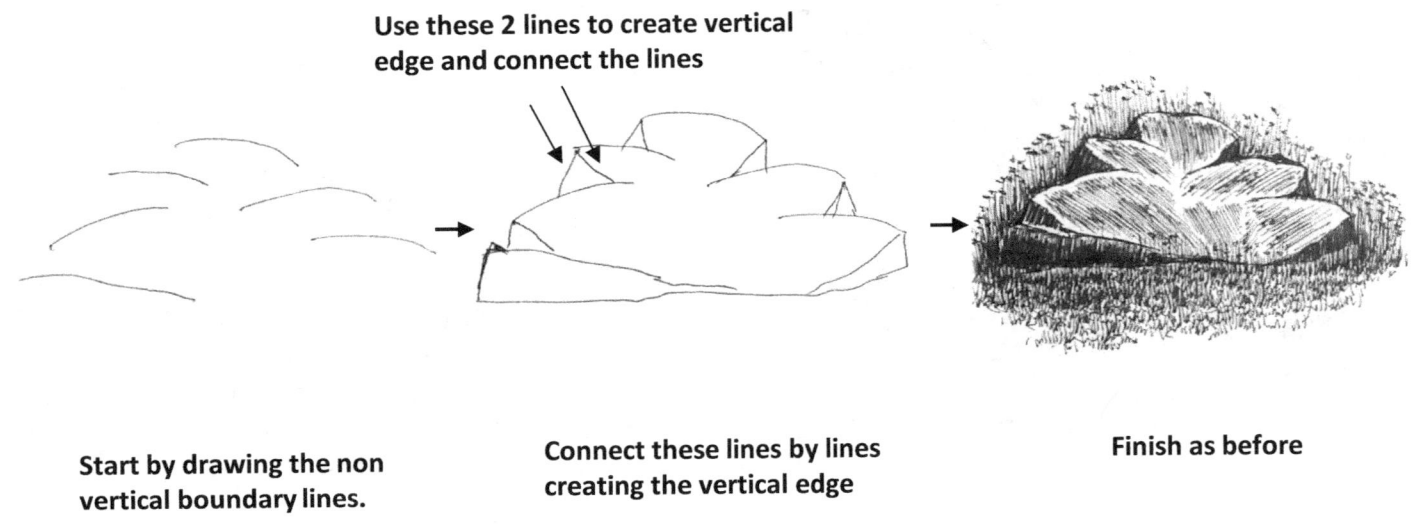

Use these 2 lines to create vertical edge and connect the lines

Start by drawing the non vertical boundary lines.

Connect these lines by lines creating the vertical edge

Finish as before

## Adding Ground Cover Around a Stone:

A stone appears grounded and much more visually appealing when grass and other ground cover is added at its base. Use following techniques to add ground cover around a stone. Drawing grass is discussed in more detail later.

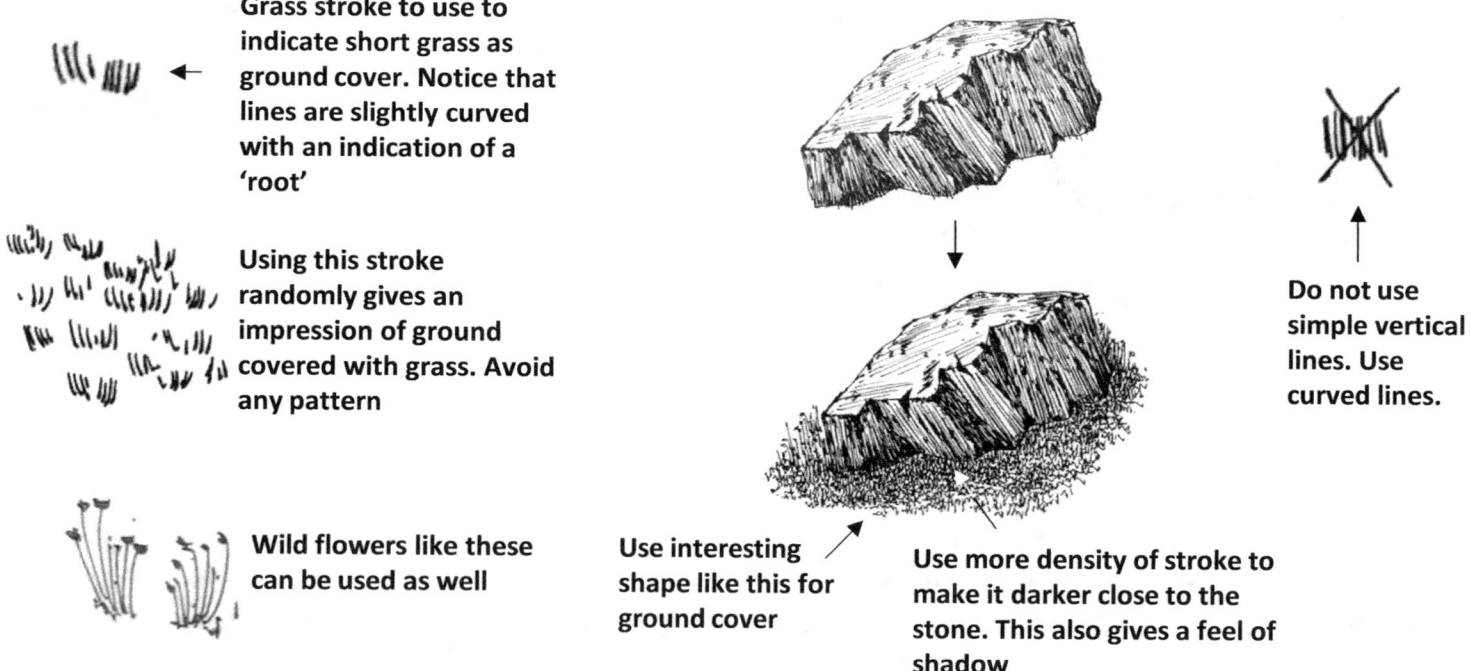

**Grass stroke to use to indicate short grass as ground cover. Notice that lines are slightly curved with an indication of a 'root'**

**Using this stroke randomly gives an impression of ground covered with grass. Avoid any pattern**

**Wild flowers like these can be used as well**

**Do not use simple vertical lines. Use curved lines.**

**Use interesting shape like this for ground cover**

**Use more density of stroke to make it darker close to the stone. This also gives a feel of shadow**

## Drawing Group of Stones:

**A set of stones is more interesting than a single stone as it conveys perception of depth in drawing and can be easily drawn as following.**

All 'height' lines end on the outline of stone in front hiding full bottom of stone behind

Part of left side is hidden here as only left side height line ends on outline of stone in front

Receding stones are made smaller

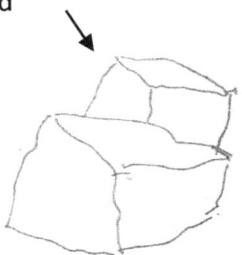

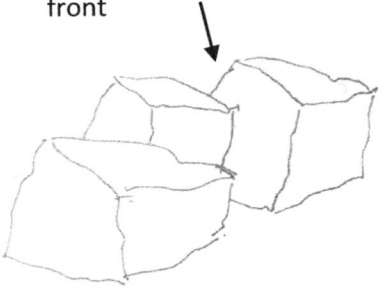

1. Always draw the stones in the front first. By hiding part of stone behind, relative order is established

2. Continue in this manner by hiding part of stones that are behind one in front

3. Make stones smaller as they go out. This establishes right perspective. Use different shapes and sizes to add interest.

## Drawing Group of Stones:

The area enclosed between stones will receive less light than if the stones were far apart and hence should be made more darker.

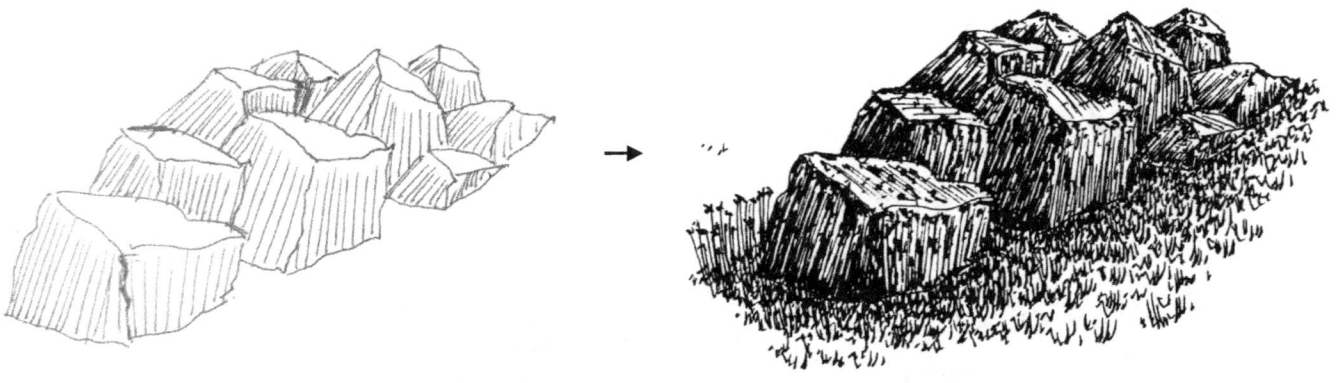

**Stones are textured as before**

# Drawing a Group of Rounded Stones:

**Here is another example of drawing group of rounded stones.**

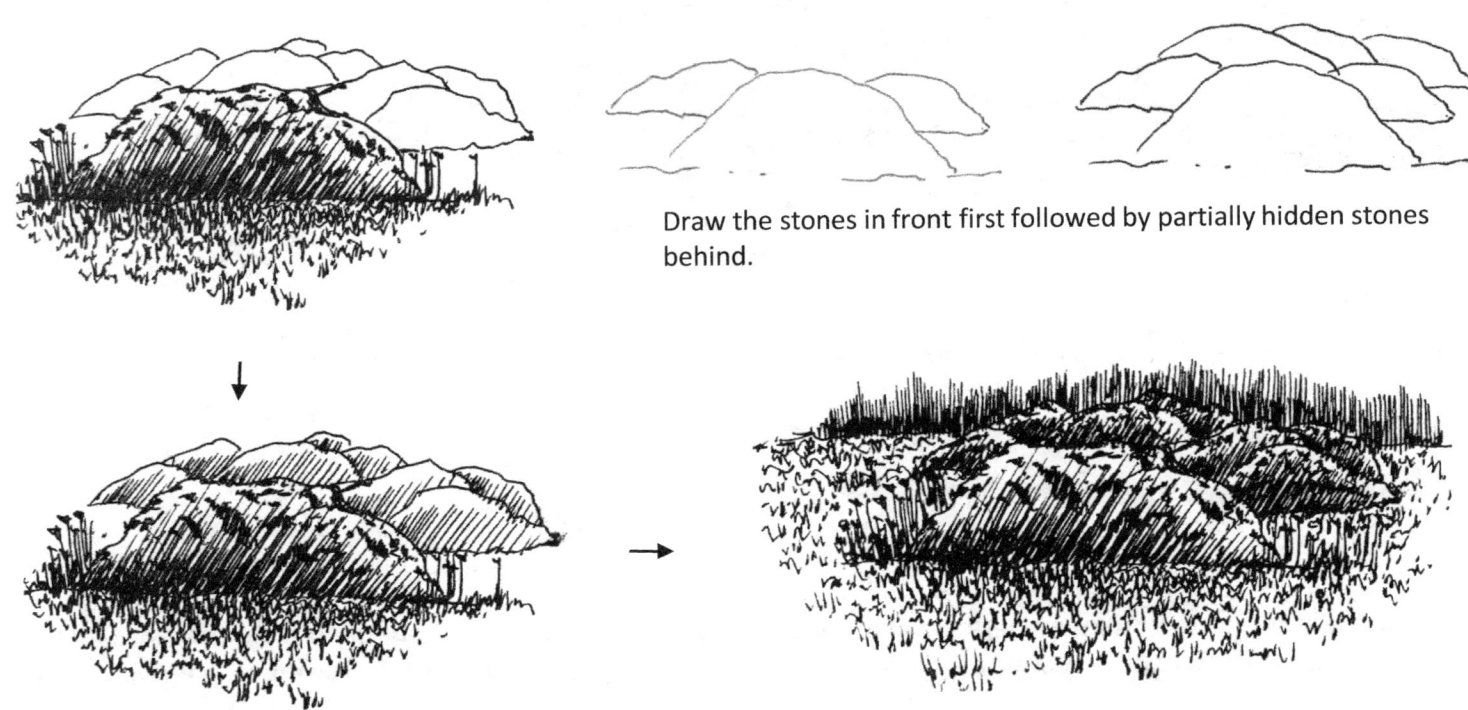

Draw the stones in front first followed by partially hidden stones behind.

# Drawing a Group of Multiple Type of Stones:

We have looked at drawing different types of stones and the power of learning to draw such stones with different feel comes out when they are used together. This adds more variety and interest to the drawing.

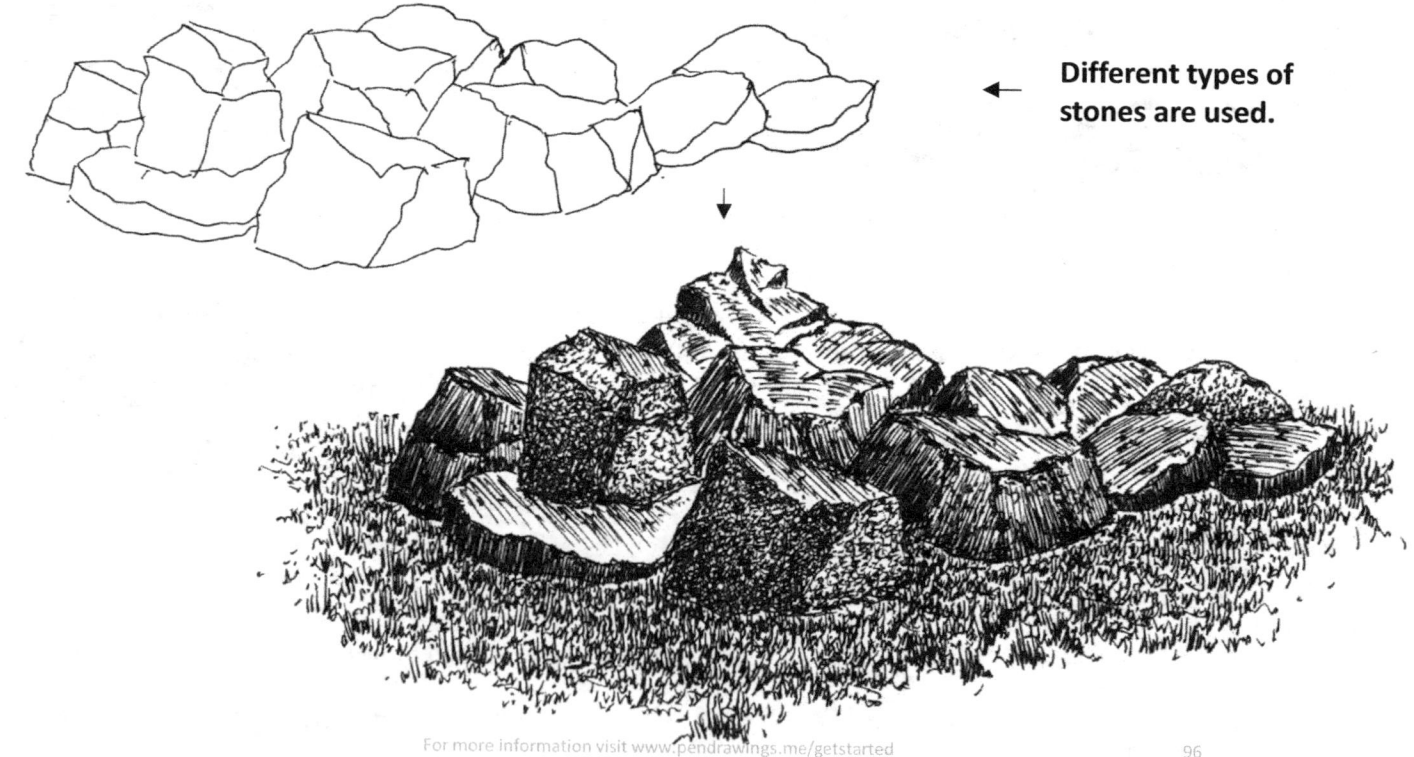

Different types of stones are used.

## Balance of Light and Dark Tone:

As we have seen, sides of a stone are usually darker than top which receives the most light. When drawing a group of stones, it is important to maintain a good balance between the light and dark tone to give it a visually pleasing appearance. This means that overall top and sides of stones should be in good proportion to achieve tonal balance.

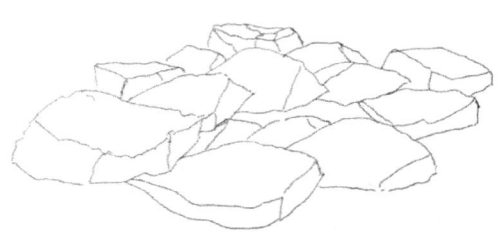

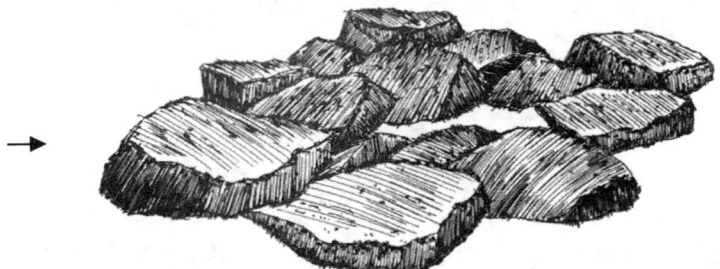

Initial Outline (again notice the use of different type of stones to add visual interest).

Notice the use of bigger top in the front stones to get lighter tone. In the back stones are smaller with less top to give it a darker tone. If I used more sides in the front too, the drawing will feel too dark.

## Avoid Adjacent Dark Tones:

In the absence of color, tonal difference between adjacent elements is very important in maintaining visual separation. For a group of stones, this means that dark side of one stone should abut lighter side of other stone. Two dark sides next to each other would lose the visual separation and make the drawing unpleasing.

Dark side of one stone is against the lighter top of another and make it look pleasing with visual separation.

Adjacent dark sides loose the visual separation of 2 stones.

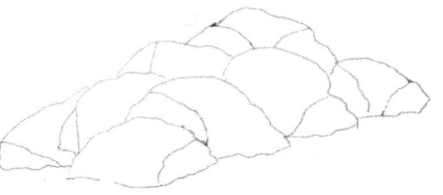

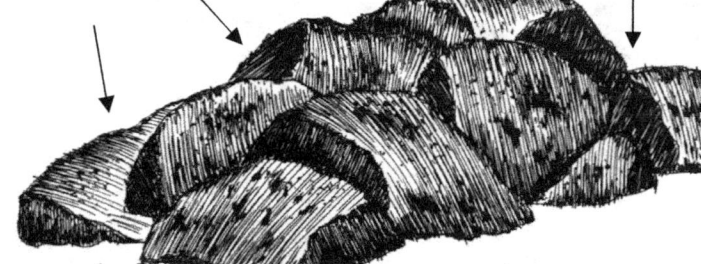

**Activity : Add different type of stones below and texture them to draw a group of stones per earlier instructions.**

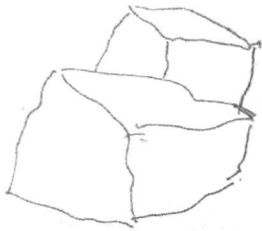

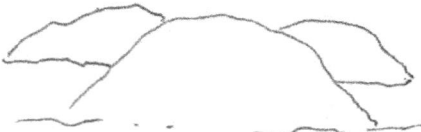

## Drawing Snow on Stones:

In a winter landscape, snow sitting on stones is a common theme. Drawing snow covered on various elements is covered in detail in other volumes in the series. Pl. visit **www.pendrawings.me/workbooks** for more information on other volumes in this series.

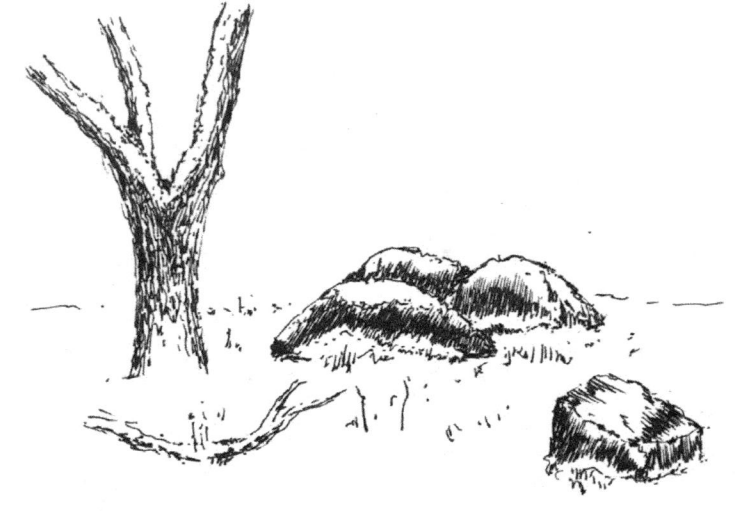

**Leave some white irregularly on top**

**Snow also accumulates on the sides and bottom of stones.**

**Leave white as shown above to indicate snow. Always keep the snow line irregular and mellow using dots and ticks.**

**Pleasing landscapes with snow are very simple and fun to draw.**

**Activity : Following is the drawing from previous page in which stones have been lightened. Texture them using the instructions provided on last page.**

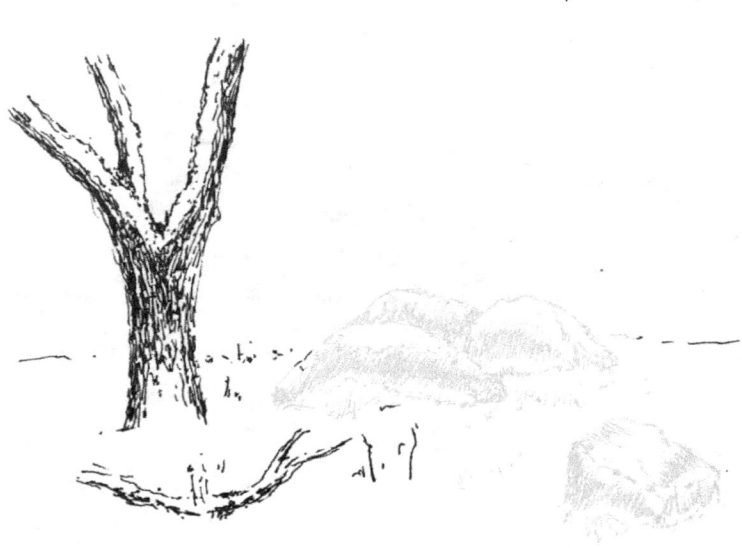

## Concept of Horizon:

If your view is not impeded, then horizon refers to the 'far out' distance where things become very small and barely discernable. 'Horizon' is where our eyes 'settle' when looking far out in the open.

In a landscape, a horizon is always 'implied', but we can make it explicit by putting down a 'horizon line'.

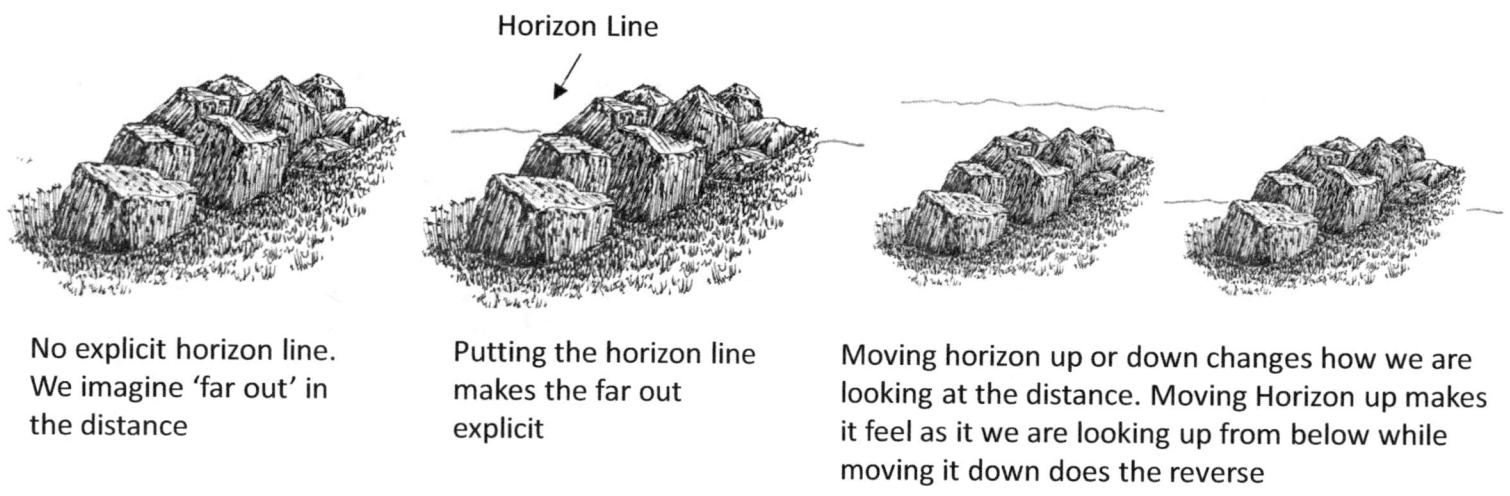

Horizon Line

No explicit horizon line. We imagine 'far out' in the distance

Putting the horizon line makes the far out explicit

Moving horizon up or down changes how we are looking at the distance. Moving Horizon up makes it feel as it we are looking up from below while moving it down does the reverse

## Drawing Interesting Horizon and Middle Ground:

**Shape of horizon sets the overall mood of the drawing. Instead of just a simple horizontal horizon, more interesting horizon gives more appeal and energy to the drawing as seen below. In addition, in middle ground, lines can be used to create interesting plains.**

Notice how this looks more pleasing than use of simple horizon on last page.

Such diagonally intersecting lines creates a pleasing horizon.

Next add such lines to create interesting middle ground.

Some more examples. Notice a sense of 'balance' between the sides. This gives more visually pleasing appearance.

# Concept of Perspective:

**Things become smaller as they go farther out from us. This 'perspective rule' should always be followed and objects closer to horizon should be smaller than similar objects away from horizon.**

objects become smaller as they get closer to horizon

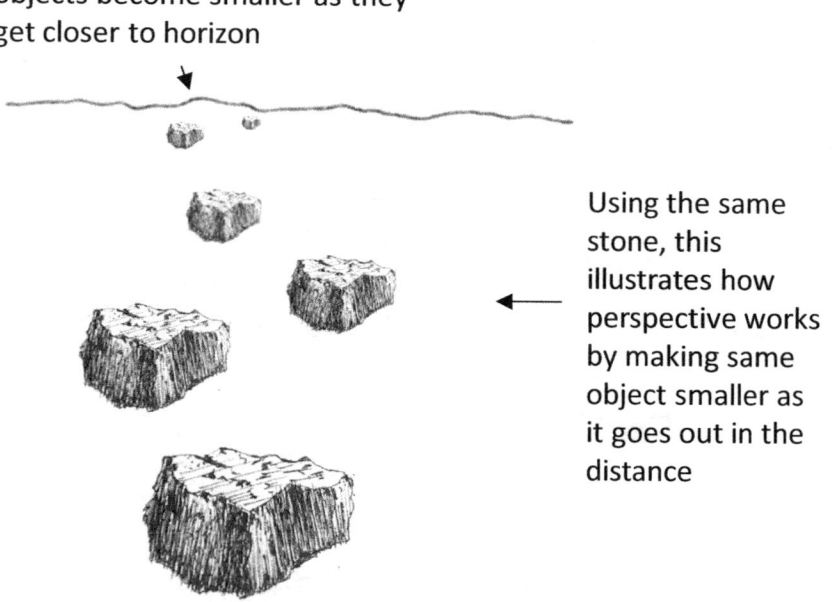

Always lay a very faint horizon line initially and draw foreground elements first

Using the same stone, this illustrates how perspective works by making same object smaller as it goes out in the distance

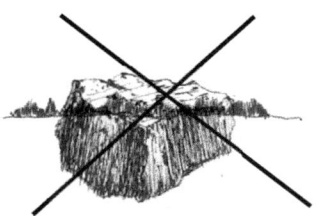

Make sure no part of horizon is visible inside a foreground element

**Activity: Put down the horizon line and draw other stones closer to horizon per perspective.**

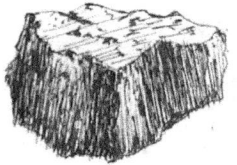 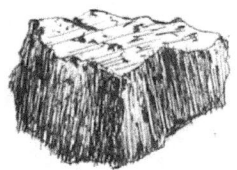 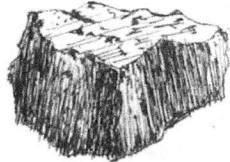

## Concept of Distant Element:

**It is usually visually pleasing to indicate something in the distance over horizon line. A distant tree line is the easiest but mountains and hills are also good choices.**

A distant tree line can be draw as a
undulating pattern of vertical lines

Smaller size of distant tree
line indicates it is further
out than one on left

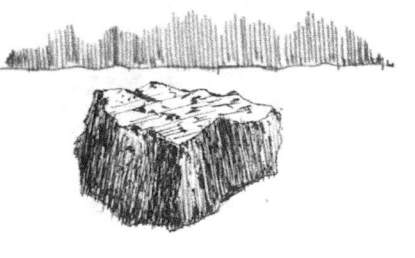

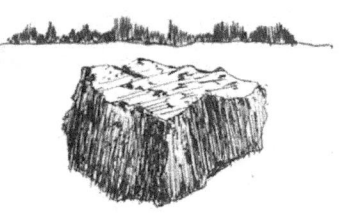

Adding a distant element
provides a place for our eyes to
rest as we view the drawing and
makes it more pleasing

The size of distant element
indicates how far we are seeing.
Smaller size of distant tree line here
indicates it is further out than one
on left

## Concept of Size Proportion:

**Our mind is used to certain sizes of different elements and they should be drawn in proportion to each other for it to be accepted and seen correct.**

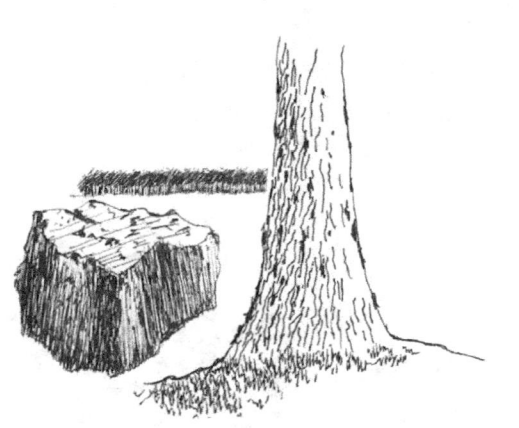

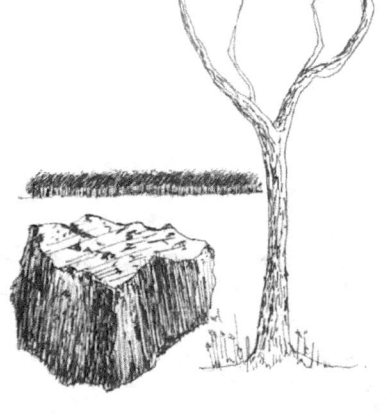

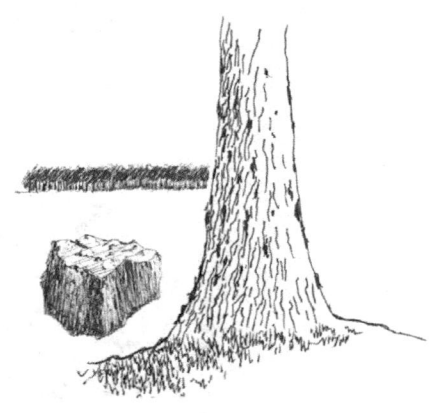

**Wrong**

**Right**

**Right**

Stone is seen as too big in relation to a mature trunk

Compared to a young tree, which is smaller in size, same size of stone conveys the right feel.

Making the stone smaller compared to a mature trunk gives the right feel/

**There is no rule for relative sizes. Just make sure that the drawing feels right.**

## Landscapes with Stones, Some Simple Examples:

Due to their size, stones are usually used in the foreground. Simple pleasing landscapes with stone consists of few stones along with other foreground elements like a wooden post or a trunk, with a backdrop of sky and a distant element along with a mountain or a hill.

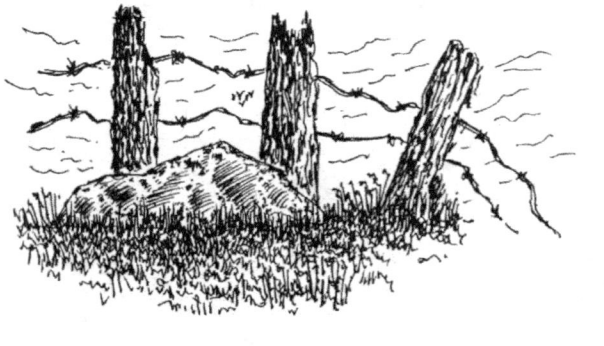

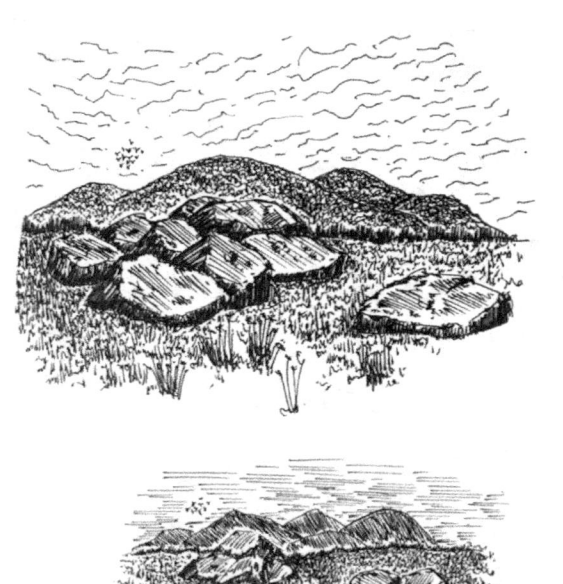

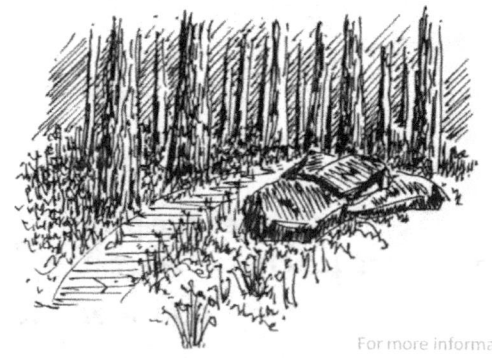

## Landscapes with Stones, Some More Examples:

Drawing other elements like wooden posts, trunks, water, mountains etc. are covered in other volumes in the series. I encourage you to consult them as well. Once you learn how to draw these different elements, you will then be able to easily combine them to create simple pleasing landscapes as shown here from your imagination.

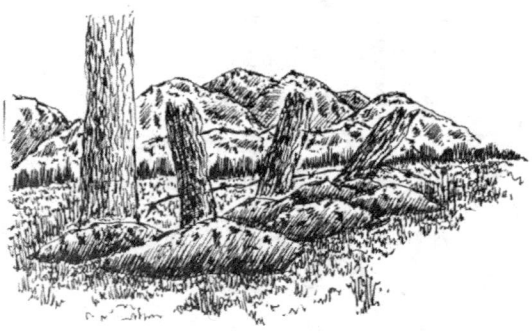

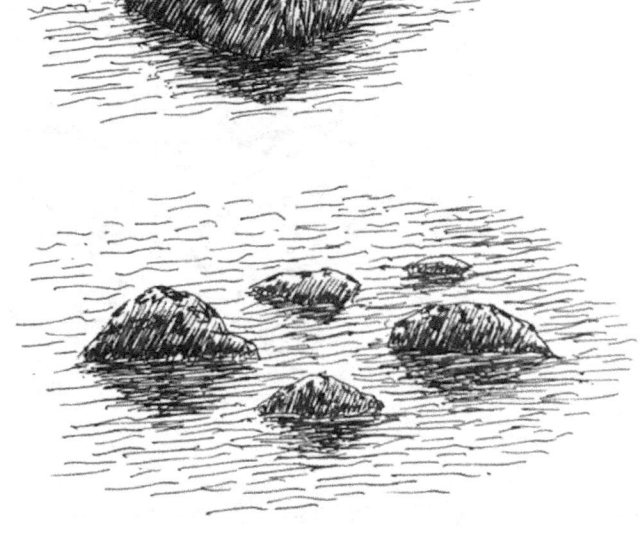

**Pl. visit www.pendrawings.me/workbooks for more information on other volumes**

**Step by Step Landscape drawing is discussed in detail later.**

Here is a drawing in which I have added other elements behind the group of stones drawn earlier. We will learn how to draw pine trees later. Drawing trunks and trees is discussed in detail in vol 1-2 of the workbooks in the series (**www.pendrawings.me/workbooks**).

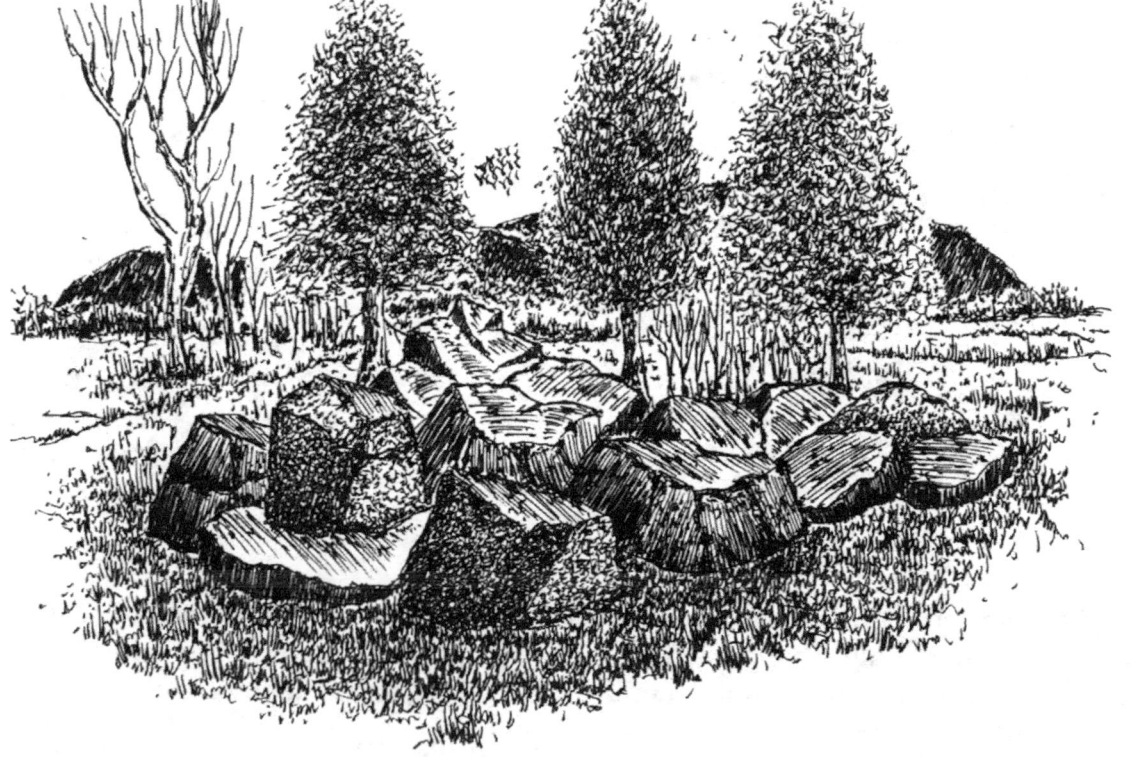

In this drawing I have added a wooded area behind a wooden wall. Such wooded areas are a great backdrop to big stones and walls in front. To learn more about drawing wooded area, pl. consult vol 5 of the workbook in the series (www.pendrawings.me/workbooks). Drawing such stone walls is discussed later.

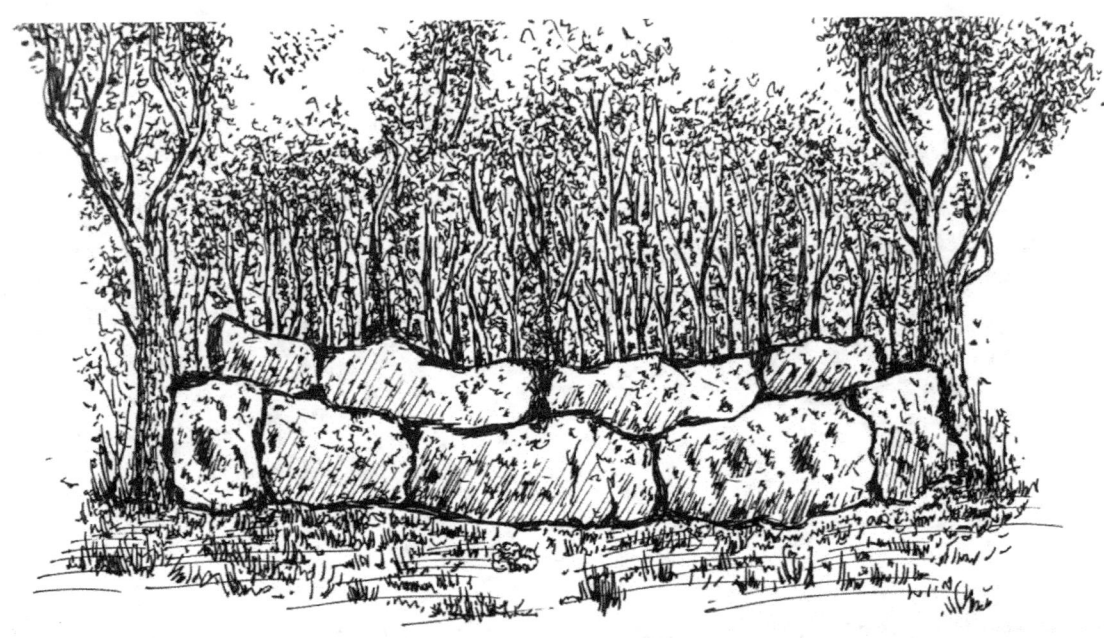

Yet another example of use of stone wall in front with a wooded backdrop. Water reflecting group of stones is also a fun composition. There is no limit to such drawings that you can do from your imagination.

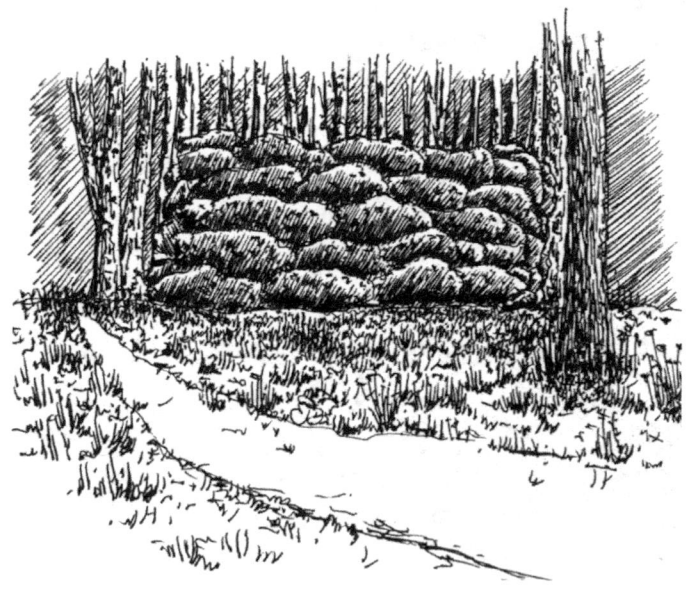

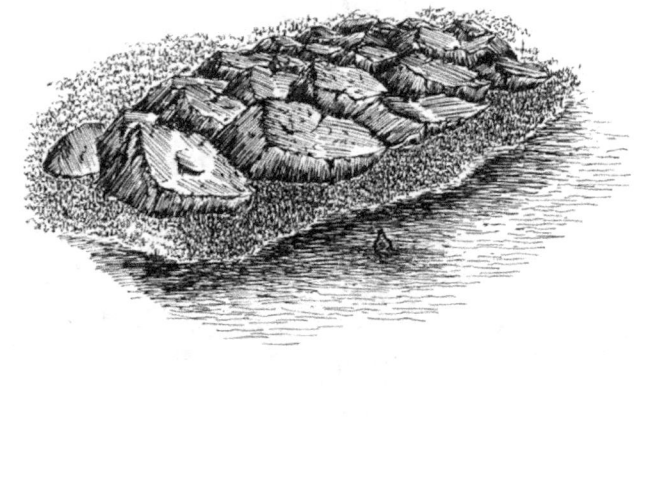

# Importance of Leaving White:

It s very important to leave some white between different elements, like between stones and hill below, to maintain visual separation between them. In the absence of color, white provides the visual separation.

**Notice a sliver of white between stones and hill. This helps to maintain visual separation between them and make the drawing more appealing**

**Loss of visual separation is often un appealing**

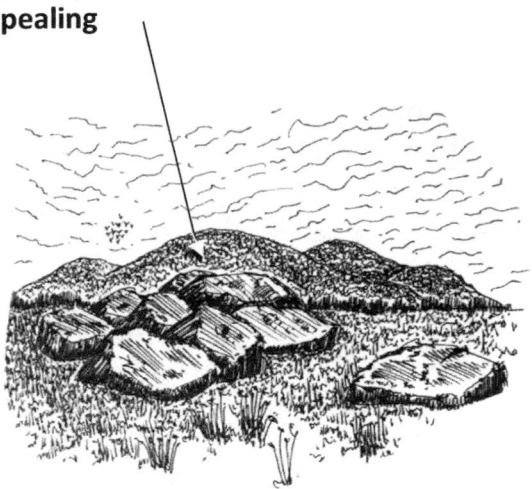 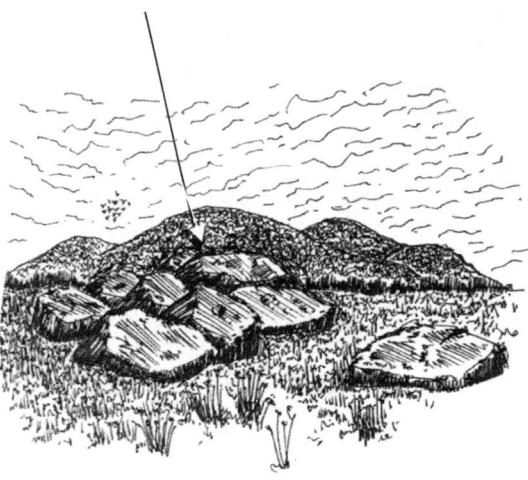

# Drawing a Stone Embankment:

**Stone embankment is a great way to add interest in any drawing and can be done using the same techniques we saw earlier for drawing group of rounded stones.**

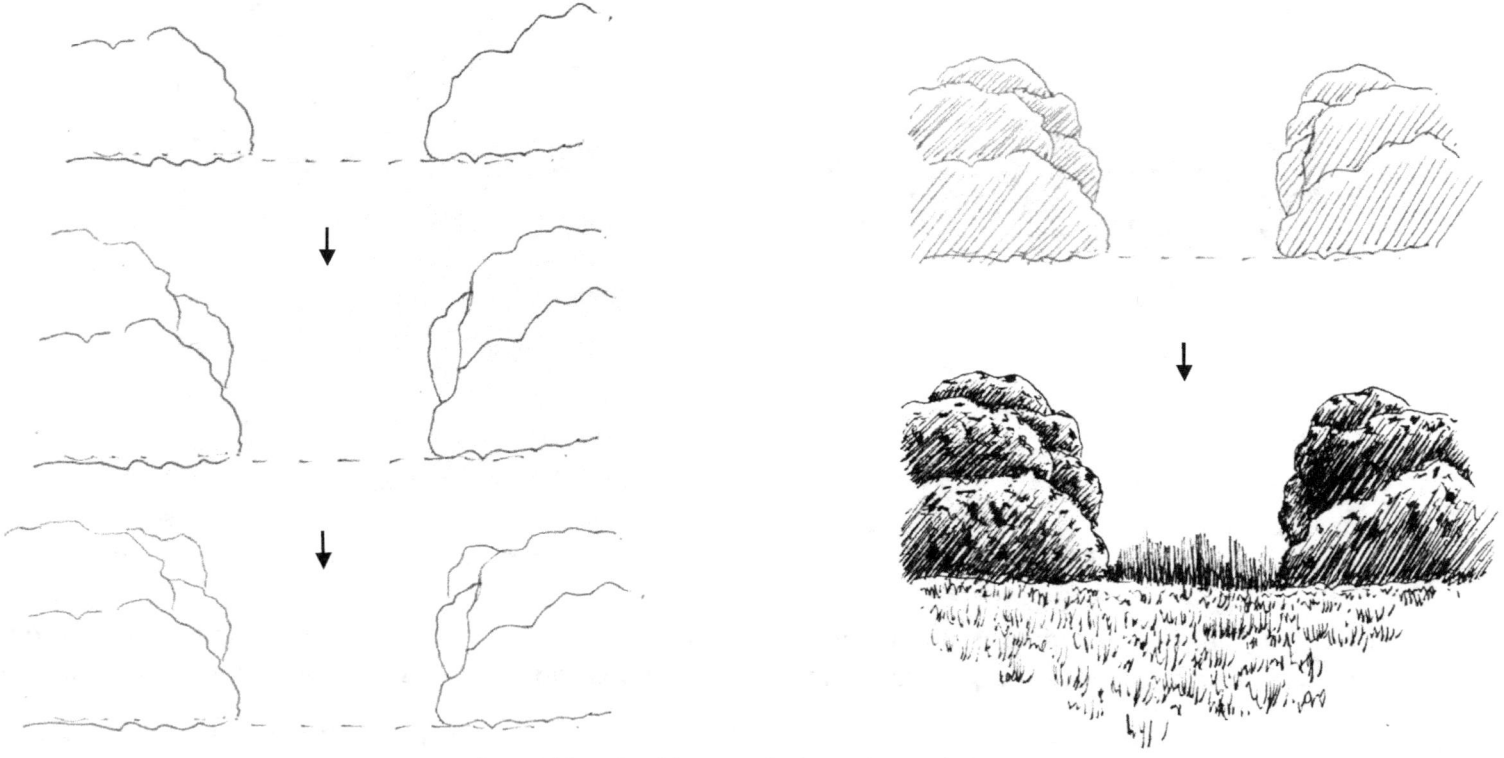

**Activity : Finish the following embankment examples per earlier instructions and texture them.**

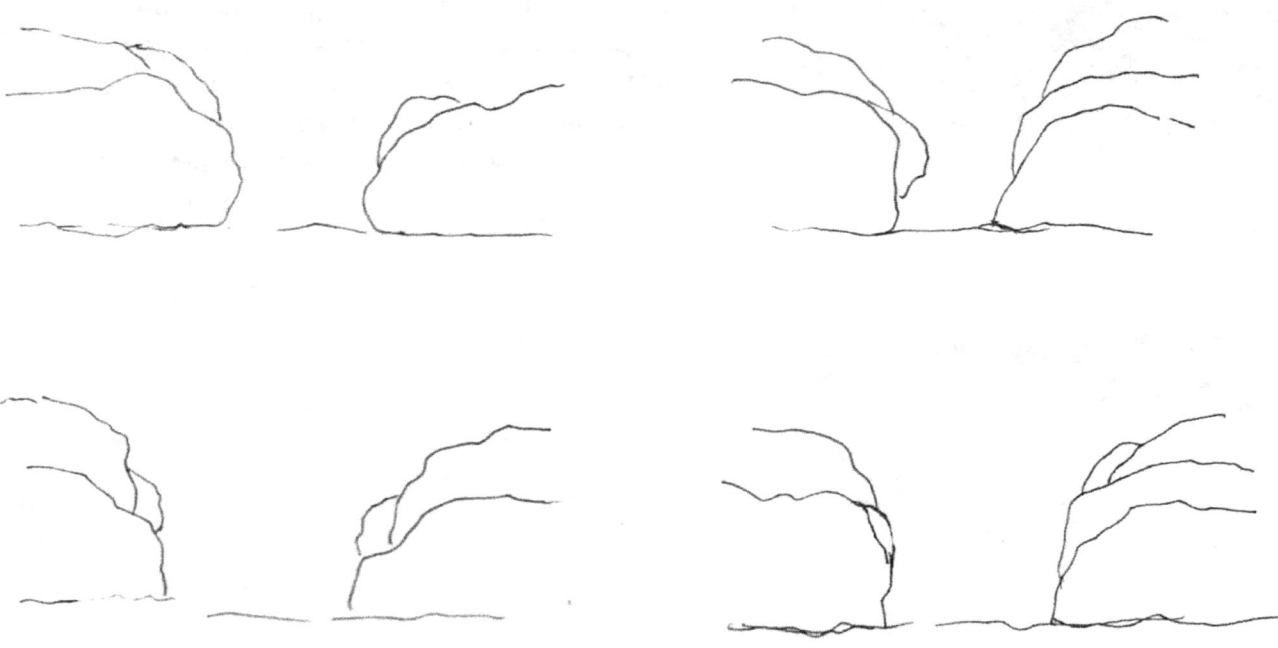

# Drawing a Stone Wall:

A stone wall can be drawn using rounded stones as shown below. Use different sizes to keep it interesting. To indicate depth, add smaller receding stones at the end.

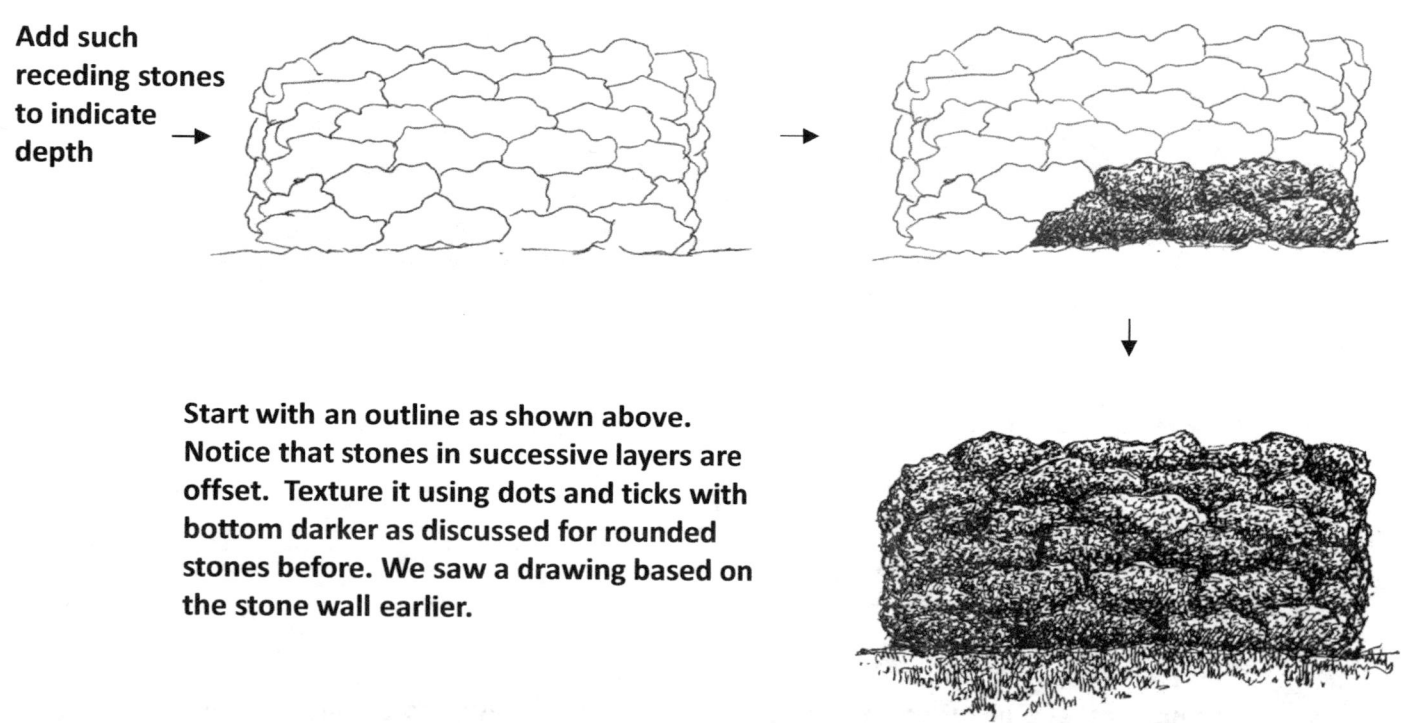

Add such receding stones to indicate depth →

Start with an outline as shown above. Notice that stones in successive layers are offset. Texture it using dots and ticks with bottom darker as discussed for rounded stones before. We saw a drawing based on the stone wall earlier.

**Activity : Texture the following stone wall outlines per earlier instructions. Draw one of your own.**

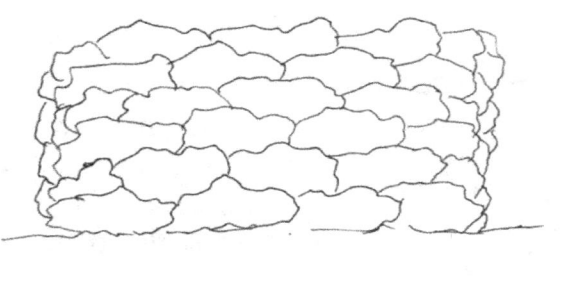

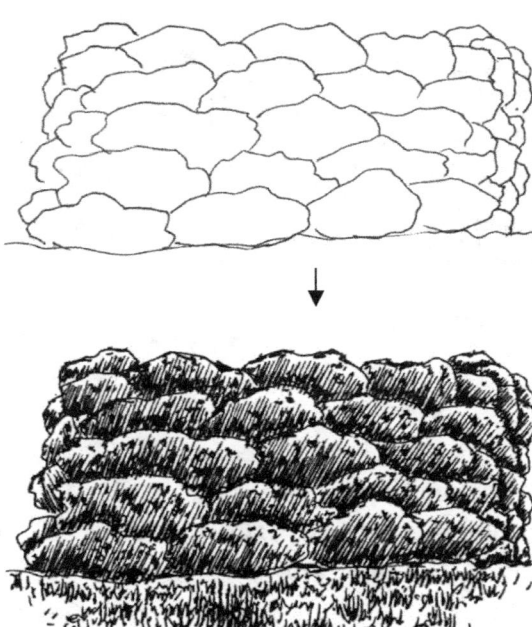

**Stone wall textured with parallel lines.**

## Drawing a Stone Wall, Another Approach:

Size of stones used gives a different feel to stone wall. Use of small stones gives a feel of stone wall used as a fence etc. as in previous example. With bigger stones, it feels heavier and comes across as a retaining wall.

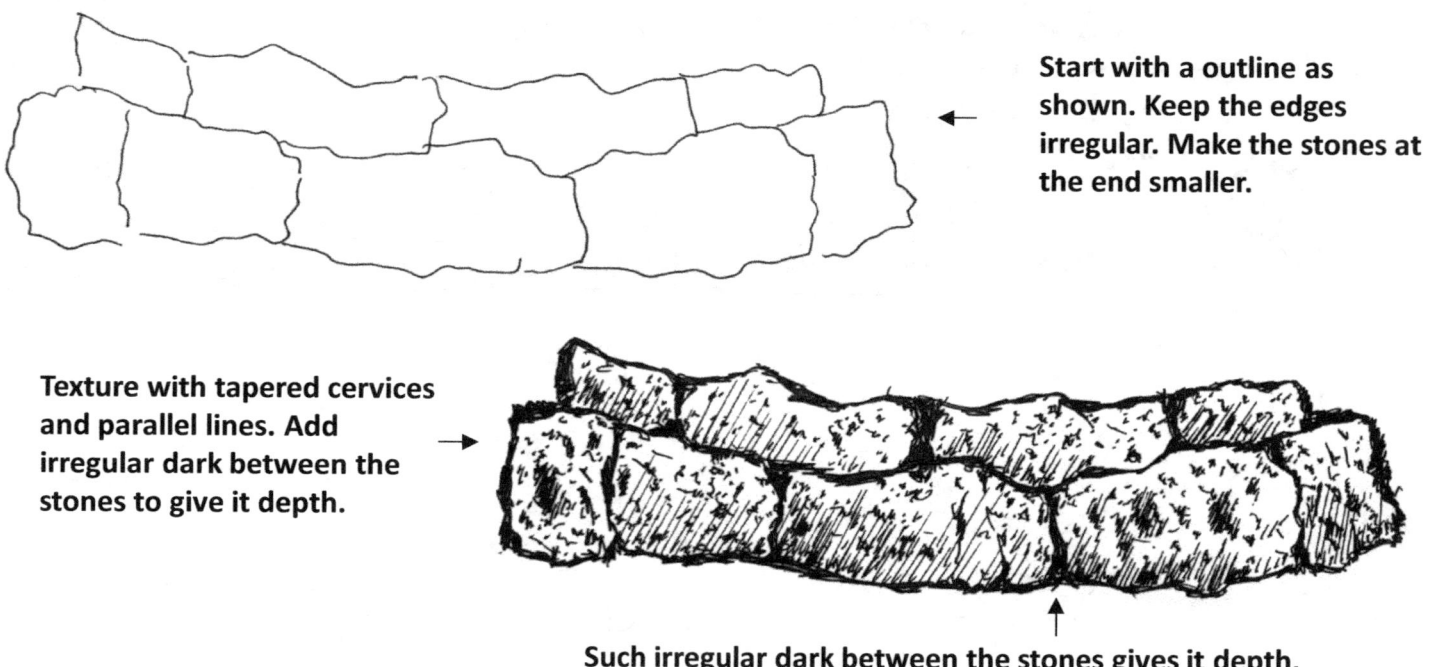

Start with a outline as shown. Keep the edges irregular. Make the stones at the end smaller.

Texture with tapered cervices and parallel lines. Add irregular dark between the stones to give it depth.

Such irregular dark between the stones gives it depth. Make sure to keep them irregular.

**Activity : Texture the following stone wall outline per earlier instructions. Draw one of your own.**

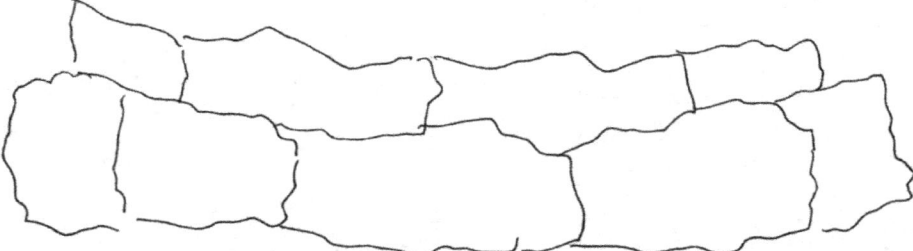

# Drawing Ground Cover:

Almost all landscapes need some ground cover. Grass and wild flowers are very easy to draw and provide a great way to add interest in any drawing. Ground cover is drawn from horizon line to the foreground

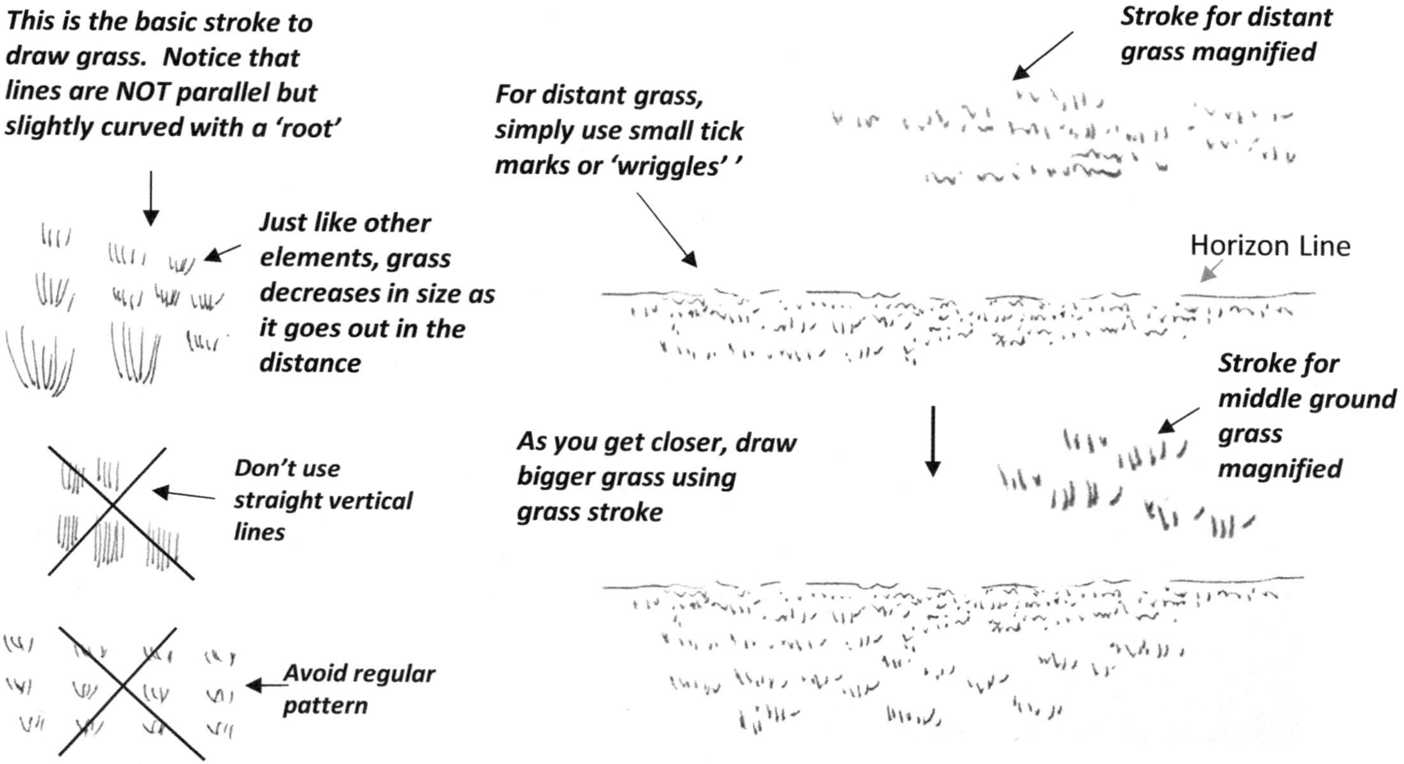

*This is the basic stroke to draw grass.  Notice that lines are NOT parallel but slightly curved with a 'root'*

*Stroke for distant grass magnified*

*For distant grass, simply use small tick marks or 'wriggles' '*

*Just like other elements, grass decreases in size as it goes out in the distance*

Horizon Line

*Stroke for middle ground grass magnified*

*Don't use straight vertical lines*

*As you get closer, draw bigger grass using grass stroke*

*Avoid regular pattern*

# Drawing Ground Cover Continued:

Continued from previous page.

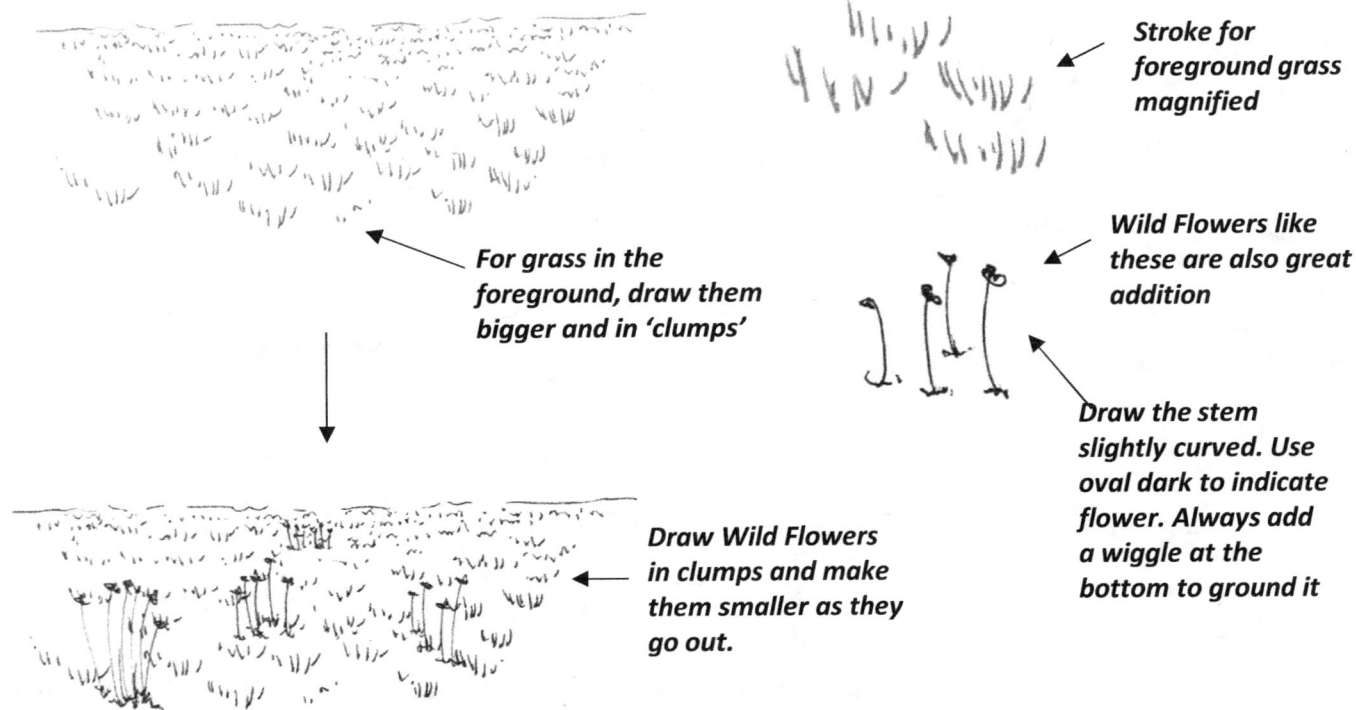

Stroke for foreground grass magnified

For grass in the foreground, draw them bigger and in 'clumps'

Wild Flowers like these are also great addition

Draw the stem slightly curved. Use oval dark to indicate flower. Always add a wiggle at the bottom to ground it

Draw Wild Flowers in clumps and make them smaller as they go out.

## Relative Intensity of Ground Cover:

Just some grass stroke is enough to give a feel of ground cover. Often explicit covering of all ground with grass is not needed. But more density of grass can be used to create different feel if needed.

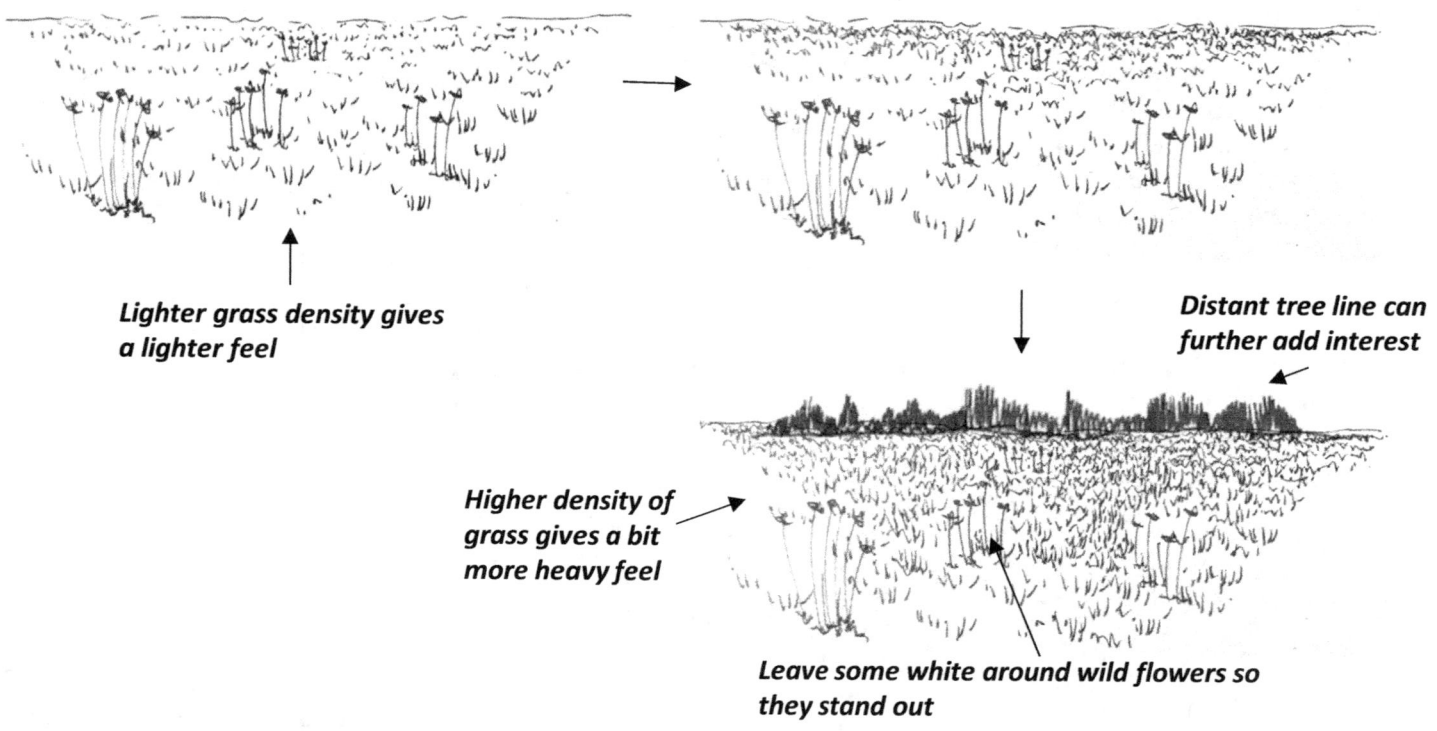

*Lighter grass density gives a lighter feel*

*Higher density of grass gives a bit more heavy feel*

*Distant tree line can further add interest*

*Leave some white around wild flowers so they stand out*

## Activity: Drawing ground cover:

**Draw grass and a distant element per earlier instructions below. Draw ground cover for earlier activities as well.**

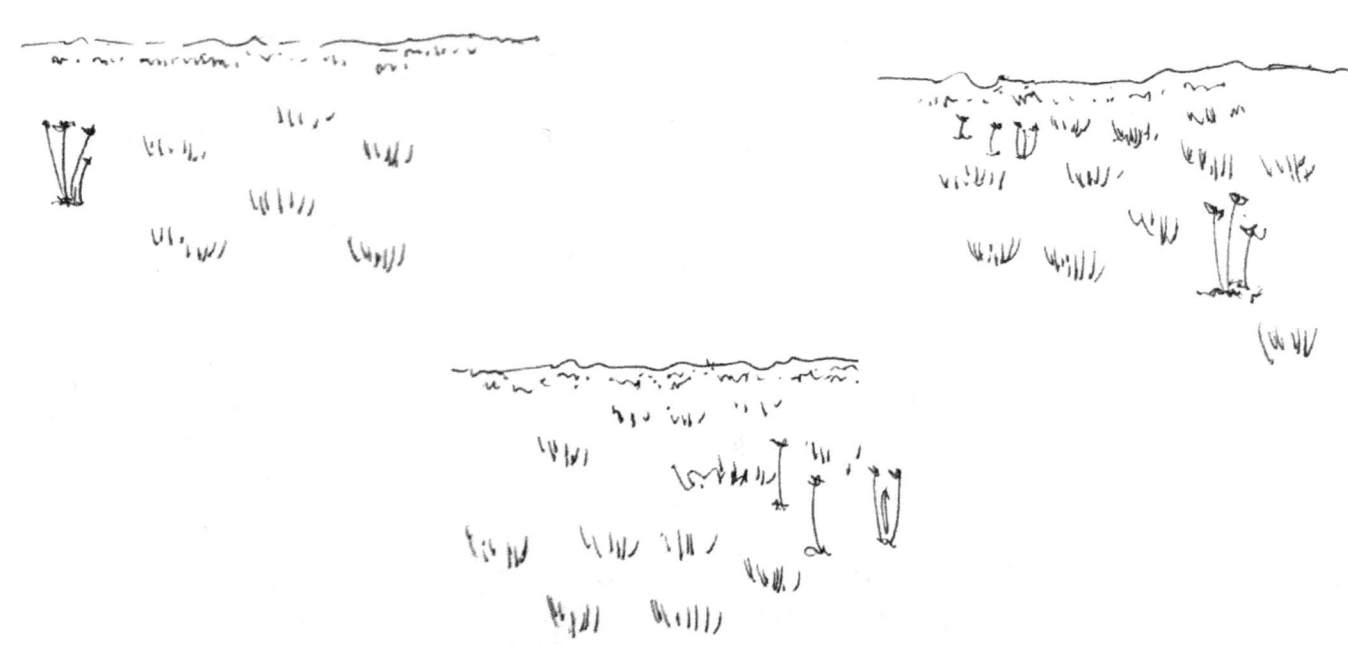

## Drawing Sky and Clouds:

We next look at how to draw sky and clouds. Clouds are thought to be tricky to draw with pen and ink, but in following pages, you will see that with right pen stroke, they are actually quite easy to draw.

The main thing to keep in mind when drawing clouds is NEVER to use a hard line. The main characteristic of clouds is their lightness and softness and a hard line conveys the opposite feeling.

Use of a broken wavering line conveys openness and softness and is ideal to convey a feel of cloud.

There are many ways to draw sky and clouds and few different techniques are presented here. For more techniques and tips, please visit www.pendrawings.me/morecontent

# How to Draw Sky and Clouds:

**There are many ways to draw sky and clouds and some techniques are presented below. Each technique gives a different feel and is appropriate for different settings.**

**Start by drawing bigger cloud strokes in the top of sky.** →

Horizon

↑

**Technique 1: Cloud Stroke used. These broken 'wandering' lines gives a feel of clouds**

**Add smaller strokes closer to horizon. Avoid any regular pattern** →

**For more techniques, pl. visit www.pendrawings.me/morecontent.**

**Add more strokes to bring out the desired feel** →

# How to Draw Sky and Clouds, Technique 1, Additional Examples:

Following are some more examples of using this technique. It is a very versatile technique and by changing size, orientation and density of these lines, different feel for sky can be obtained.

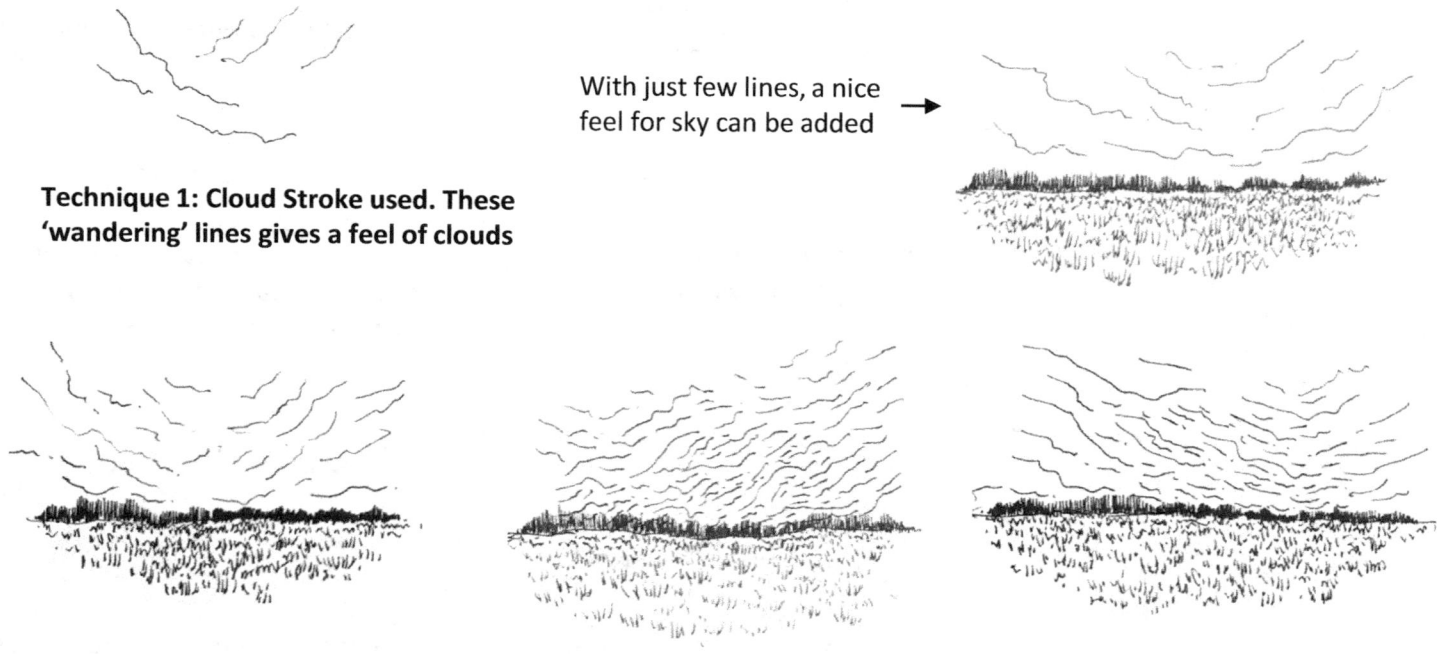

**Technique 1: Cloud Stroke used. These 'wandering' lines gives a feel of clouds**

With just few lines, a nice feel for sky can be added →

# How to Draw Sky and Clouds, Technique 1, Additional Examples:

**Flow of lines in this technique can be used very effectively to create interesting cloud formations. Below are 2 examples where the flow of lines adds energy and dynamism to the drawing.**

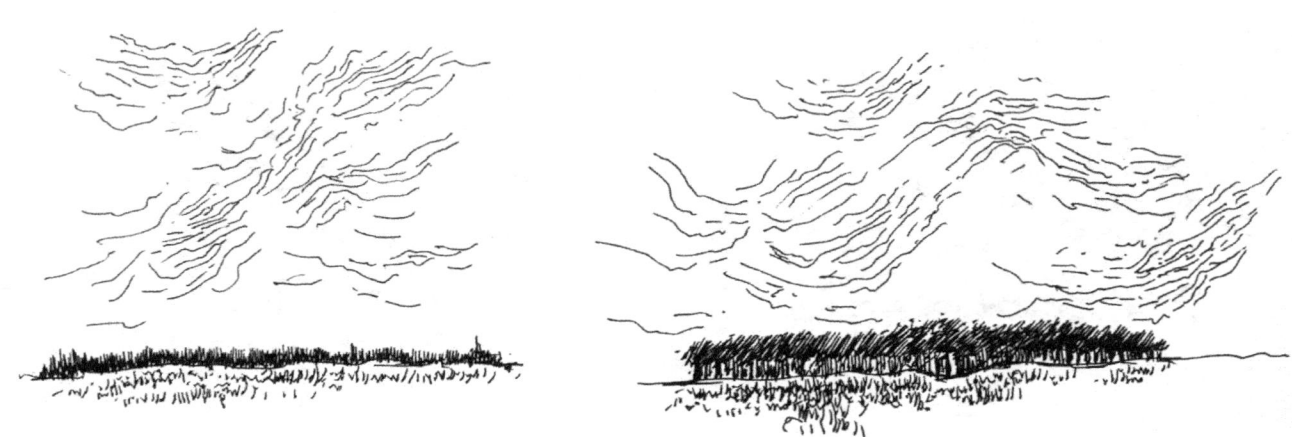

## Using Intensity of Lines to create Mood:

Darker clouds and Sky usually imply and create a more foreboding mood. Intensity of lines can be adjusted to bring out the desired feel. In 2 earlier drawings, I have added more intensity below to create a heaver mood.

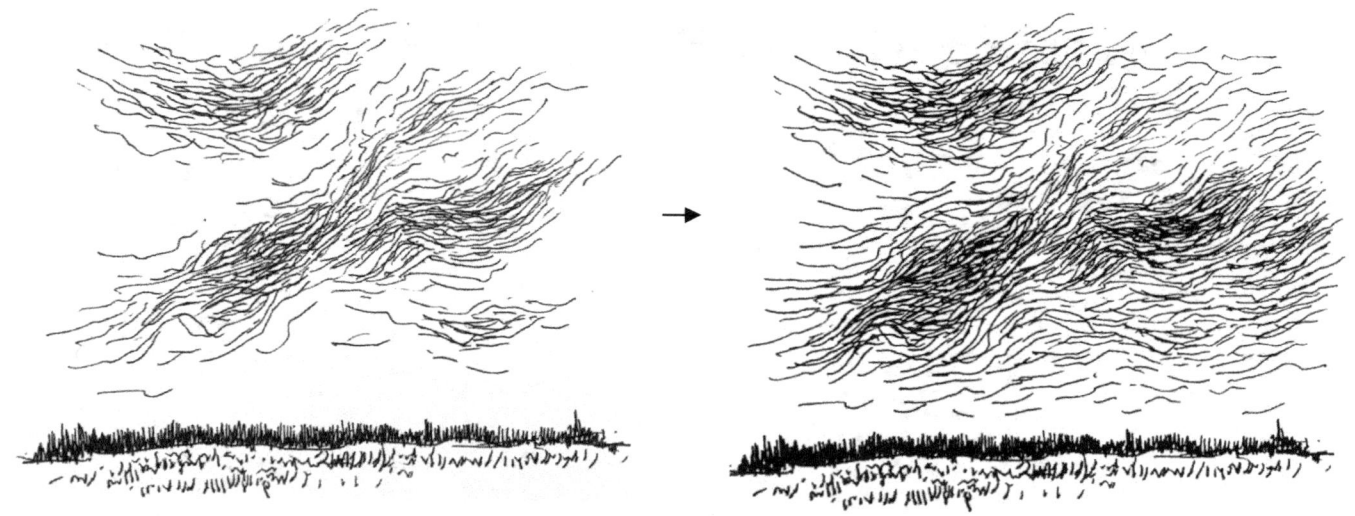

## Drawing Nightscapes:

This technique is ideally suited for drawing a night sky. Drawing night sky and nightscapes is fully covered in vol. 7 of my pen and ink drawing workbook series (www.pendrawings.me/workbooks). Please consult that volume for more detailed explanation on drawing a night sky.

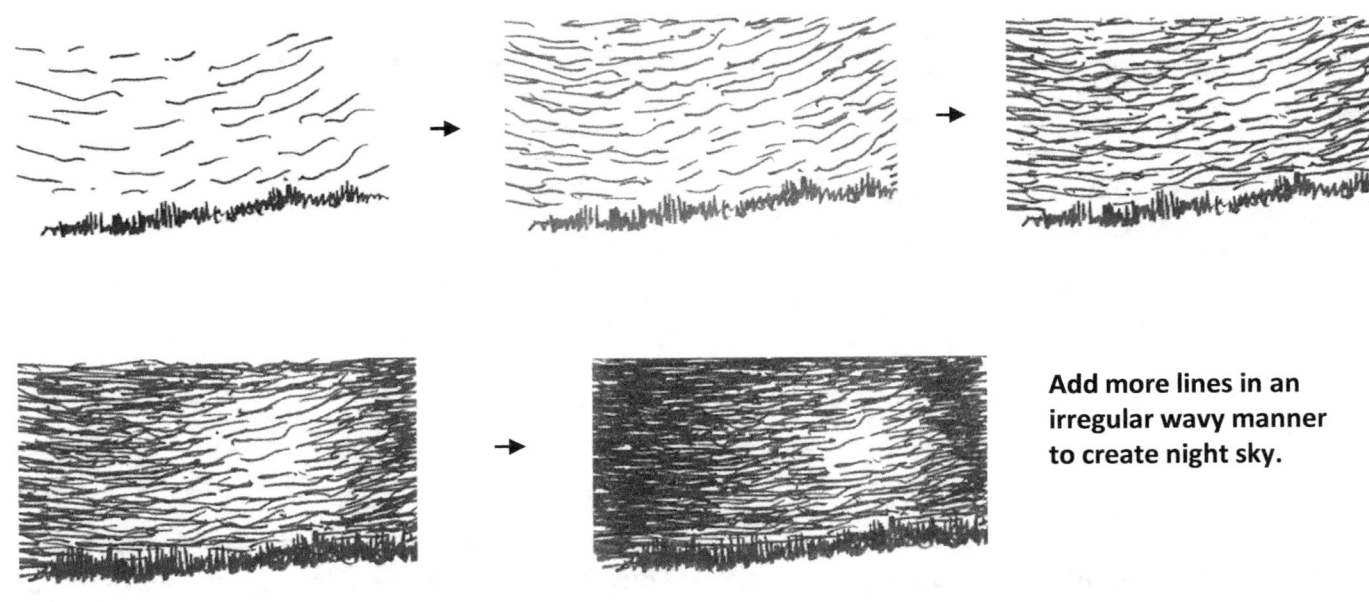

Add more lines in an irregular wavy manner to create night sky.

## Combining Lines with Dots and Dash:

Dots and dash can also be used along with line as shown below. This brings out still more mellow feel. Density of stroke can be changed to bring out the desired feel as in the second drawing.

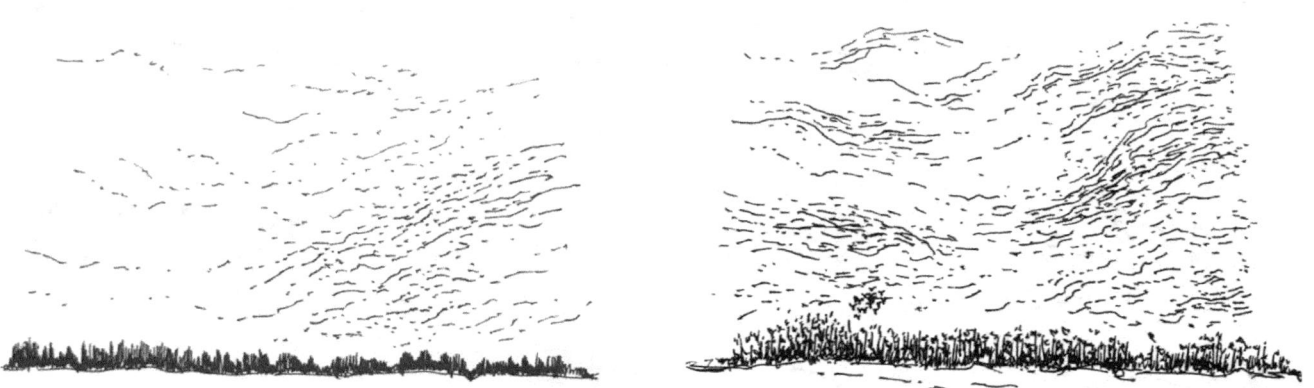

Use of dots and dash along with line give more gentle feel. By changing the density of strokes, intensity and feel of sky can be controlled.

**Activity: Practice drawing sky and clouds per earlier instructions. Vary the intensity to set different moods.**

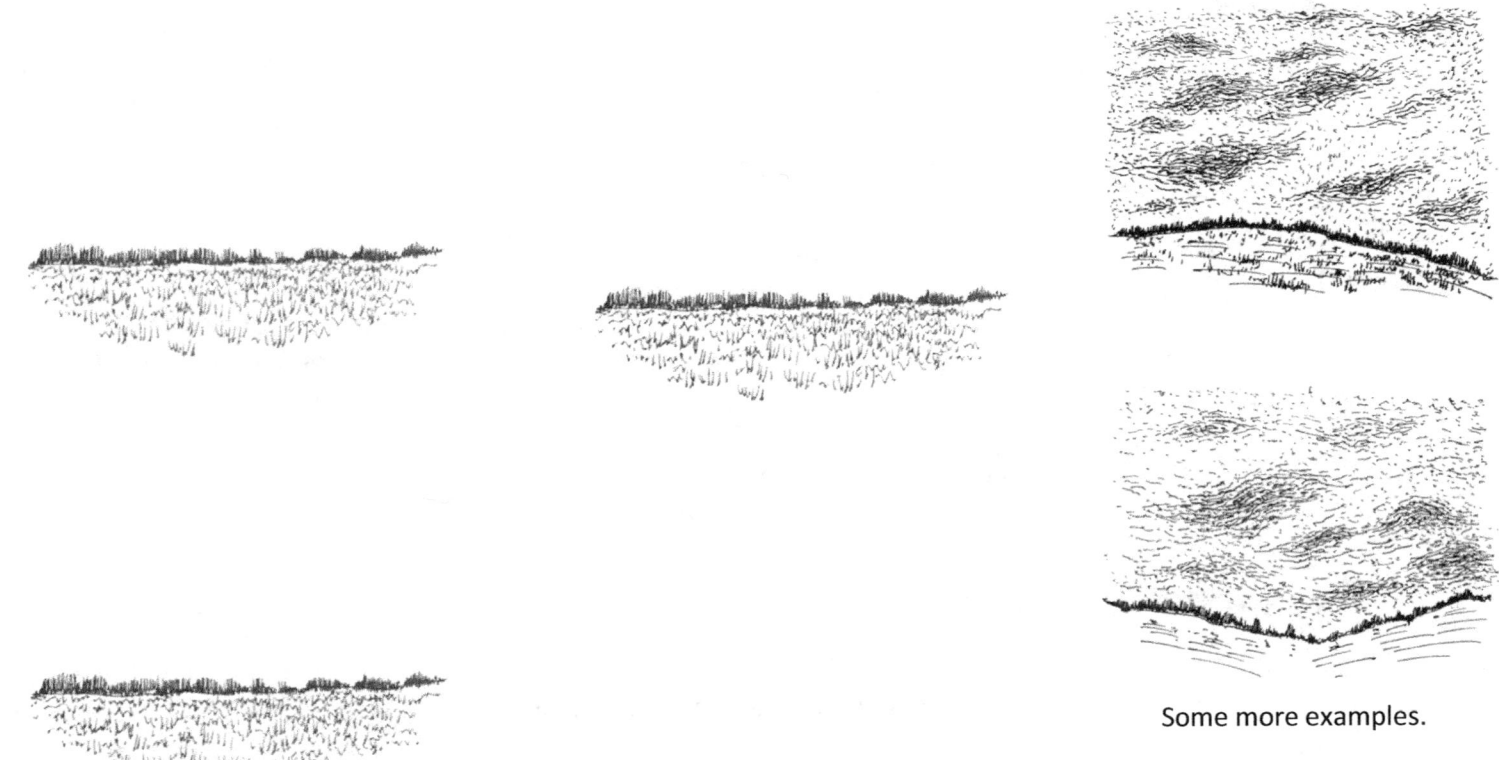

Some more examples.

# How to Draw Sky and Clouds, Technique 2:

**In this technique, explicit outline of clouds is drawn using 'broken' lines.**

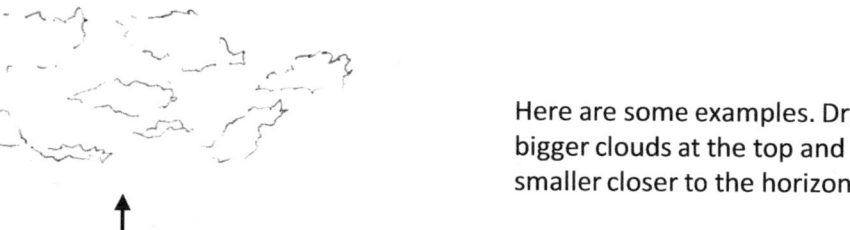

**Technique 2: Cloud outline using broken lines.**

Here are some examples. Draw bigger clouds at the top and smaller closer to the horizon.

Cloud lines from previous technique can be used as well, especially for small clouds closer to horizon

**For more techniques, pl. visit www.pendrawings.me/morecontent.**

## How to Draw Sky and Clouds, Technique 2, Continued:

**Dots and ticks can be used to fill the outline as well to create a different feel. Darken one side of cloud more as shown below to bring out the form of cloud.**

Use different sizes of clouds
with pleasing distribution

Darken one side to
bring out the form.

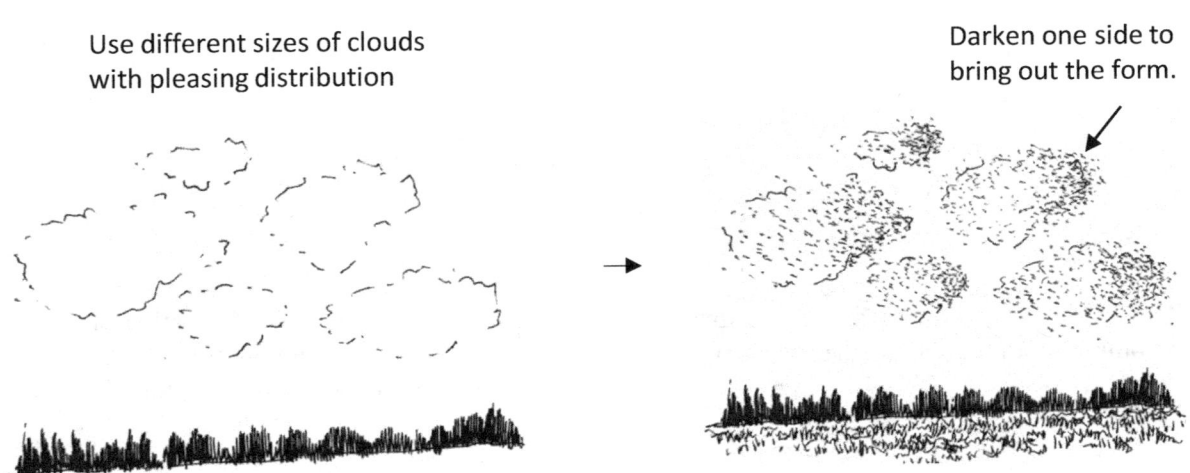

# How to Draw Sky and Clouds, Technique 2, Continued:

Dots and ticks can be used by themselves to indicate clouds as well. Omitting a broken outline creates more mellow feel for the clouds. Different techniques presented here create different feel for the clouds and Sky. Choose the one based on feel you intent to create in your drawing.

Outline for cloud is omitted. This creates a very mellow, fluffy feel for the clouds

Another option is to not use cloud outline but indicate sky in this manner.

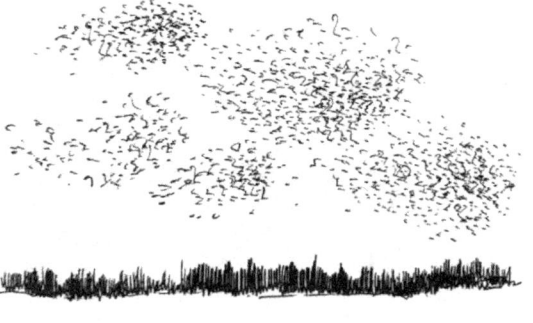

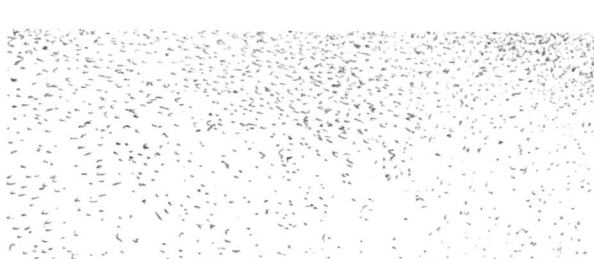

Here is a drawing that uses dots and ticks to draw a gentle back drop of clouds. Notice the use of different sizes and slightly varying tones to add interest to the clouds.

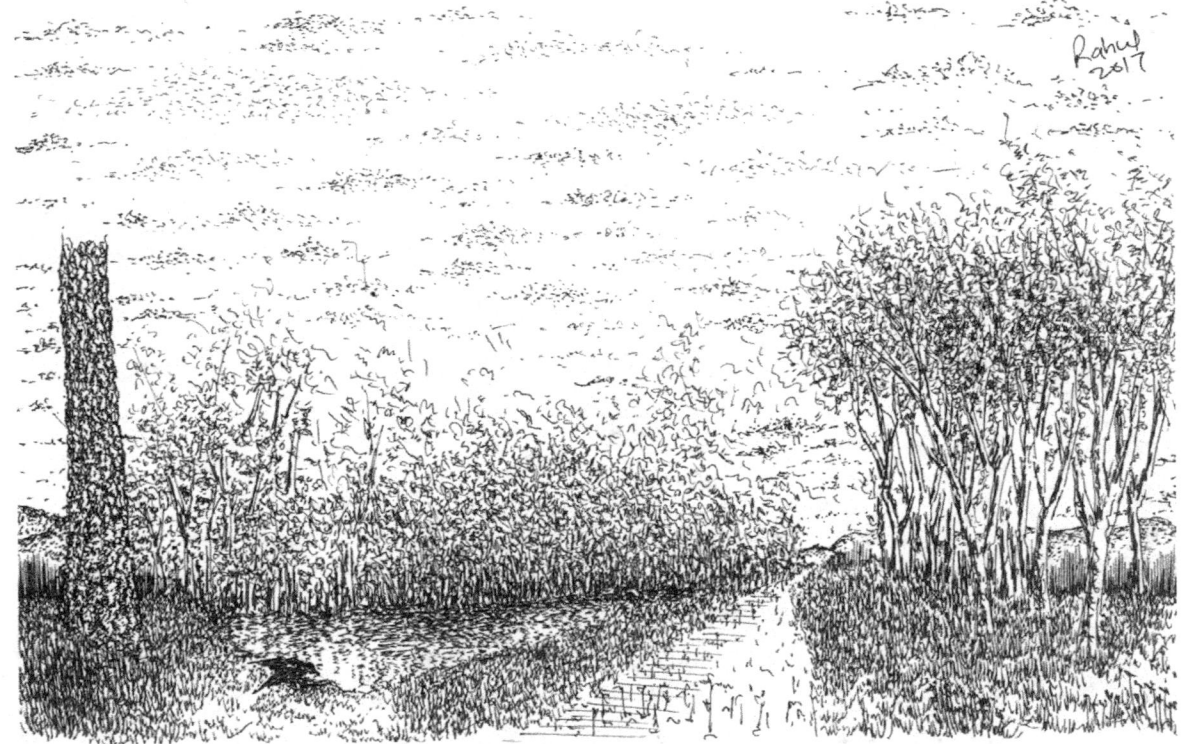

Here is an example of use of dots and ticks to texture sky. I used this technique to create a soft and warm feel against the gentleness of snow. Sky can be textured in limitless ways with this technique.

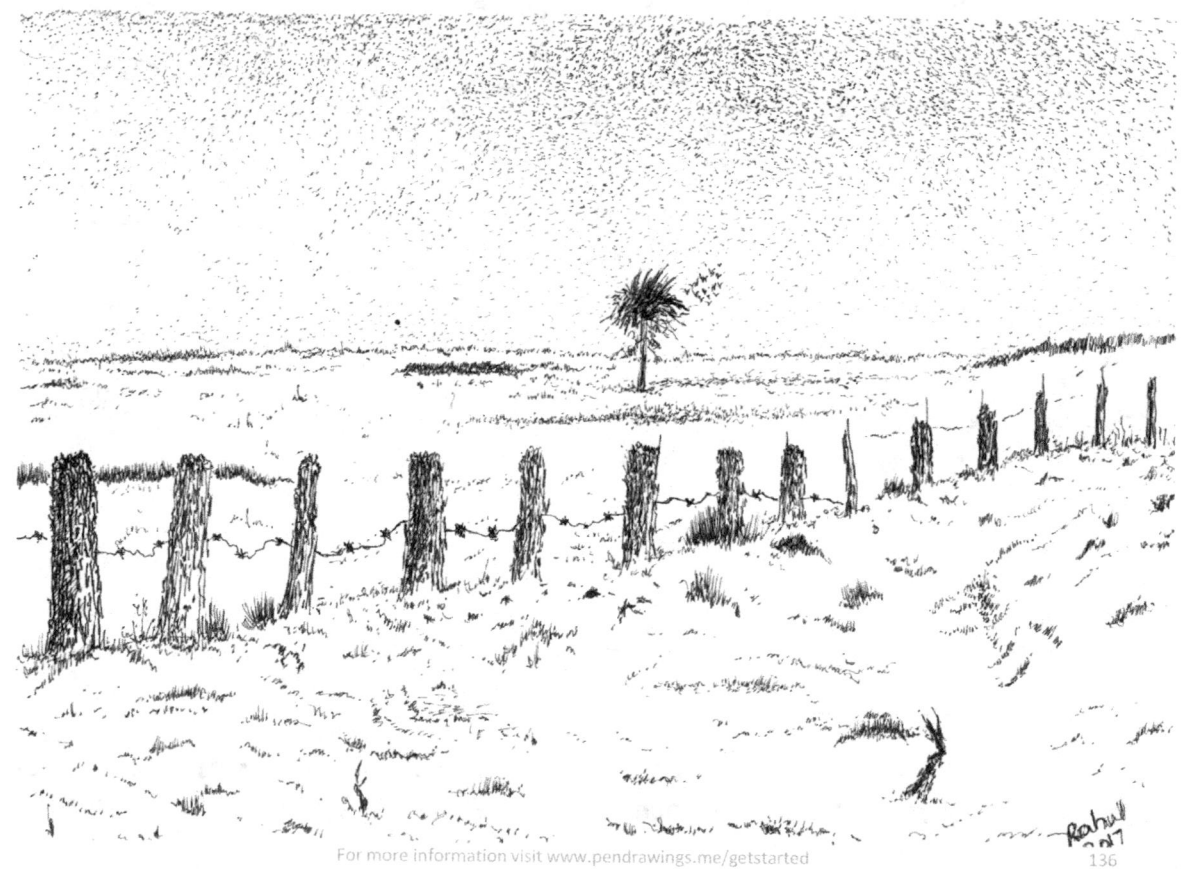

Here is yet another example of use of dots and ticks. Notice that darker tone is usually up with lighter tone towards the horizon.

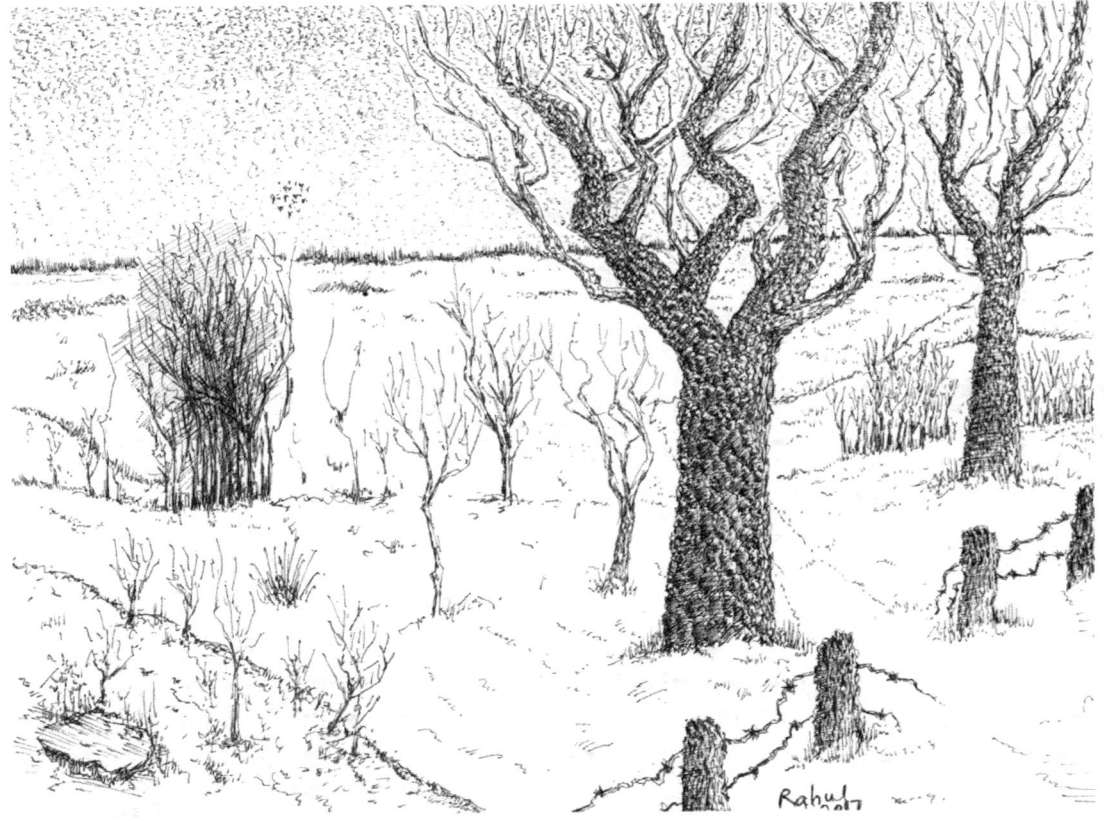

## Drawing Night Sky with Dots and Ticks:

**Different kinds of night sky can be easily done with dots and ticks as well. Drawing night sky and nightscapes is fully covered in vol 7 of my pen and ink drawing workbook series (www.pendrawings.me/workbooks). Please consult that volume for more detailed explanation on drawing a night sky.**

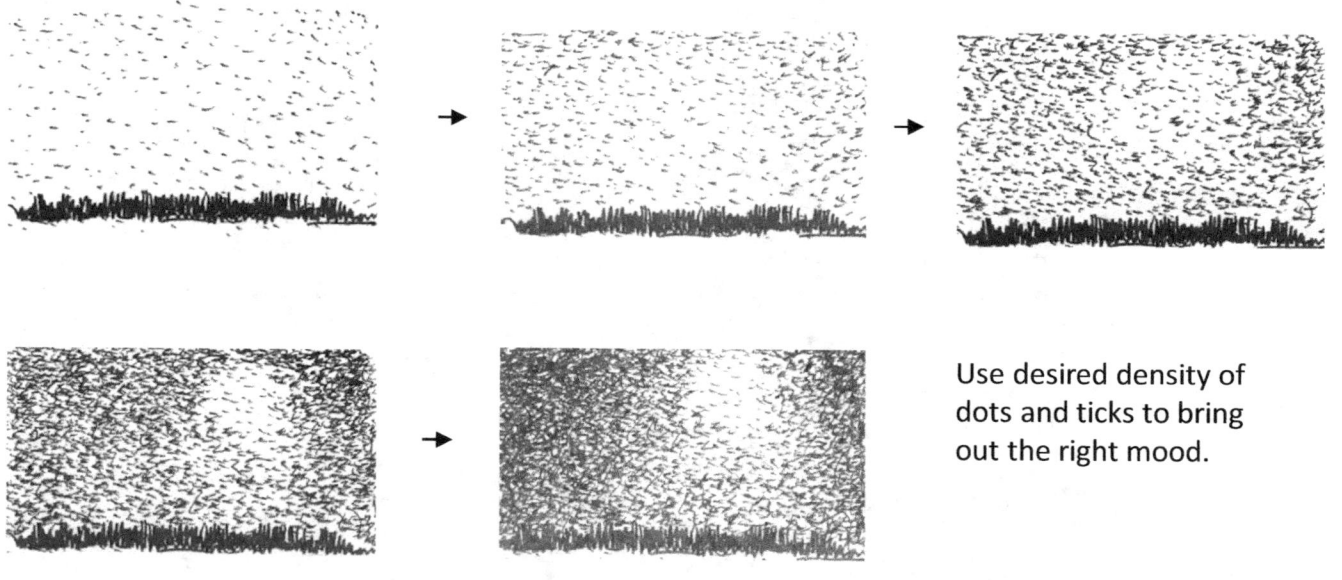

Use desired density of dots and ticks to bring out the right mood.

**Activity: Practice drawing sky and clouds using dots and ticks per earlier instructions. Vary the intensity to set different moods.**

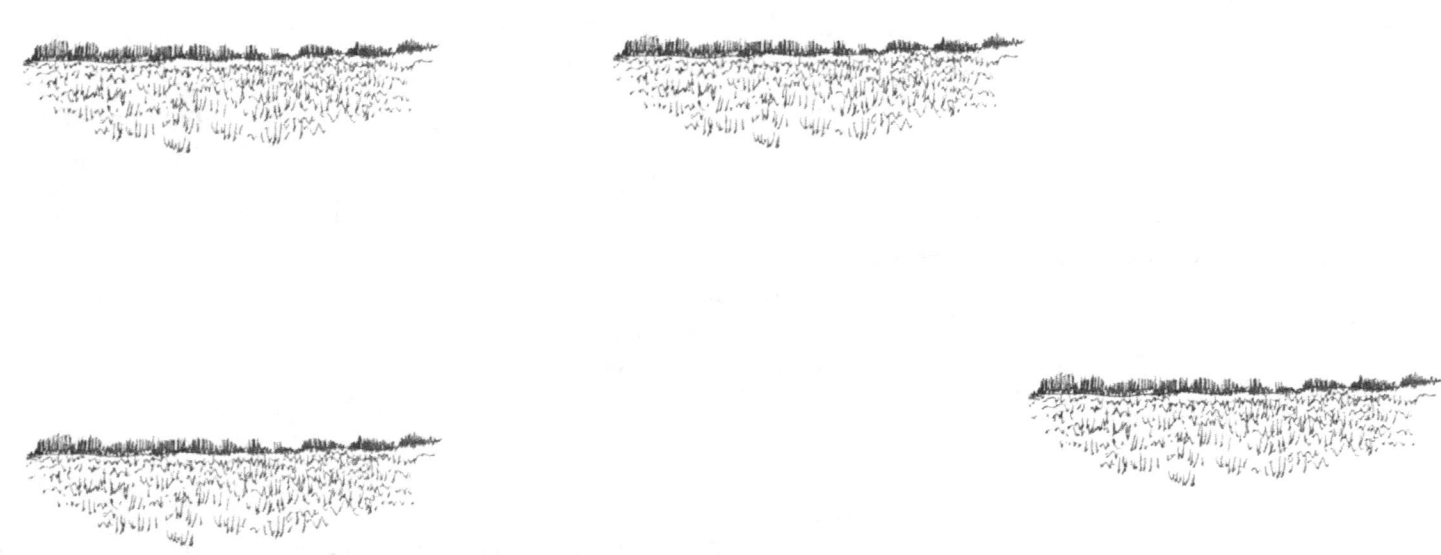

# How to Draw Sky and Clouds, Technique 3:

**In this technique, parallel lines in a wavy manner are used.**

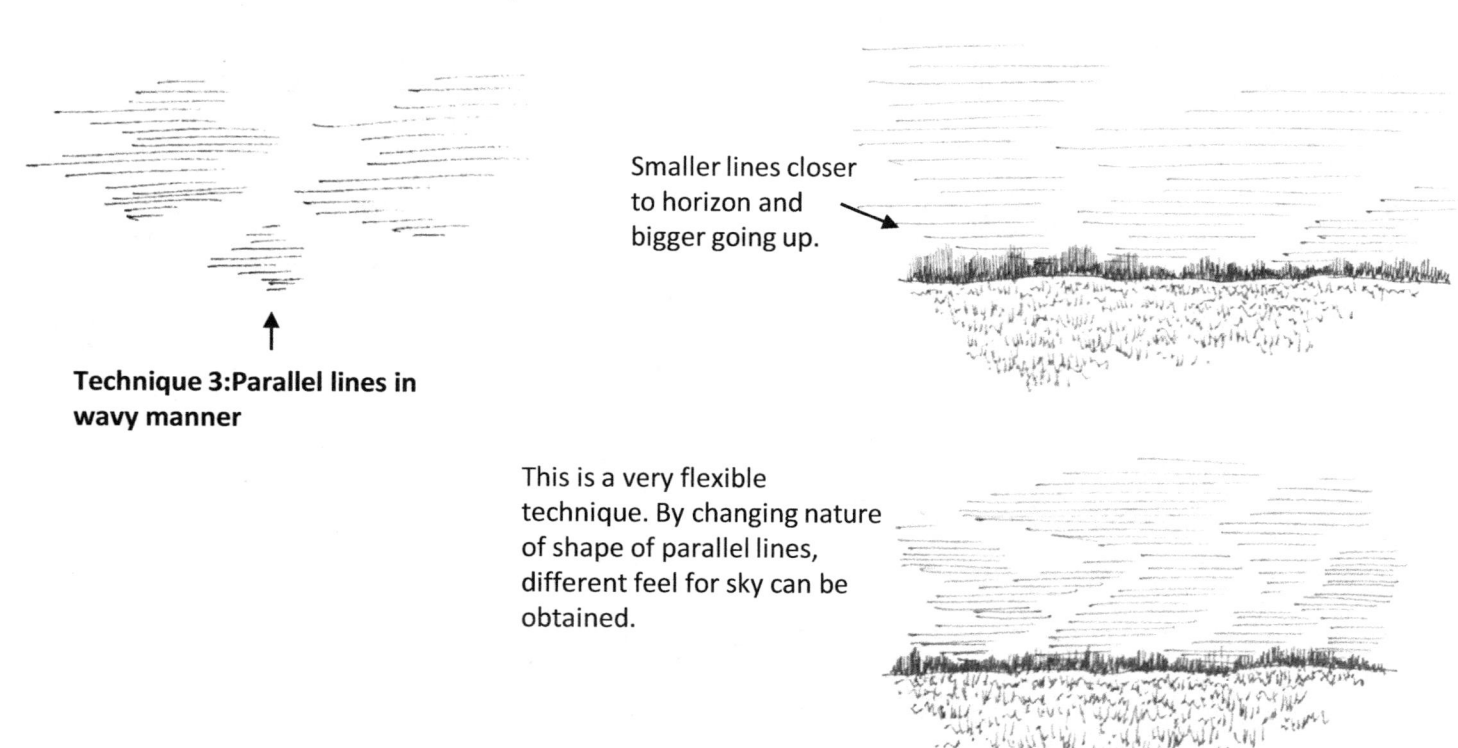

**Technique 3:Parallel lines in wavy manner**

Smaller lines closer to horizon and bigger going up.

This is a very flexible technique. By changing nature of shape of parallel lines, different feel for sky can be obtained.

# How to Draw Sky and Clouds, Technique 3, Additional Examples:

**Following are some additional examples. By using different layout and sizes for these lines, limitless variations can be done to bring out different mood.**

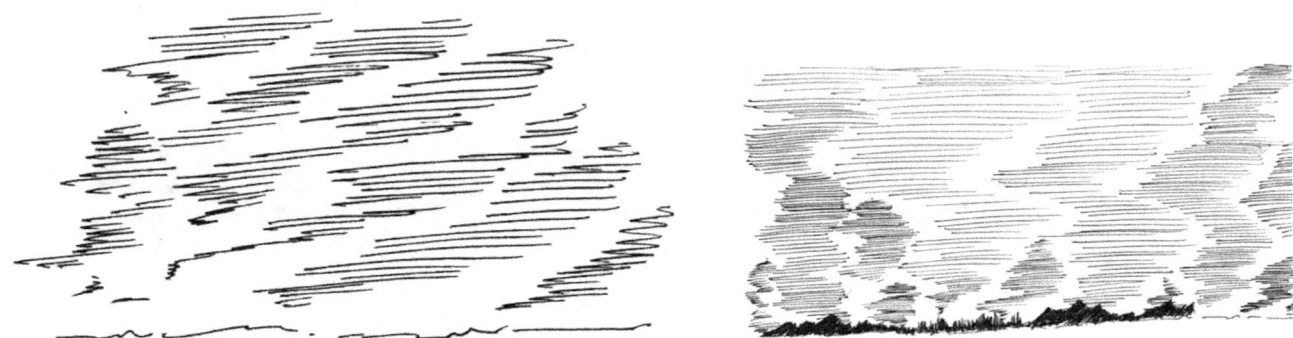

Here is an example of use of technique 3. Notice how the cloud lines directs the viewers attention to horizon. By focusing the attention of viewer to appropriate focal points, this technique can add great visual interest.

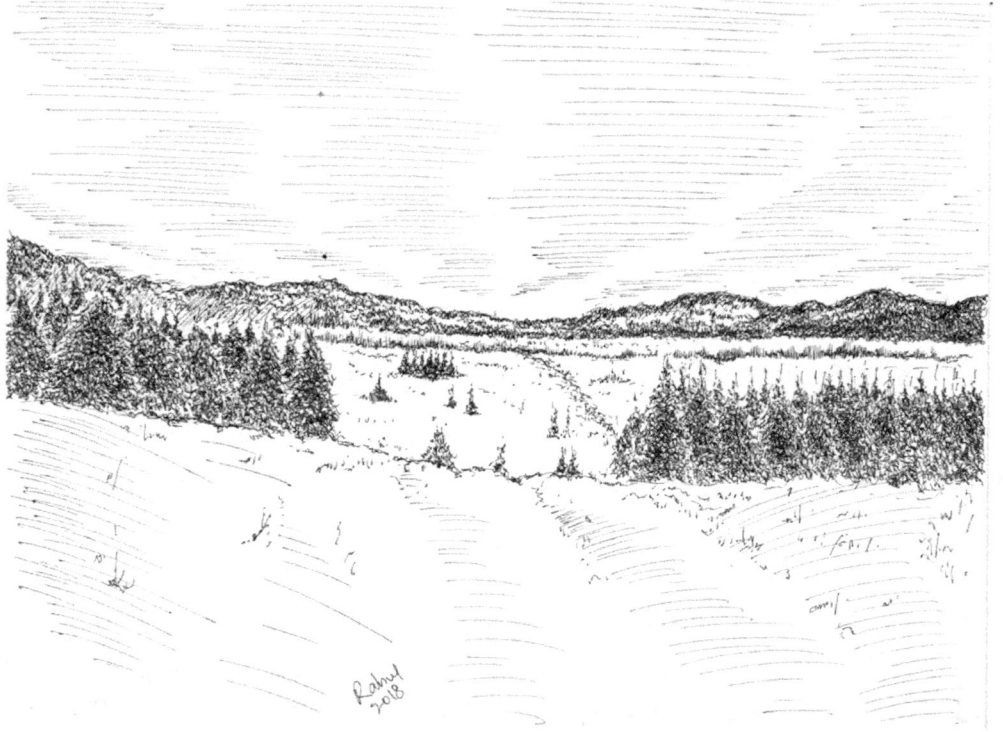

**Another example of use of technique 3. This technique is very useful in establishing a focal point in distant horizon and guiding viewer to it.**

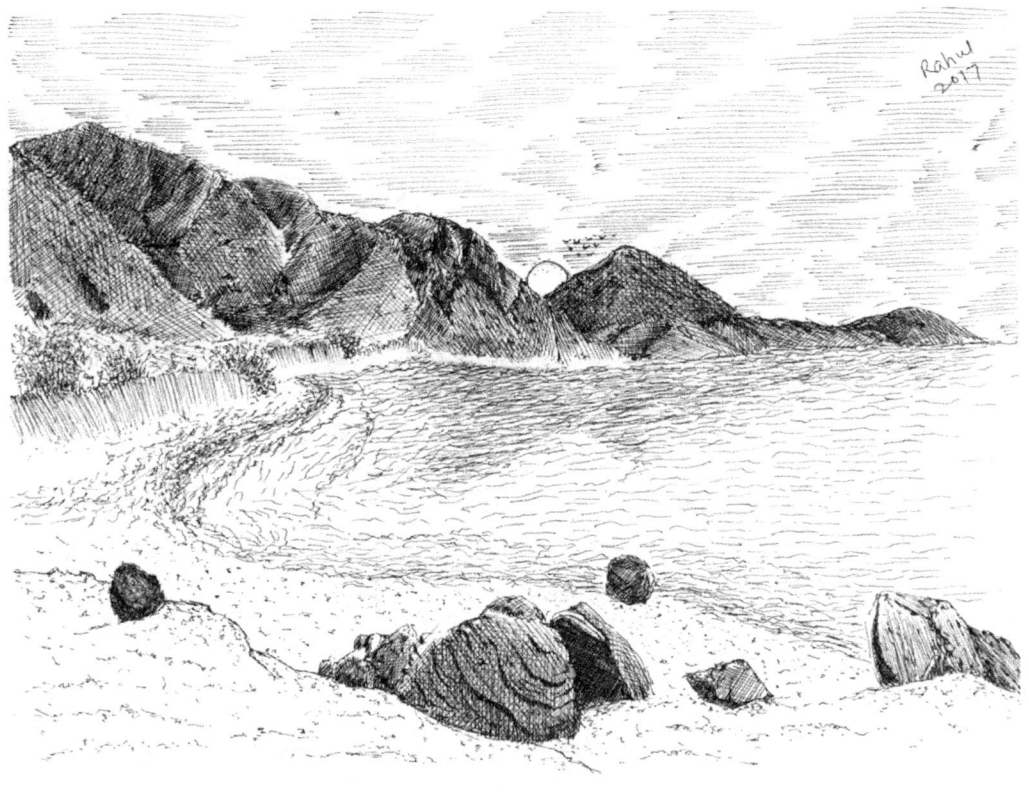

**Yet another example. I use this technique quite a lot in my drawings. For more examples. Pl. visit www.pendrawings.me.**

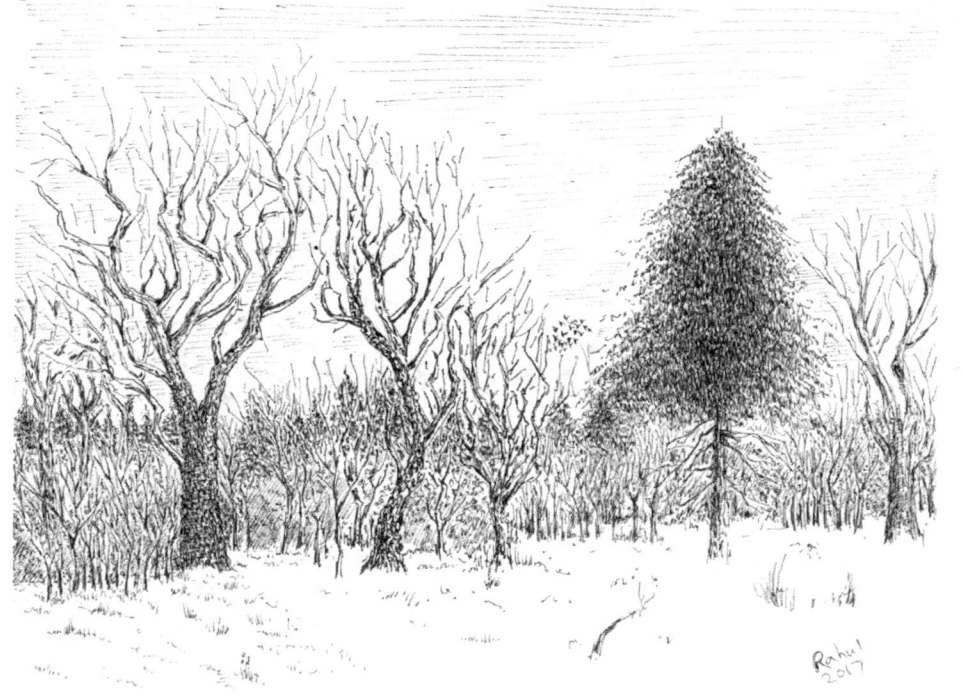

## Using Tone to set Mood:

**By using darker tones for parallel lines, an intense mood can be established. Darker clouds then becomes focal point and draws attention to themselves.**

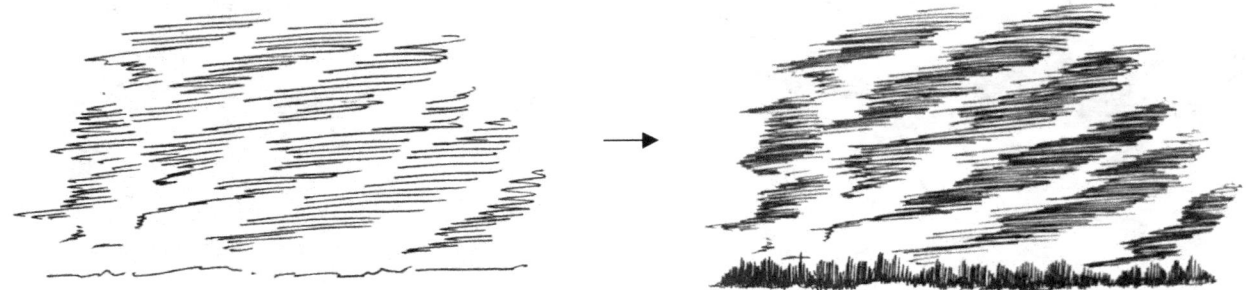

## Using Tone to Set Mood, Continued:

Here is another example of transitioning to darker tone to set intense mood. If you have good control of drawing parallel lines to lay down tone, then you can create any specific desired mood by controlling the intensity of these lines in this technique.

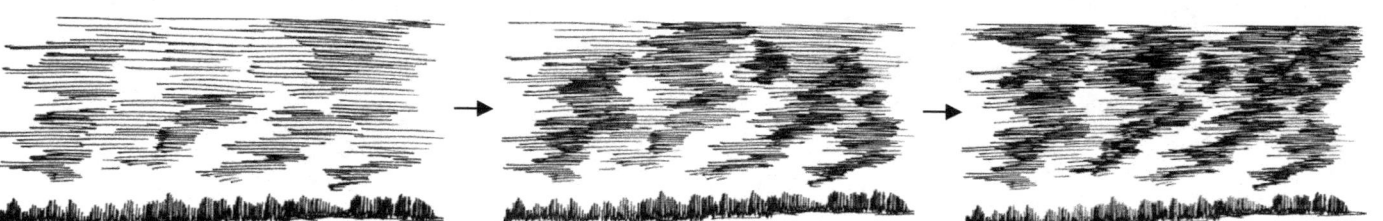

Add darker tone in an irregular manner. Do not fully darken but leave some lighter tones overlaid with darker tones to set the mood.

## Drawing Intense Clouds:

Following are some more examples of intense clouds using darker tones with explicit cloud outlines. Notice that there is a range of tones in the clouds to give them depth.

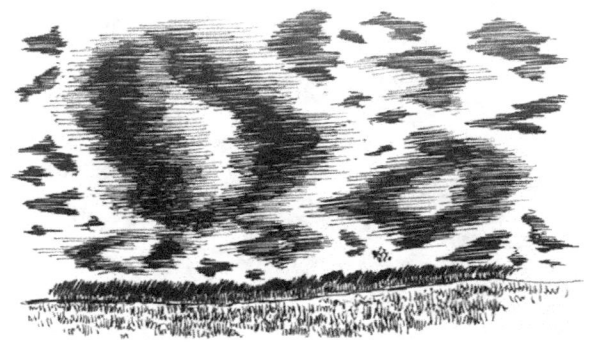 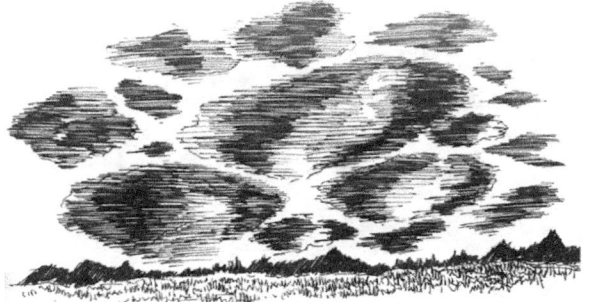

# Drawing Layered Clouds:

**Layers of Clouds can be drawn as shown below and textured with parallel lines to create more depth.**

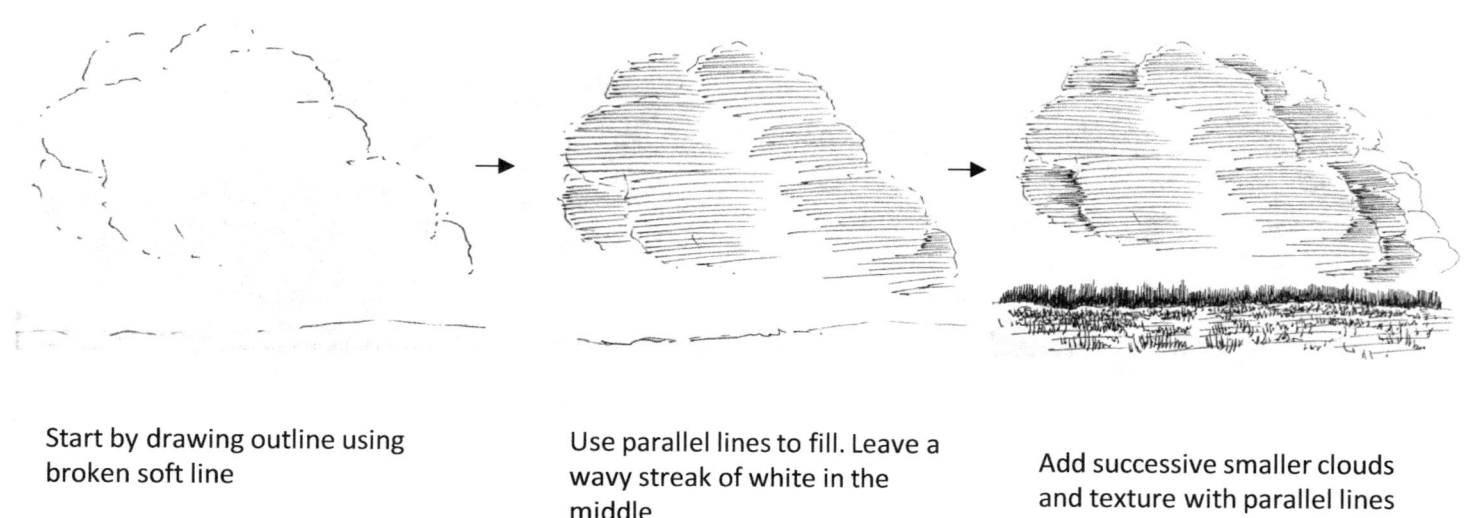

Start by drawing outline using broken soft line

Use parallel lines to fill. Leave a wavy streak of white in the middle

Add successive smaller clouds and texture with parallel lines

# Drawing Layered Clouds, Continued:

**This technique creates more involved clouds. Use it when you want to make them center of attention.**

Darken slightly the edge
between 2 layers

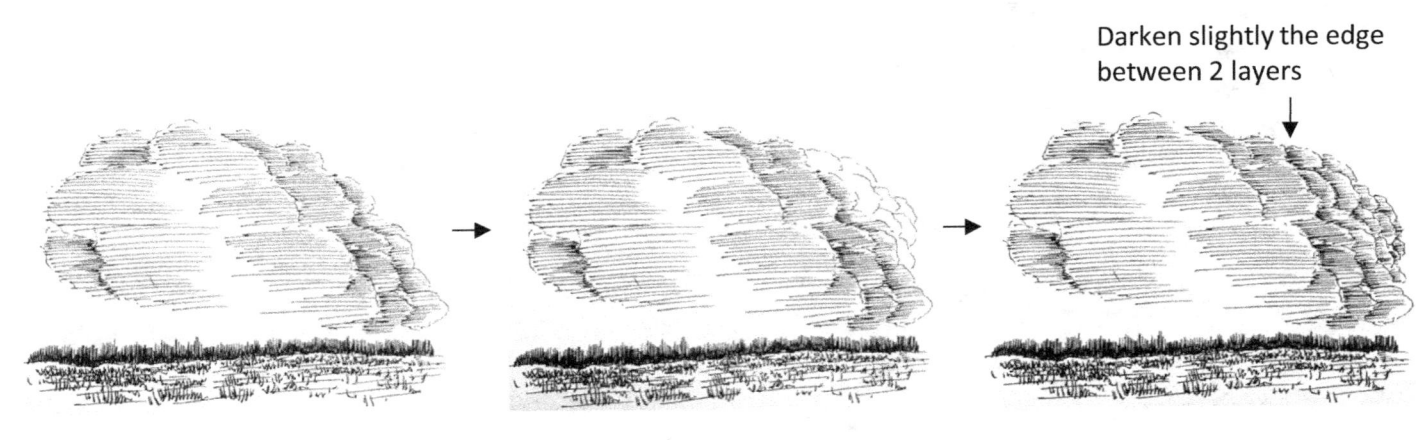

Add more smaller layers to give it more depth     Adjust the tone to your liking

# Drawing Layered Clouds, Additional Examples:

Here are some more examples of this technique.  Notice how the edges are broken and irregular to bring  out feel of clouds.

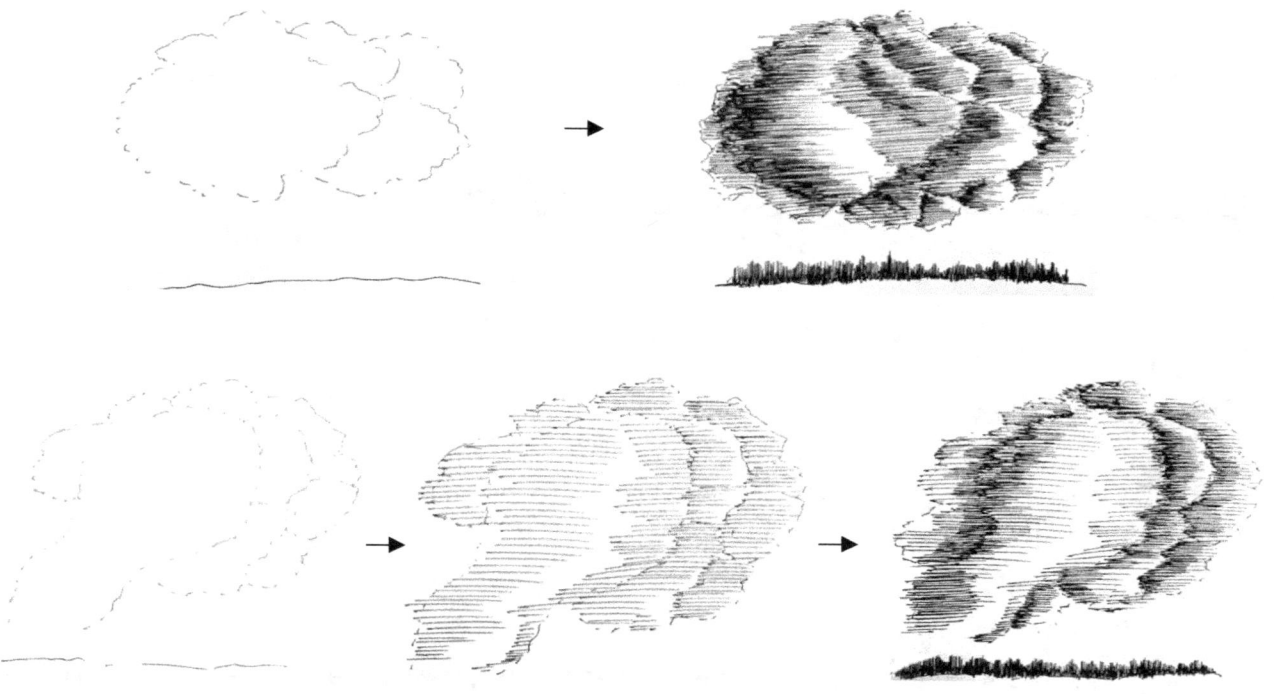

# Drawing Layered Clouds, Additional Examples:

By using darker tones, very intense mood can be set. Following are some more examples.

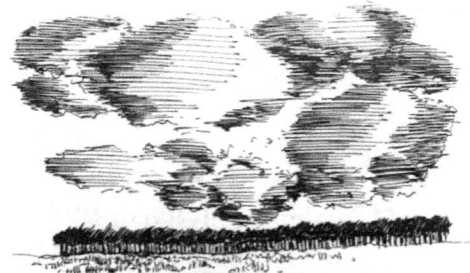
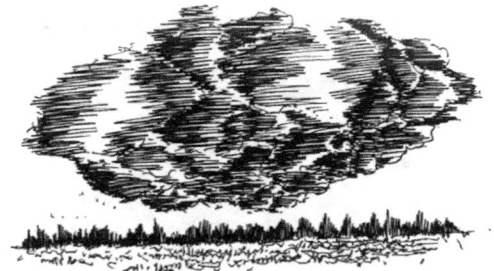
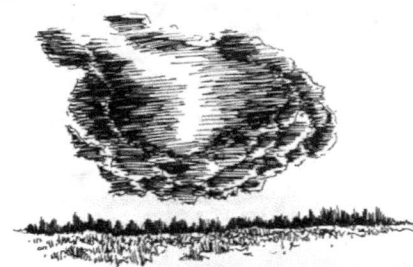

# How to Draw Sky and Clouds, Technique 4:

**This technique is a variation on last technique where wavy lines resembling clouds are draw as shown below.**

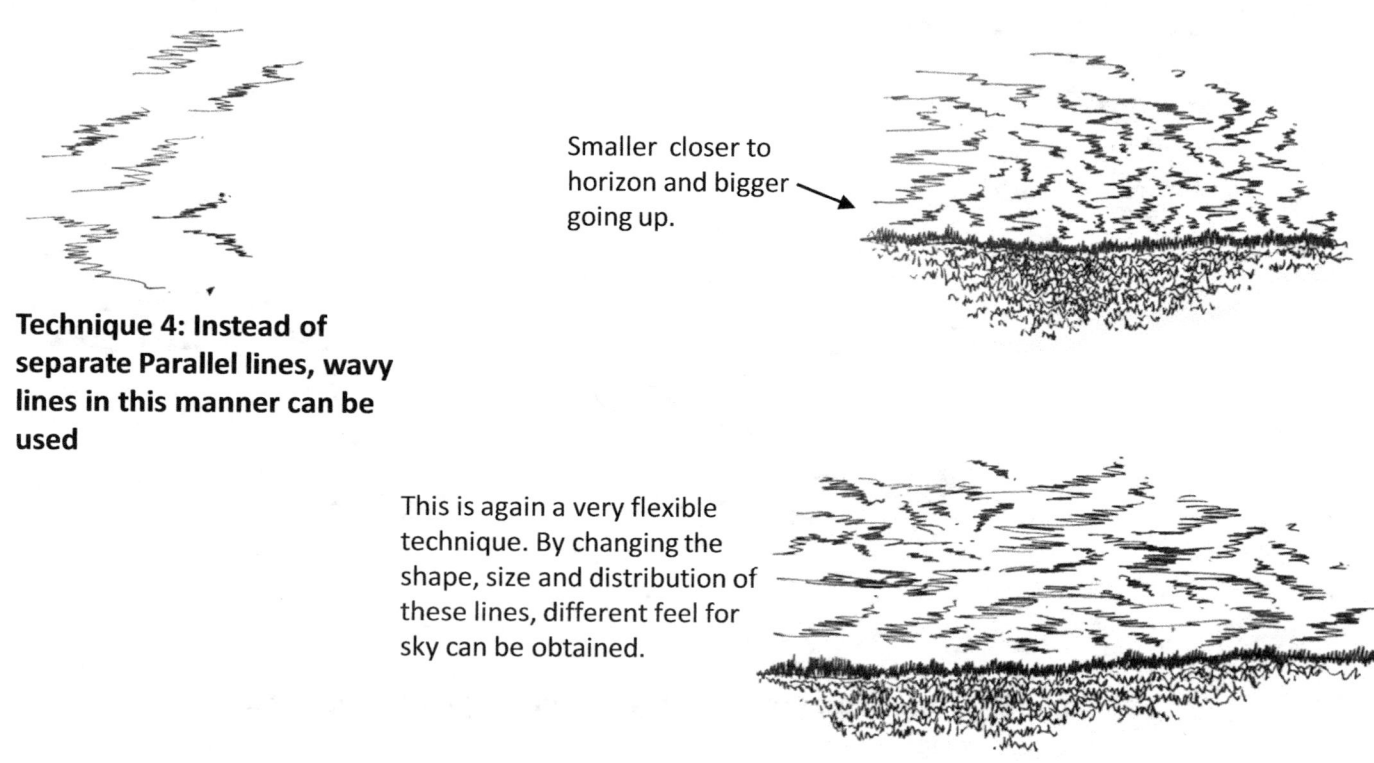

Smaller closer to horizon and bigger going up.

**Technique 4: Instead of separate Parallel lines, wavy lines in this manner can be used**

This is again a very flexible technique. By changing the shape, size and distribution of these lines, different feel for sky can be obtained.

Here is an example of use of this technique in a drawing. By controlling the volume of such lines, you can control how much attention they draw to themselves.

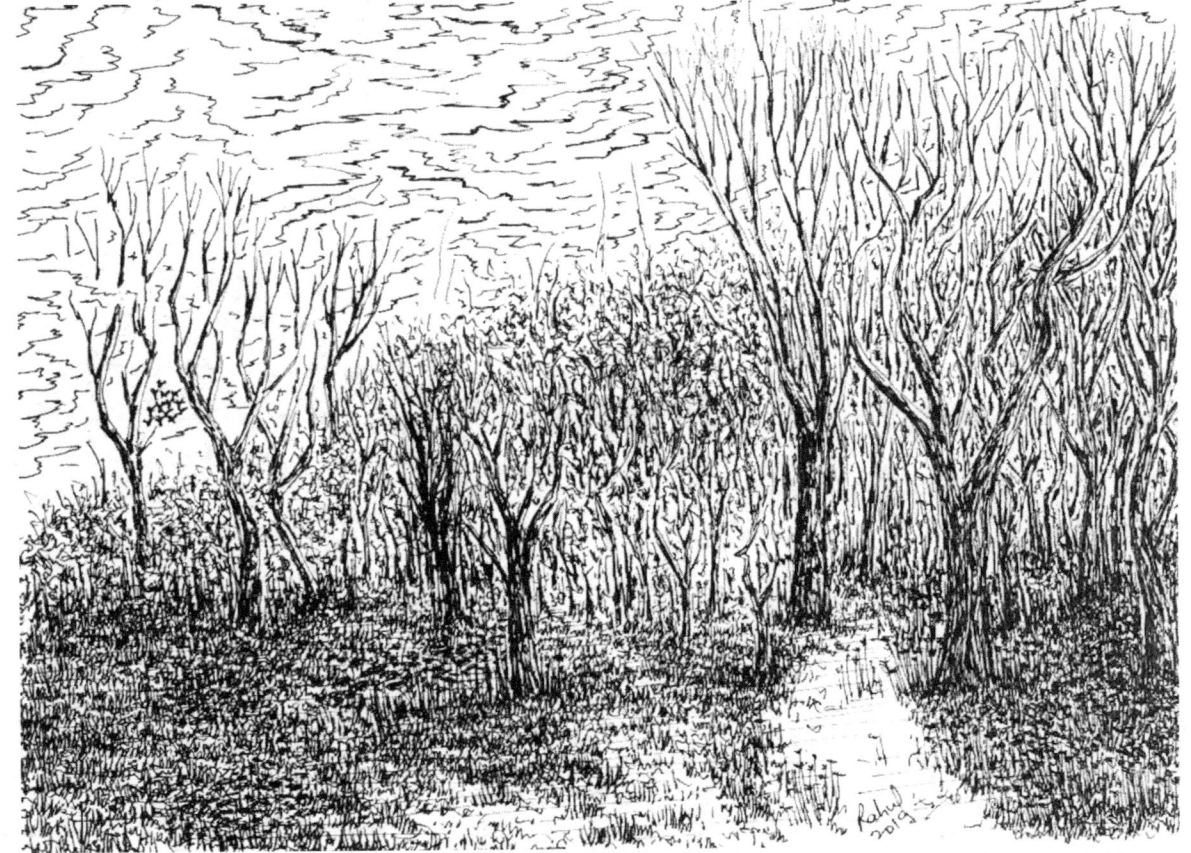

Here is an example where I have used a mix of techniques to create the backdrop. Mix and match different techniques to see the mood they set. Experiment with different techniques and evolve your own.

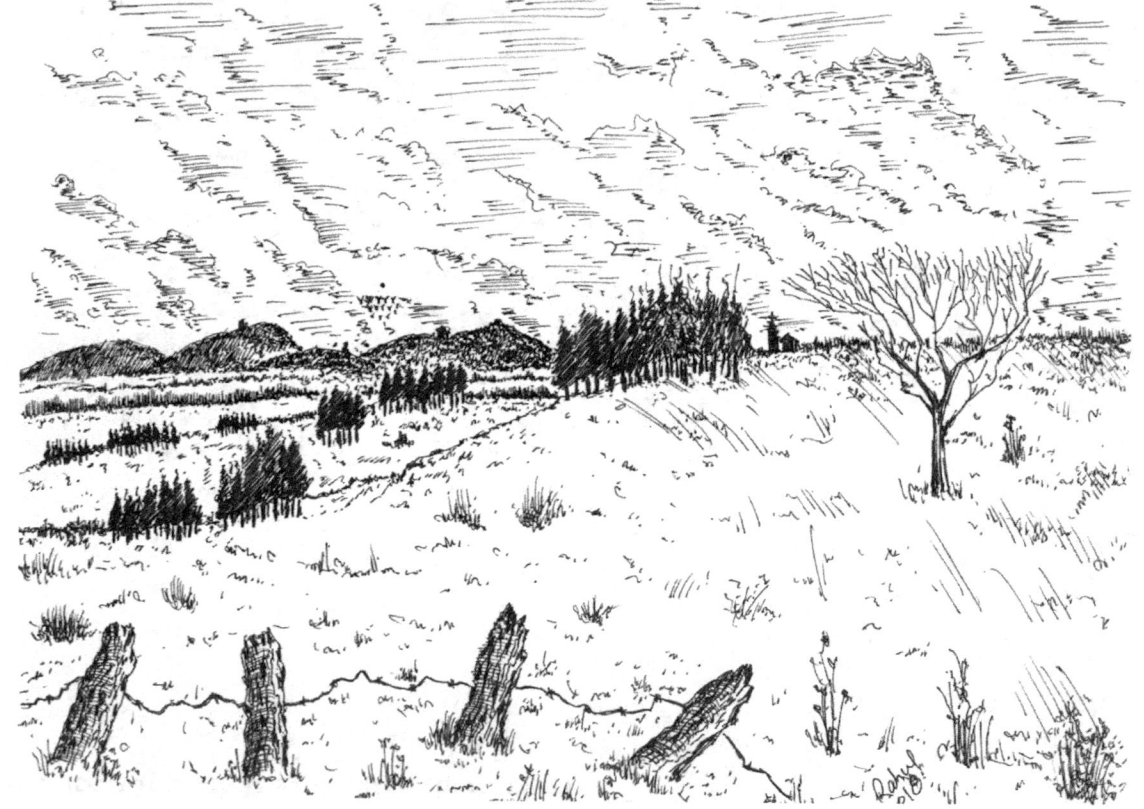

**Here is yet another way to do sky/clouds.**

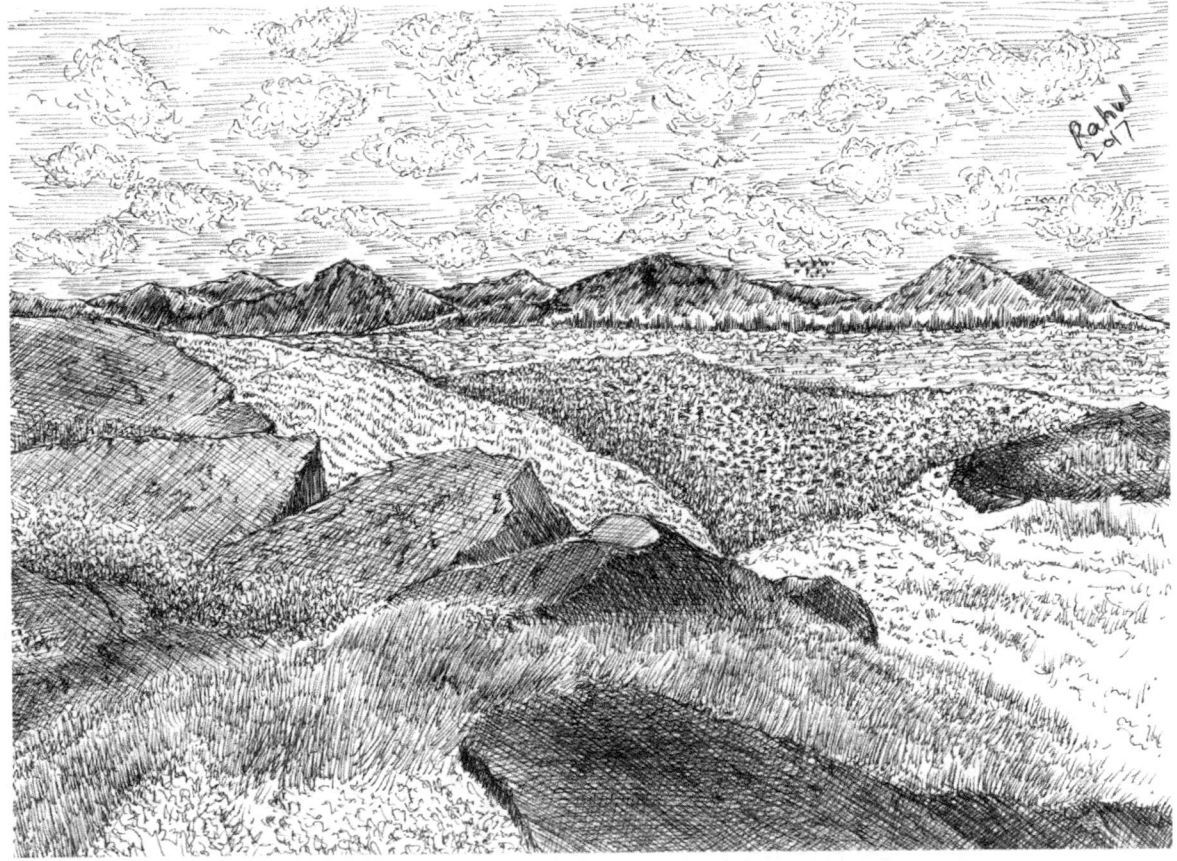

**Yet another technique. Always study and learn from any good pen and ink drawing you come across.**

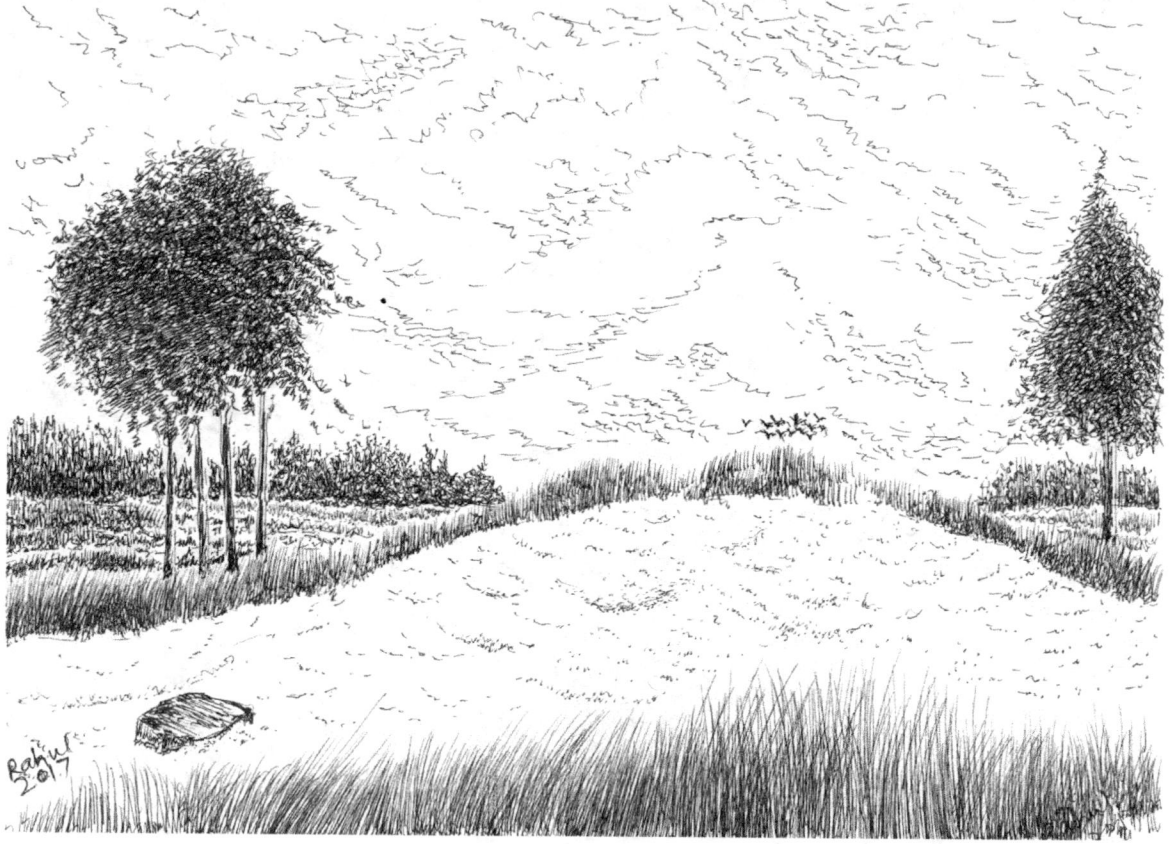

## Activity: Drawing Sky and Clouds:

*Following are the starting points to draw clouds. Draw Distant element and ground cover as well.*

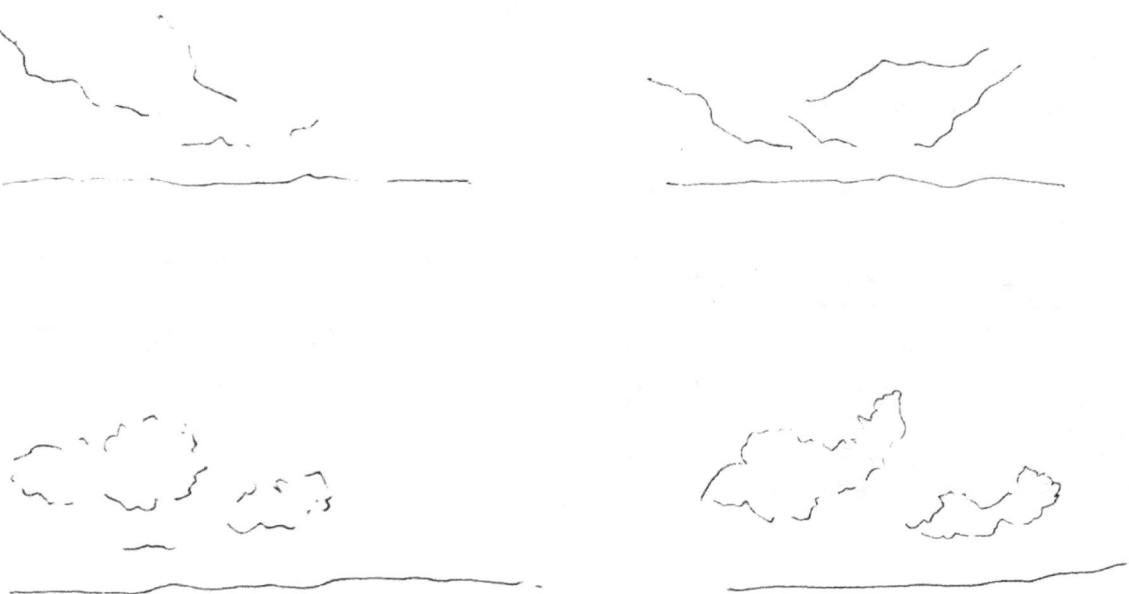

## Sky and Clouds as Negative Space:

So far we have looked at strokes to draw sky and clouds. Another option is to use negative technique, i.e. lave the clouds white while texturing the backdrop. This gives a different feel as seen below.

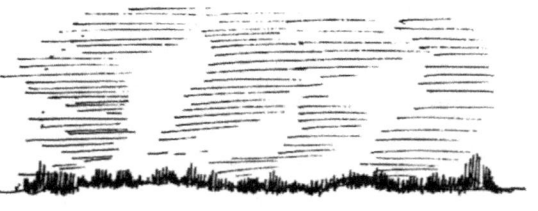

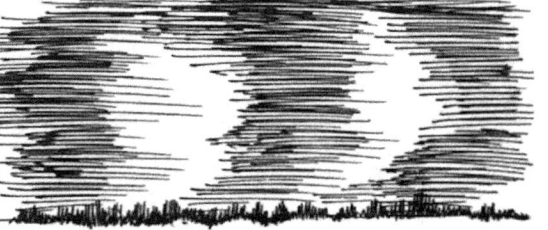

Here the parallel lines are used to provide background tone with irregular white of negative space indicating clouds.

Background tone can be changed to set the overall mood as well.

If you are not comfortable drawing longer parallel lines, dots and ticks can be used to render background as well. →

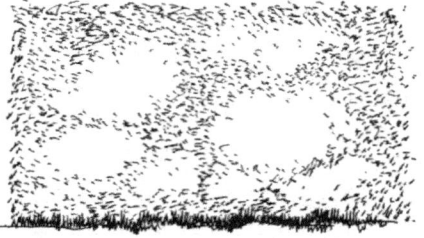

## Negative Space vs. Other Techniques:

Shown below is comparison of 2 techniques that can be used in negative approach and to actively draw sky/clouds. The difference is in the manner of usage of these strokes but a very different feeling is evoked.

Leave more white when using negative approach in an irregular manner to make negative space focus of attention.

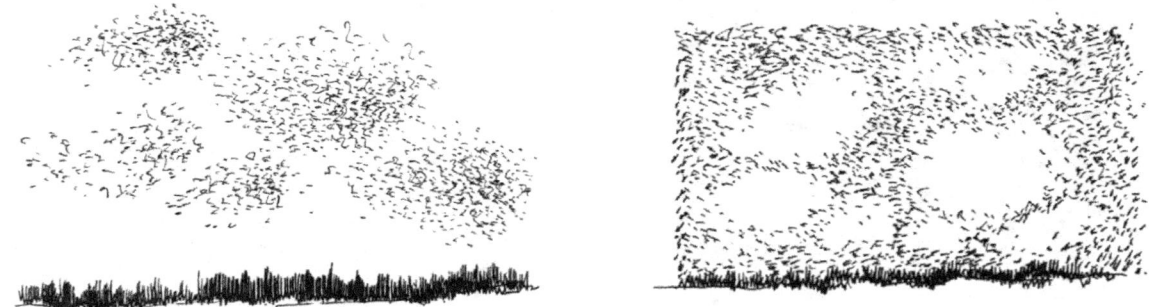

Use of dots and ticks in negative approach usually results in more tonal presence in Sky/Clouds.

Here is a drawing incorporating negative approach for Sky/Clouds. Against other dark elements, the white of negative space provides nice contrast without interfering with it.

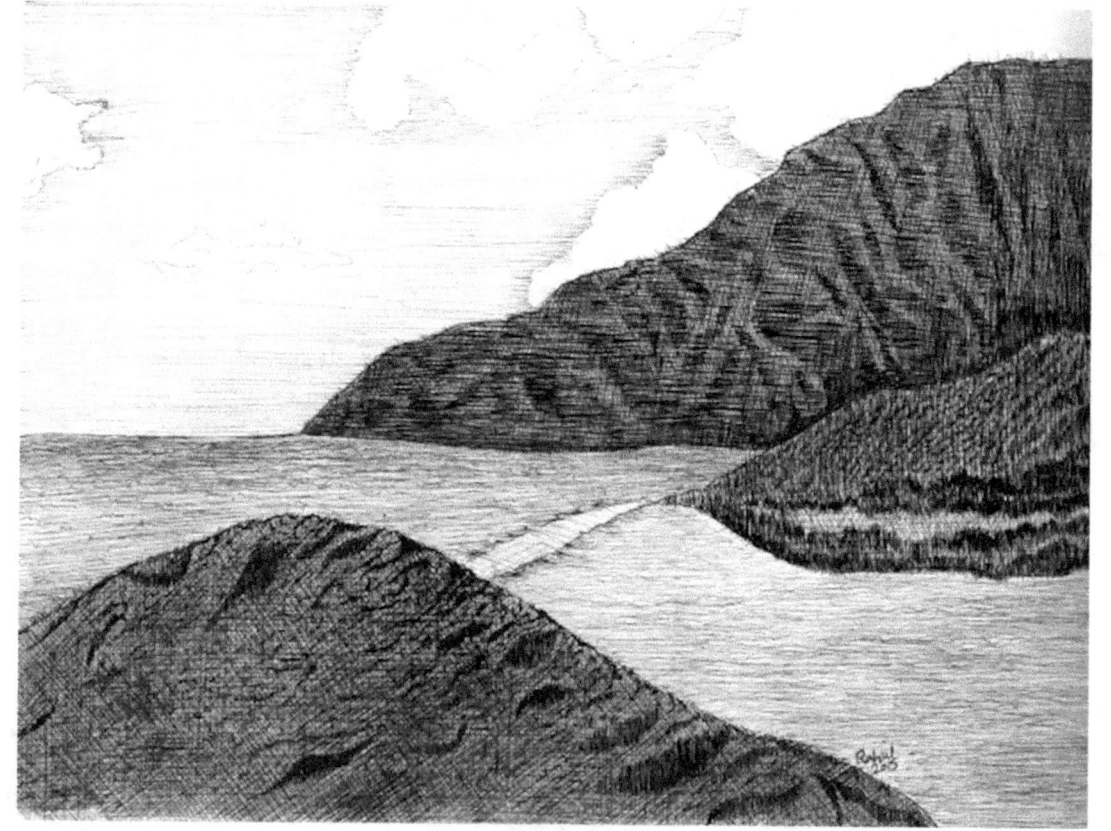

**Activity: Practice drawing sky and clouds using Negative technique in the space below.**

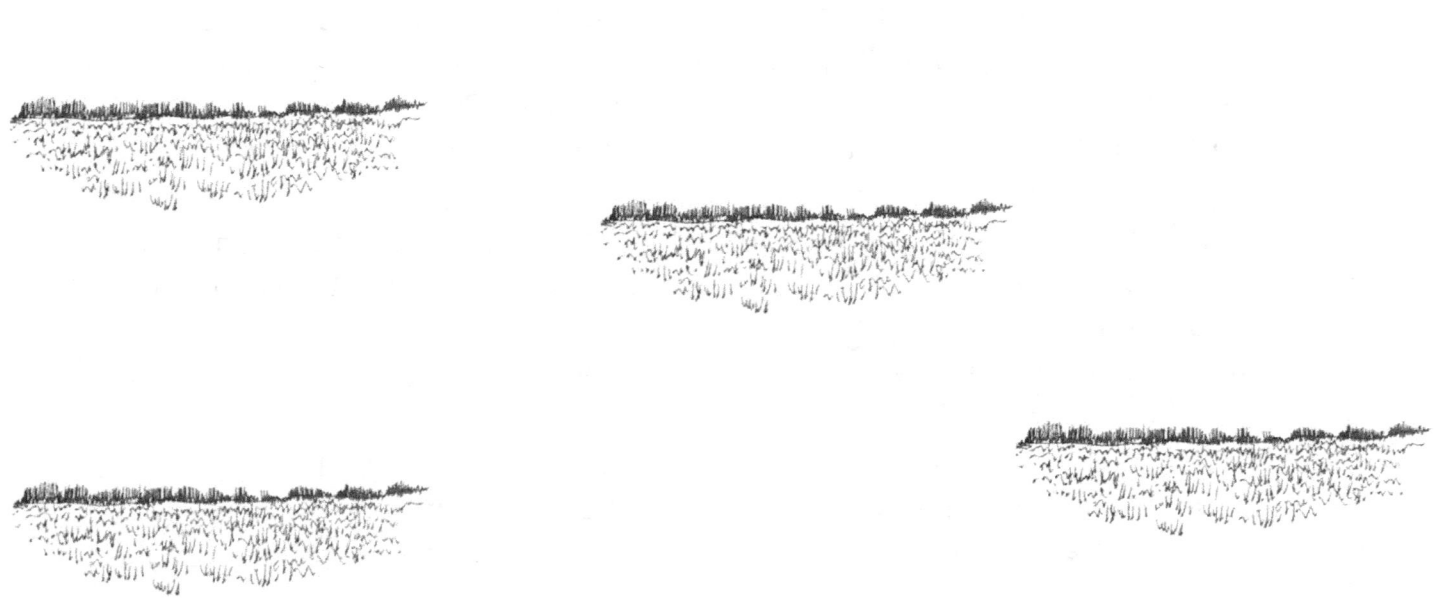

**Drawing Coniferous Trees:**

Coniferous or Pine trees are a great addition to any landscape. Very pleasing landscapes can be drawn with smattering of pine trees at different distances from the viewer as discussed later.

The main thing to keep in mind when drawing Pine trees is that there should be a change in tone from center to edges when drawing a dense pine tree. There are usually more needles in the center and this gives a darker feel to the center. Edges have far fewer density of needles and so should be kept lighter.

To convey the feel of needles, different strokes can be used and some of them are presented in following pages. Distance also makes a big difference. For pine trees that are drawn closer to viewer and hence bigger, their needles need to be made more explicit as more details of bigger trees are visible. For smaller trees at a distance, it is their shape that primarily conveys their feel.

Drawing deciduous trees is covered in another volume of the workbook.

# Drawing Coniferous Trees:

Steps to drawing a typical pine tree.

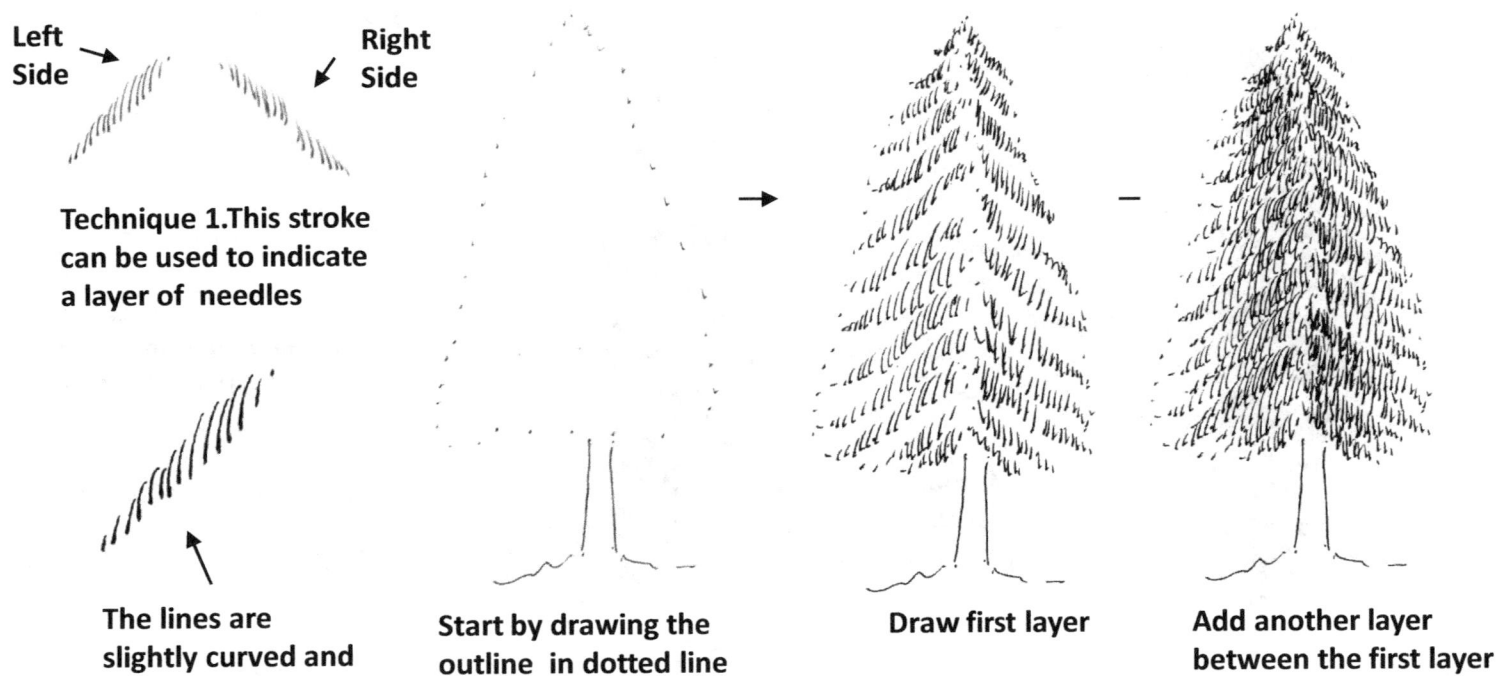

**Left Side**

**Right Side**

**Technique 1. This stroke can be used to indicate a layer of needles**

**The lines are slightly curved and tapers to the edge**

**Start by drawing the outline in dotted line**

**Draw first layer**

**Add another layer between the first layer**

# Drawing Coniferous Trees:

**Steps to drawing a typical pine tree.**

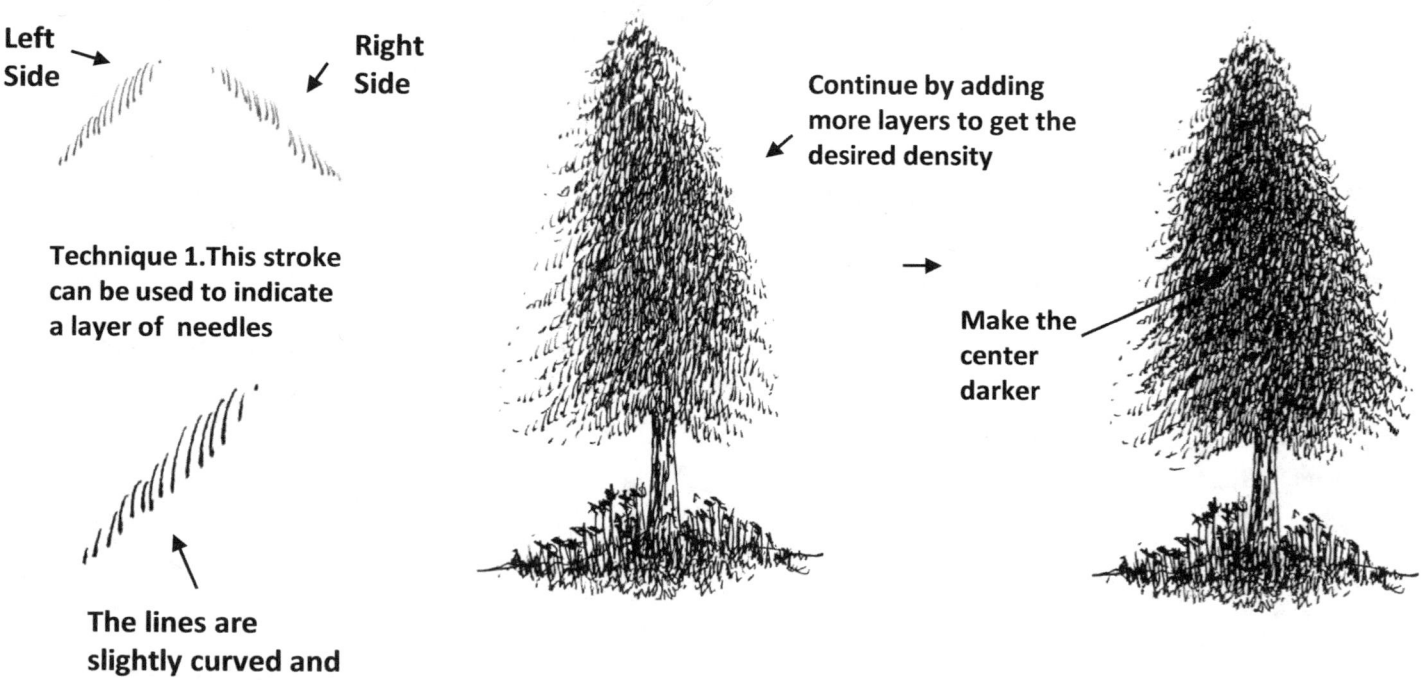

**Left Side**

**Right Side**

**Technique 1.This stroke can be used to indicate a layer of needles**

**The lines are slightly curved and tapers to the edge**

**Continue by adding more layers to get the desired density**

**Make the center darker**

# Drawing Coniferous Trees, More Examples:

Here are some more examples of drawing coniferous trees with technique shown on last page. There is no limit to the trees you can draw in this manner by varying their size, shape, layout of needle foliage etc.

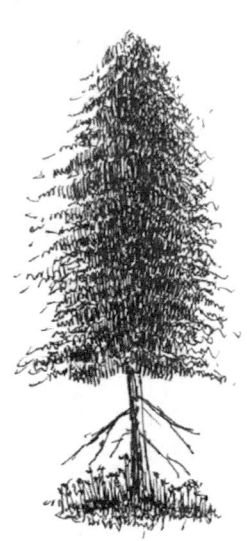
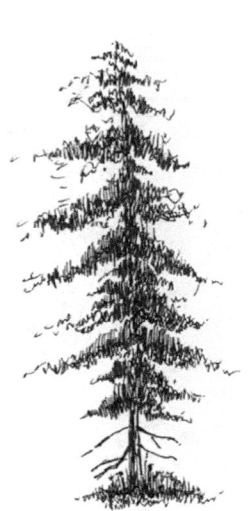
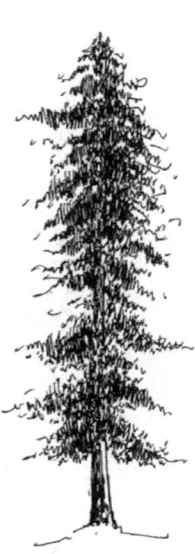

# Drawing Coniferous Tree, Technique 2:

**Steps to drawing a typical pine tree.**

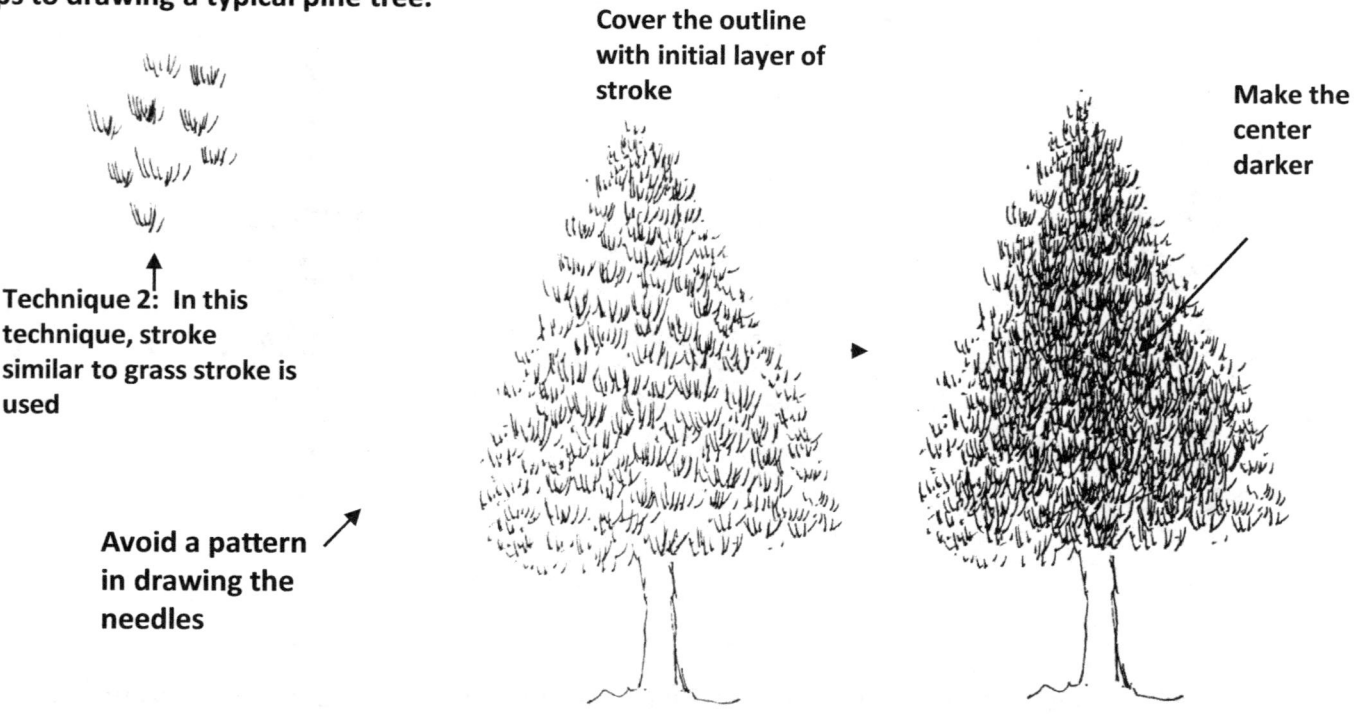

**Cover the outline with initial layer of stroke**

**Make the center darker**

**Technique 2: In this technique, stroke similar to grass stroke is used**

**Avoid a pattern in drawing the needles**

# Drawing Coniferous Tree, Technique 2:

**Steps to drawing a typical pine tree.**

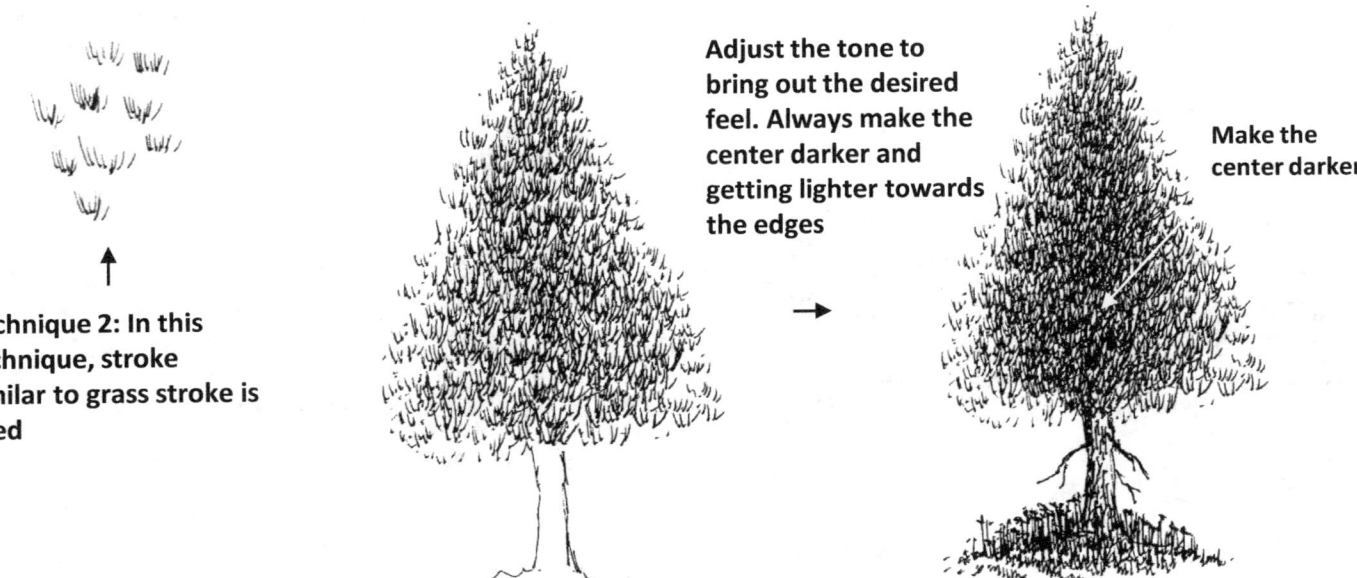

**Adjust the tone to bring out the desired feel. Always make the center darker and getting lighter towards the edges**

**Make the center darker**

**Technique 2: In this technique, stroke similar to grass stroke is used**

# Drawing Coniferous Tree, Technique 2:

Layers of needle foliage often adds visual interest and can be indicated by alternate layers of light and dark needle foliage as shown below.

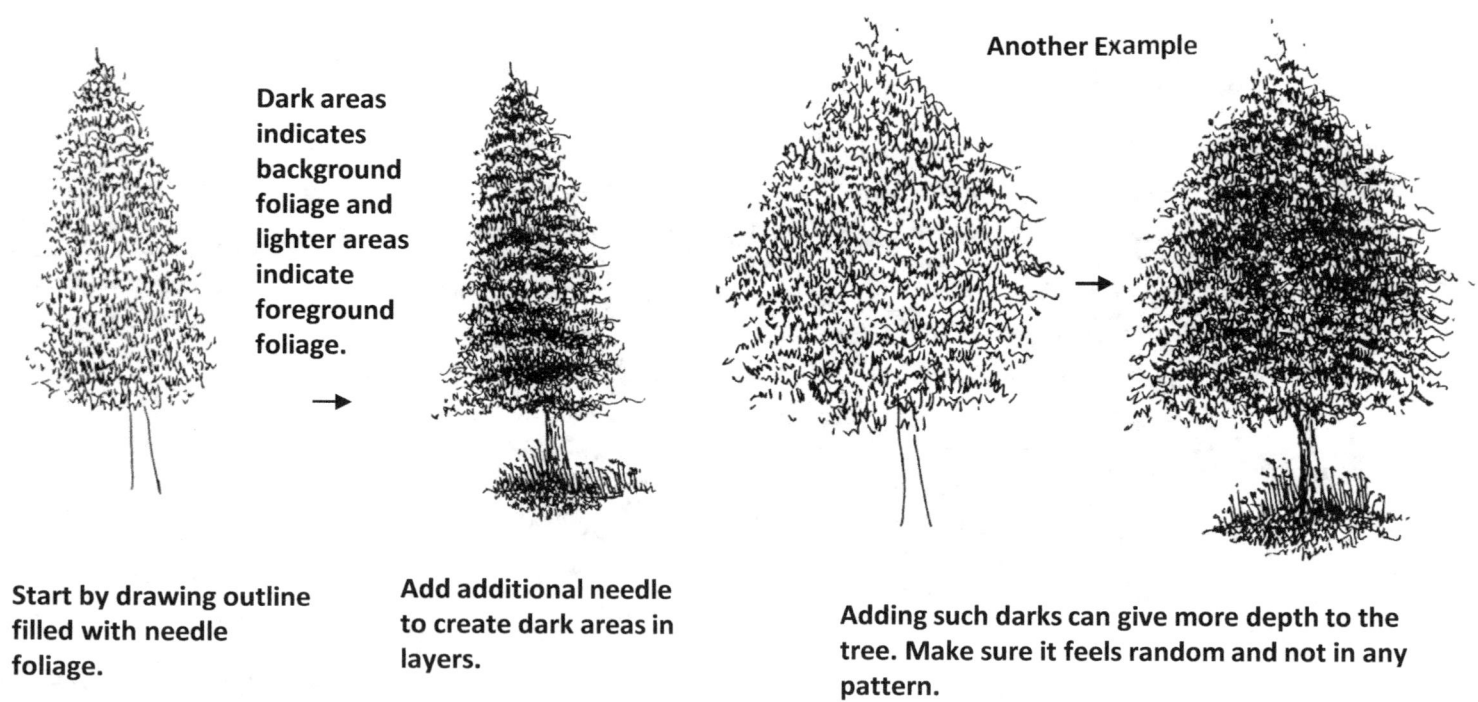

Dark areas indicates background foliage and lighter areas indicate foreground foliage.

**Another Example**

Start by drawing outline filled with needle foliage.

Add additional needle to create dark areas in layers.

Adding such darks can give more depth to the tree. Make sure it feels random and not in any pattern.

## Activity: Drawing Pine Trees:

Finish the following coniferous trees per earlier instructions.

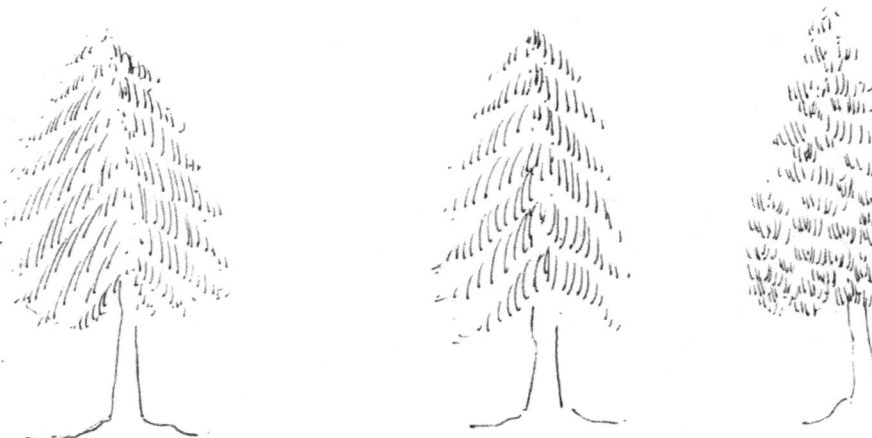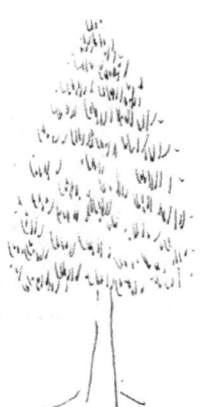

## Drawing Coniferous Tree, Technique 2, continued:

So far we have drawn pine trees with no visible branches. This is most often used approach and is usually sufficient. But branches can be drawn and needle foliage depicted on them to give a different feel as well.

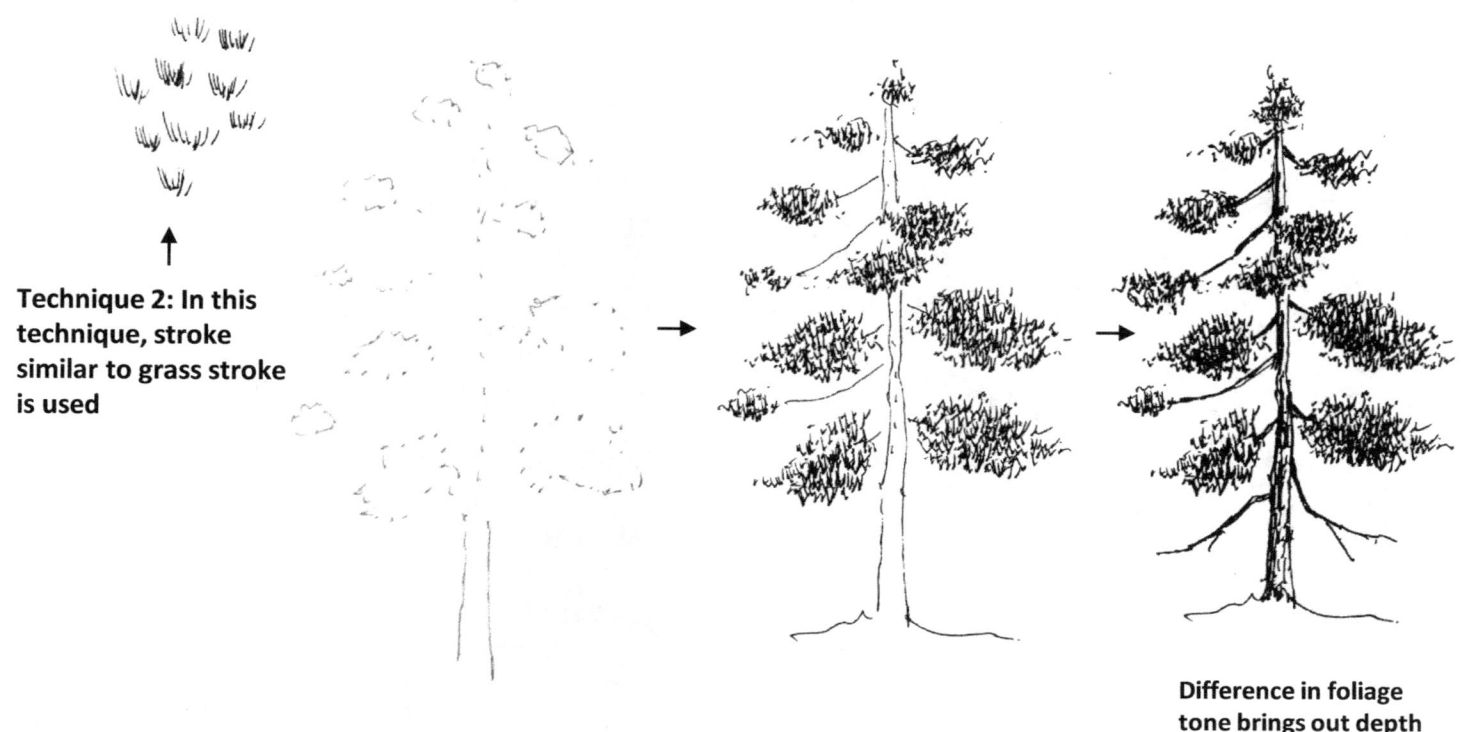

**Technique 2: In this technique, stroke similar to grass stroke is used**

**Difference in foliage tone brings out depth**

# Drawing Coniferous Tree, Technique 2, Some More Examples:

**Some foliage is in front (trunk not visible) and some behind (trunk visible). This adds to depth perception.**

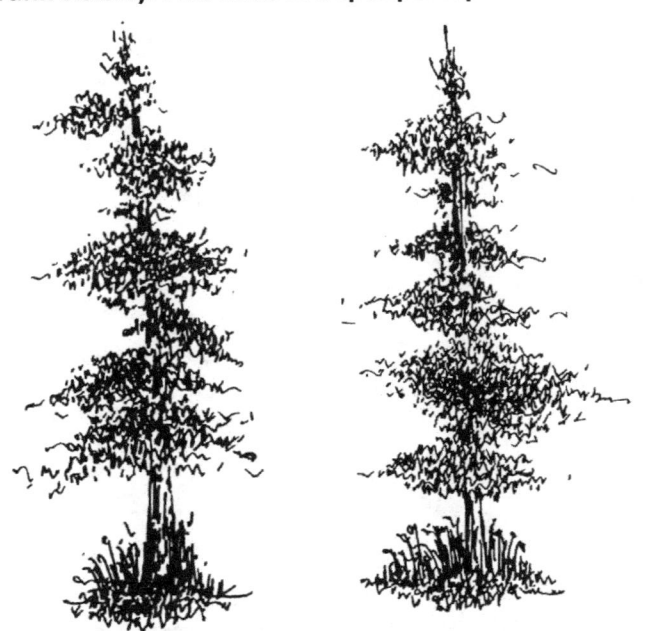

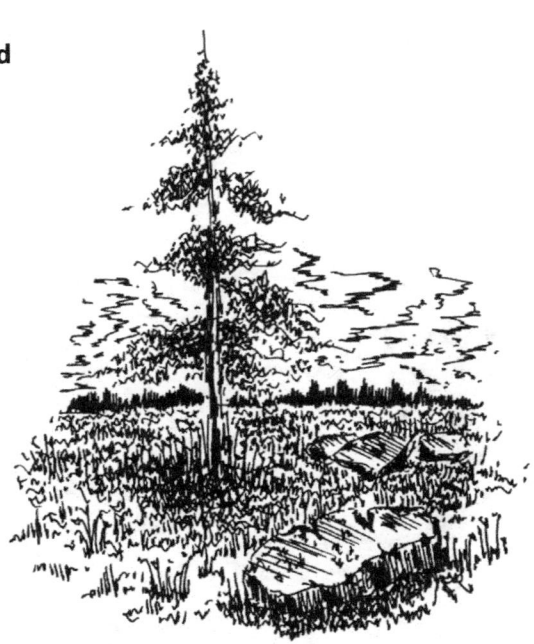

**Pleasing landscapes like this with pine tree and other foreground elements like stone, posts etc. can be easily drawn from imagination any time.**

# Drawing Coniferous Tree with Branch Structure:

Yet another option is to draw branch structure and then add needle foliage to it as shown below. By using different branch structures, limitless variations on this can be drawn. Needle foliage can be depicted using upwars or downward stroke as we have seen earlier.

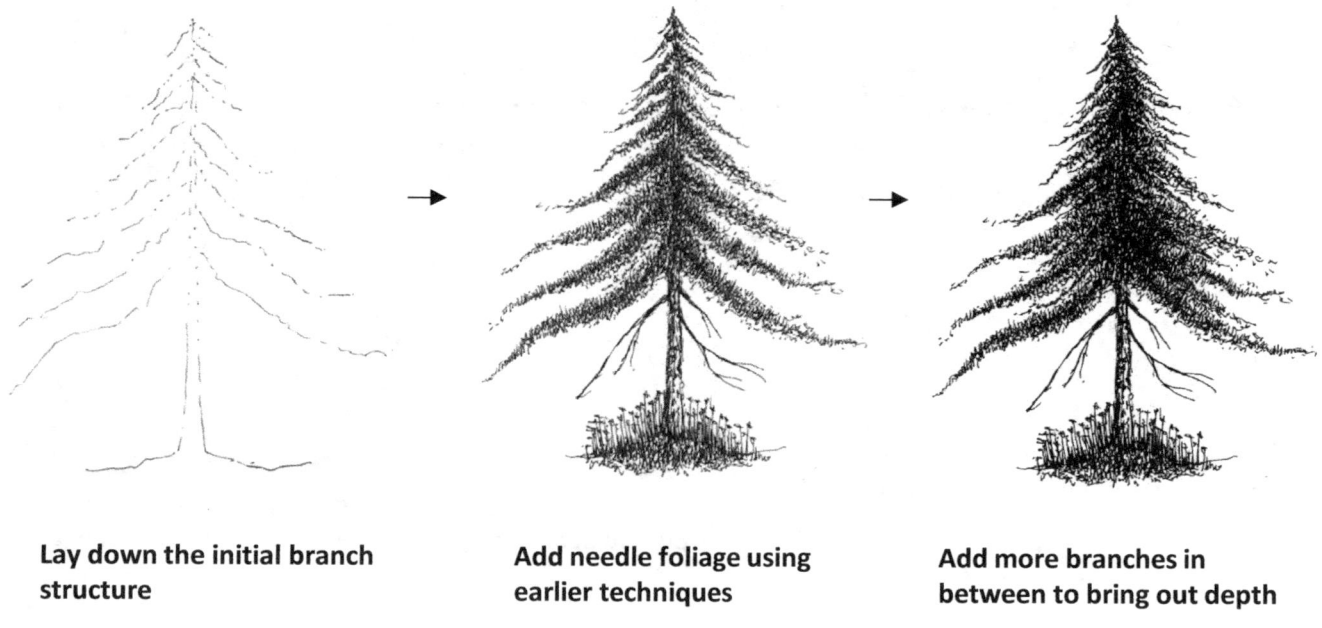

**Lay down the initial branch structure**

**Add needle foliage using earlier techniques**

**Add more branches in between to bring out depth**

# Drawing Coniferous Tree with Branch Structure, Additional Examples:

**Following are some more examples. Try one of your own.**

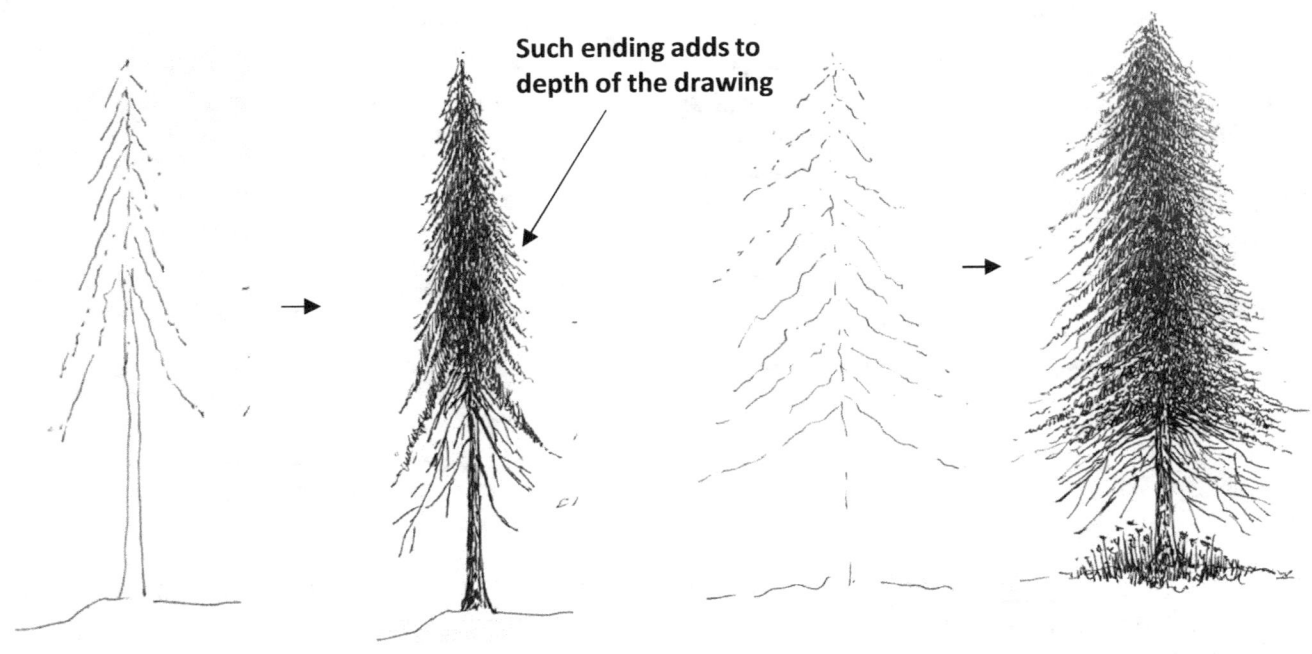

**Such ending adds to depth of the drawing**

# Drawing Coniferous Tree, Technique 3:

So far we looked at 2 strokes which gives the feel of needles oriented in a particular way. This is not necessary and in fact any ticks and wiggles as shown below can be used to indicate needle foliage. When used in sufficient density along with typical shape of coniferous trees, it conveys the right feel.

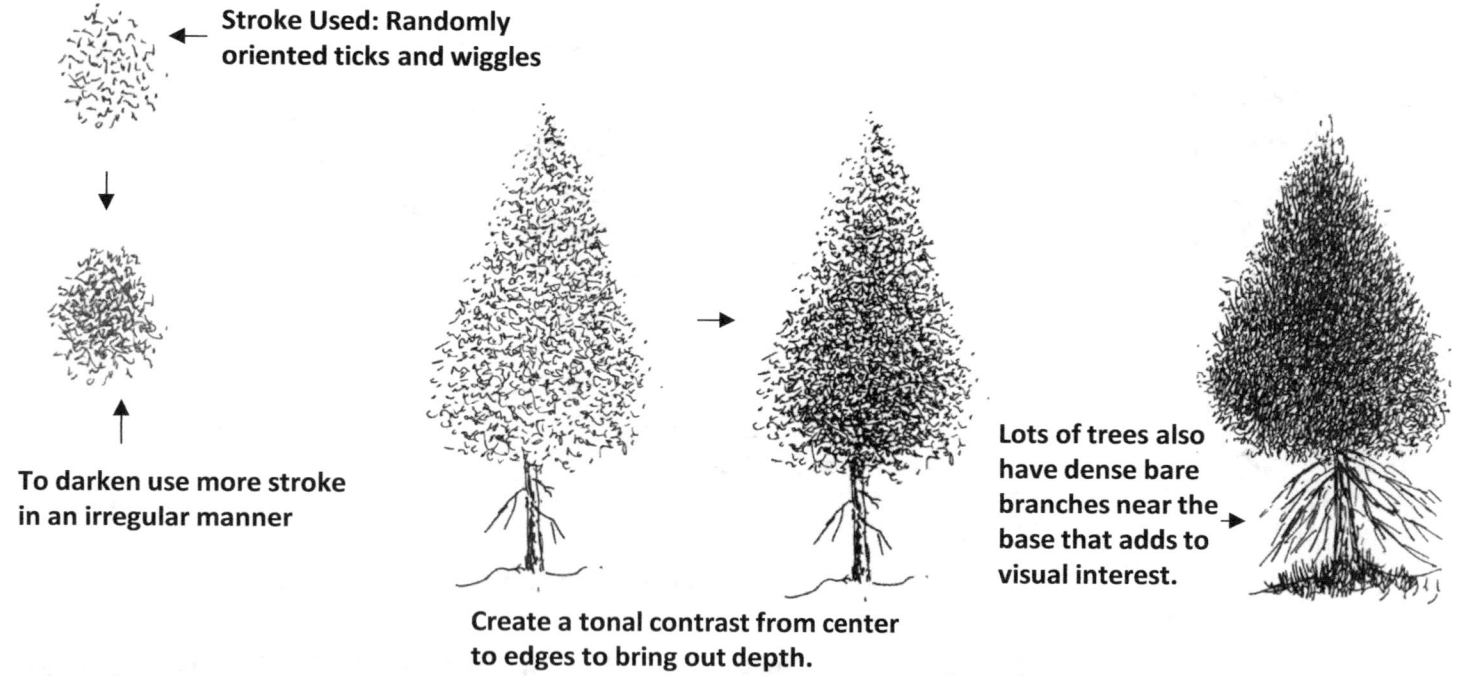

**Stroke Used: Randomly oriented ticks and wiggles**

To darken use more stroke in an irregular manner

Create a tonal contrast from center to edges to bring out depth.

Lots of trees also have dense bare branches near the base that adds to visual interest.

# Drawing Far Away Coniferous Trees:

**In this technique use the wiggle lines as shown below to give a feel of needle foliage. This works best when the pine trees are drawn smaller in size, i.e. not too close.**

Use Wriggly lines like these to show needle foliage at a distance

Darken the center more using more stroke. Center is always darker than edges.

Always leave some white between the trees to make them apart.

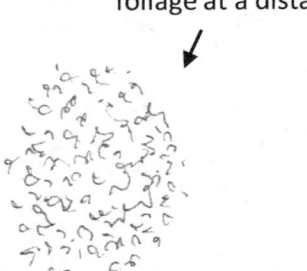

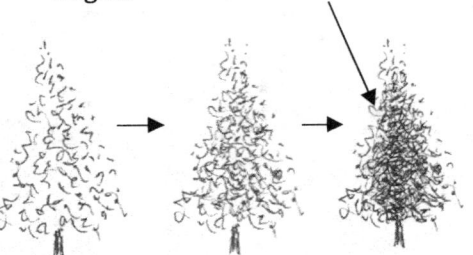

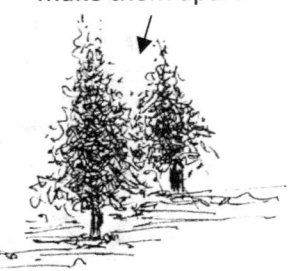

Once you learn to draw coniferous trees, you can use them in your compositions in very powerful way. Think about using mix of close and far away trees. Due to their dark tone, they can be very effectively used as a focal point. Here is a drawing I did.

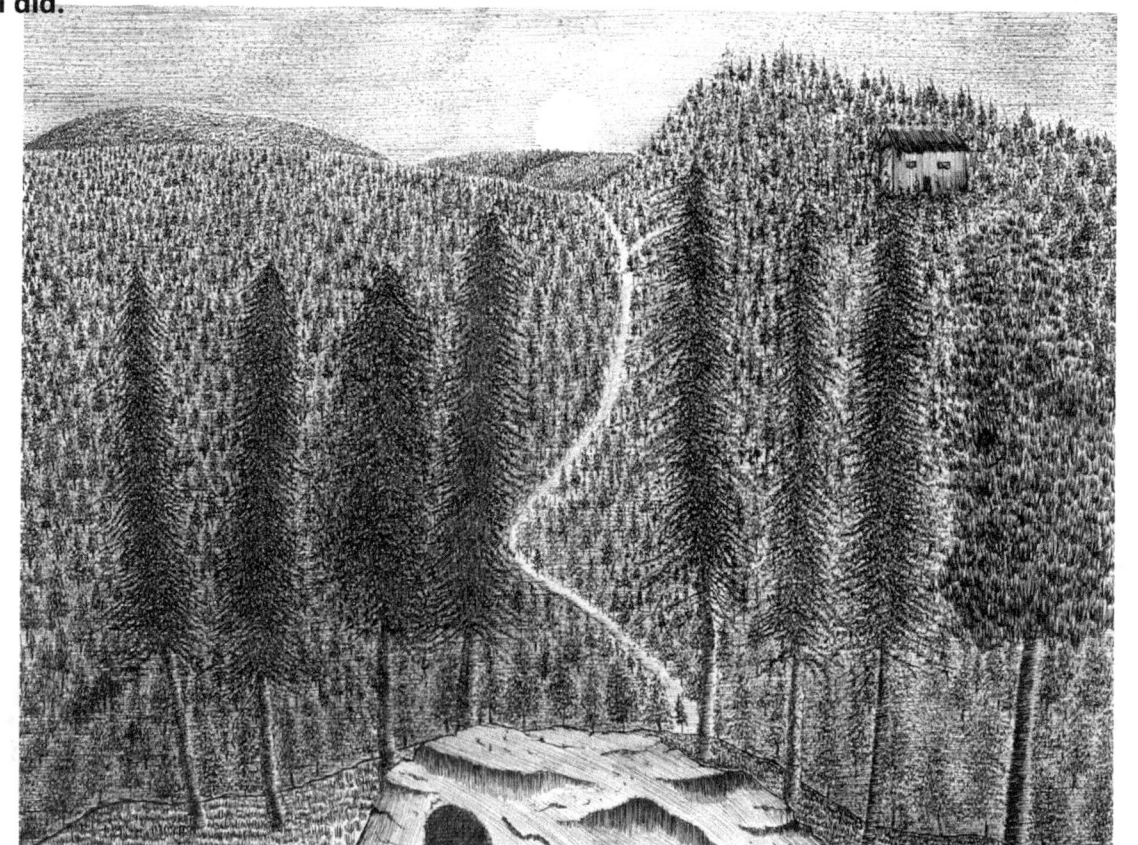

In this drawing, coniferous trees are used in the middle ground to add different texture and help viewer move from foreground to the distant horizon. The group of stones is what we drew earlier.

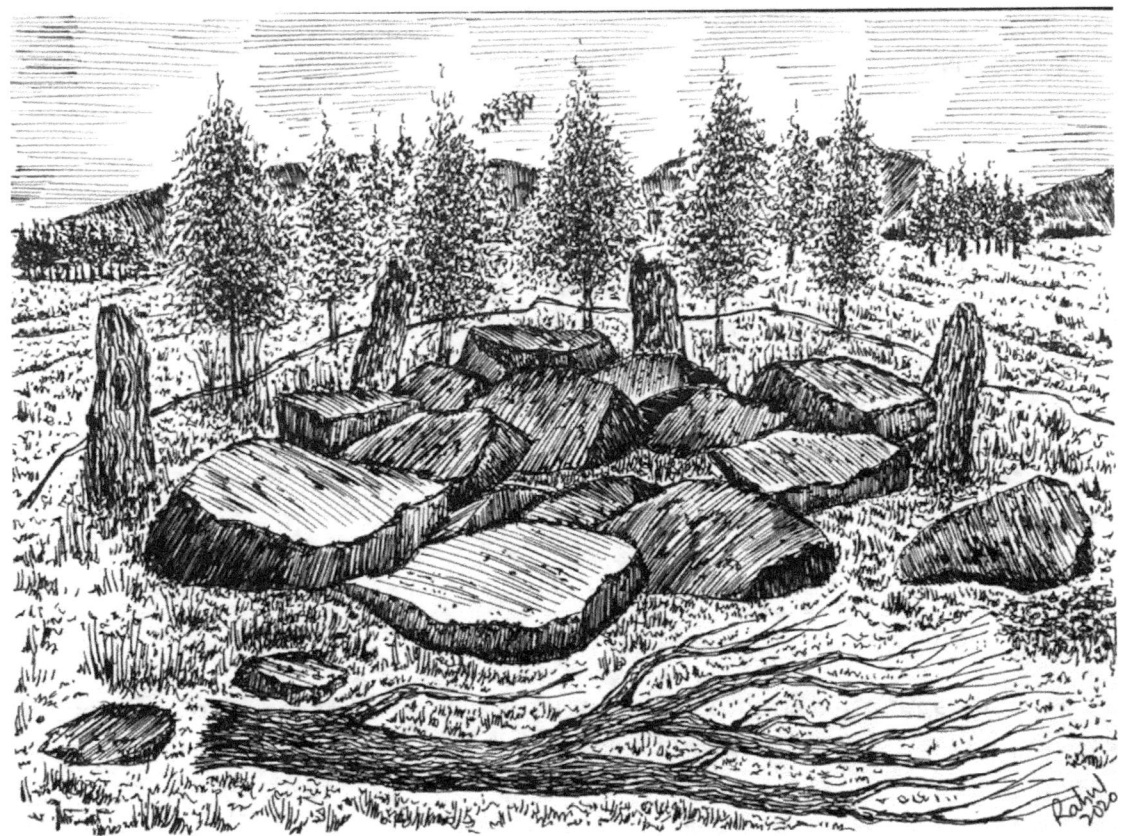

## Drawing Snow Covered Pine Trees:

Snow covered pine trees are a part of any winter landscape and can be easily drawn using ticks and wiggle marks. The white of paper comes across as snow when properly surrounded by other texture.

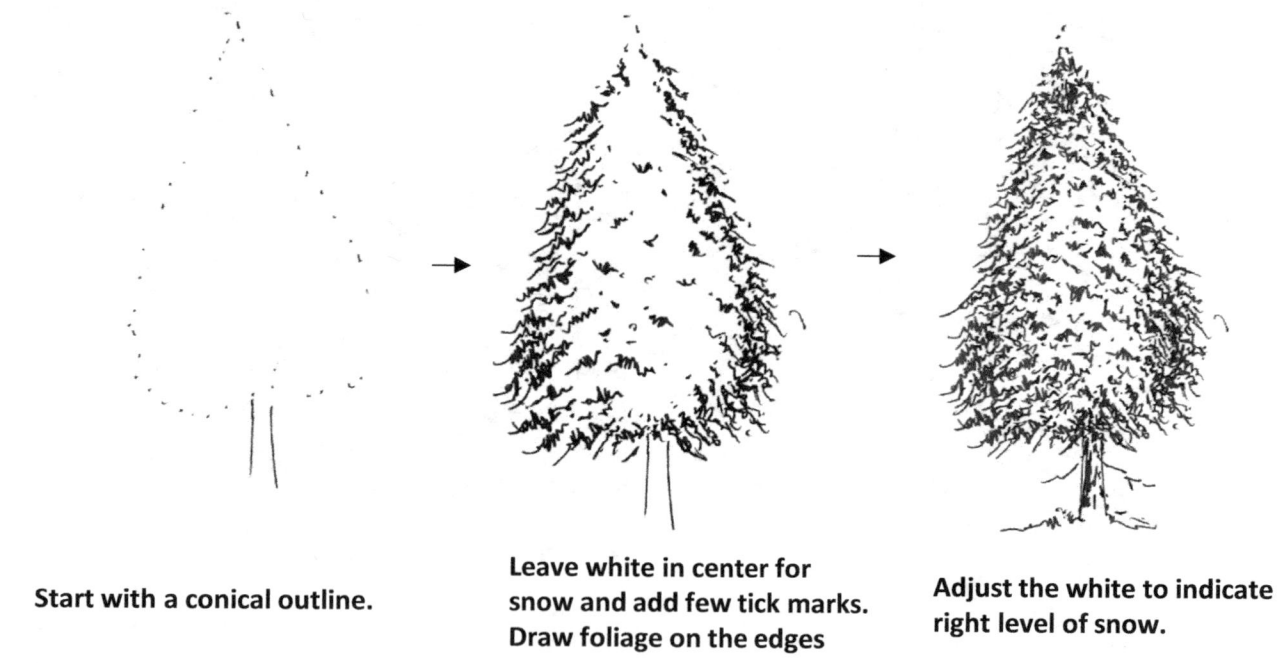

Start with a conical outline.

Leave white in center for snow and add few tick marks. Draw foliage on the edges

Adjust the white to indicate right level of snow.

## Drawing Snow Covered Pine Trees, Continued:

To properly bring out feel of snow, make its outline in a tapered irregular manner. There is usually a small break in snow cover and tapered darks that are added indicate that.

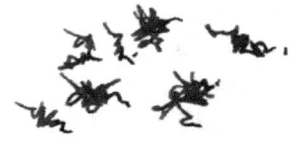

**Use such shapes against white of paper to indicate snow**

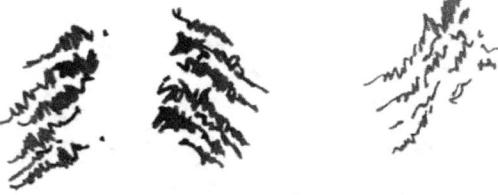

**Add strokes like these along the edges to indicate foliage not covered with snow.**

**A drawing with snow covered pine trees. When combined with bare winter trees (discussed in another volume), they really set the winter mood.**

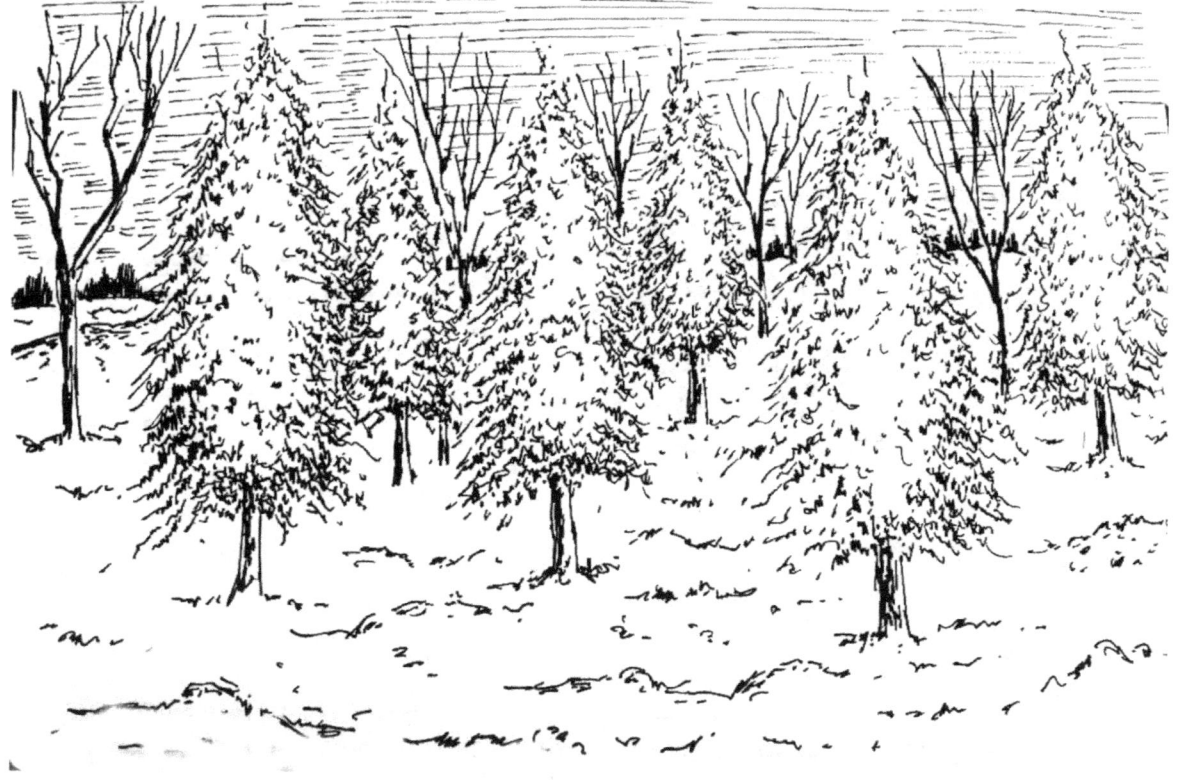

**A more detailed drawing. As you grow in confidence with practice, you can attempt such drawings.**

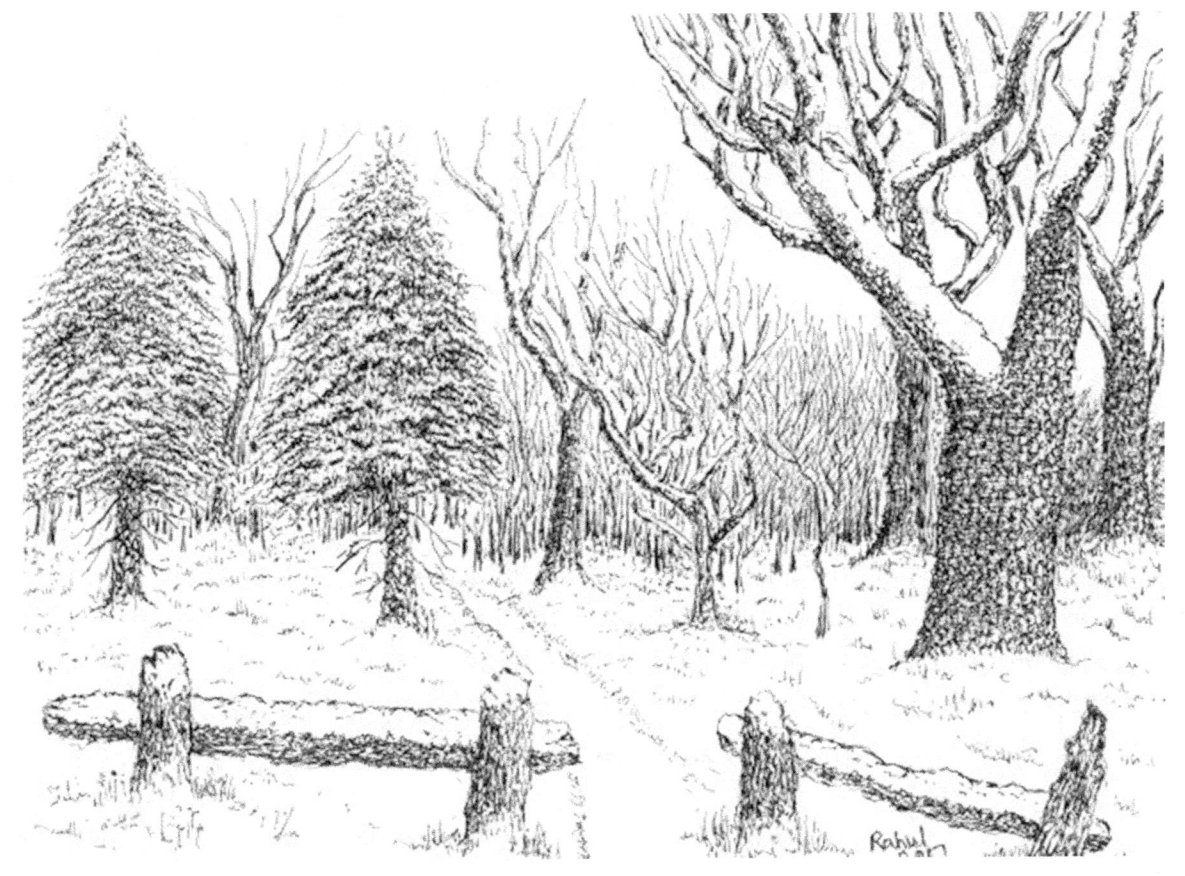

**Putting a Landscape Together:**

So far we have looked at drawing individual elements of nature in detail, specifically stones, sky and cloud, ground cover and coniferous trees. We also saw simple landscapes that can be done with these elements. Next we will look in detail how these elements can be combined to create a pleasing landscape. Different choices for use of these elements and there manner of usage is discussed in detail. This will help you start putting your own landscapes together based on the ideas presented here.

We start by looking at the basic elements of a simple landscape. Other details and choices that can add to the charm of the drawing are discussed in detail next.

Great thing about landscapes is that you will never run out of ideas for them. Once you learn the 'theme' or core concepts behind the use of these elements, you will be able use them in different ways to bring your imagination to fruition. Don't be afraid to experiment. Practice often and you will be able to draw these landscapes in no time.

## Step by Step Landscape Composition:

We now look at steps involved in a typical landscape composition. This will help you understand how to do your own compositions. Drawing different elements that are used in a typical landscape are covered in this and other volumes (www.pendrawings.me/workbooks). A typical landscape will have the following elements.

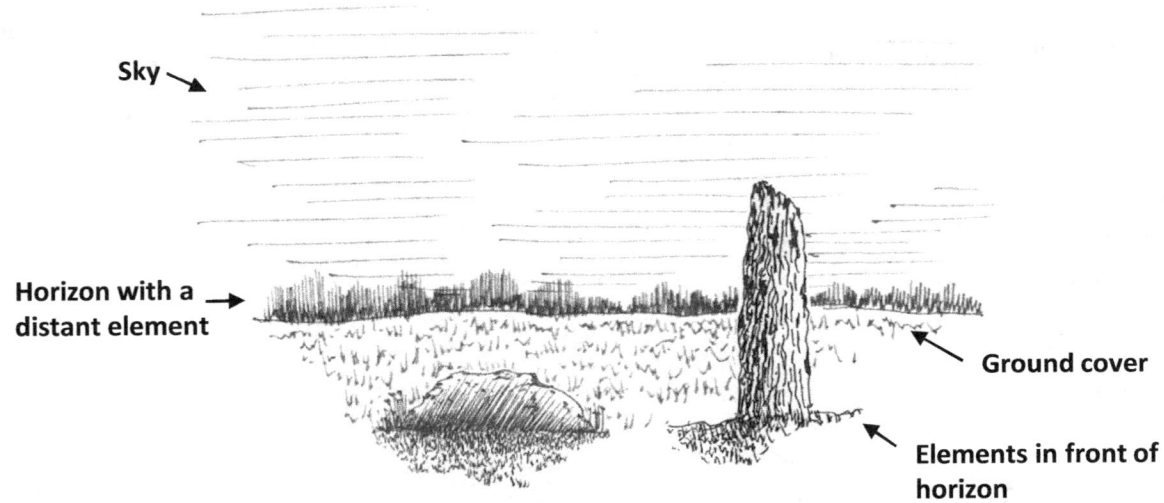

With different choices for these elements, pleasing simple landscapes can be easily drawn. In a smaller composition like this, the 'middle ground' is omitted. Later we will see how interesting middle ground can be used for relatively larger sized drawings to bring out more visual interest.

# Typical Steps for a Landscape Composition:

**As there is no erasure in pen and ink, outlines for a pen and ink drawing are typically put from front to back.**

Faint horizon line is hidden when foreground element that crosses it is textured

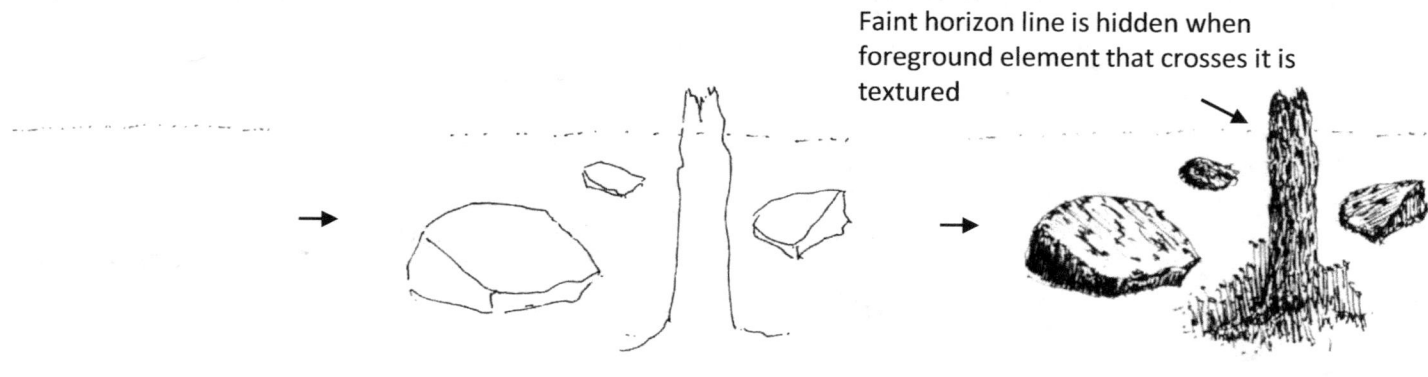

**1. Start by laying down a faint horizon line**

**2. Outline the foreground elements and texture them.  Make elements closer to horizon smaller and use right size for different elements so they appear in proportion.**

## Typical Steps for a Landscape Composition :

In a small drawing with foreground elements like this one the focus is squarely on them.

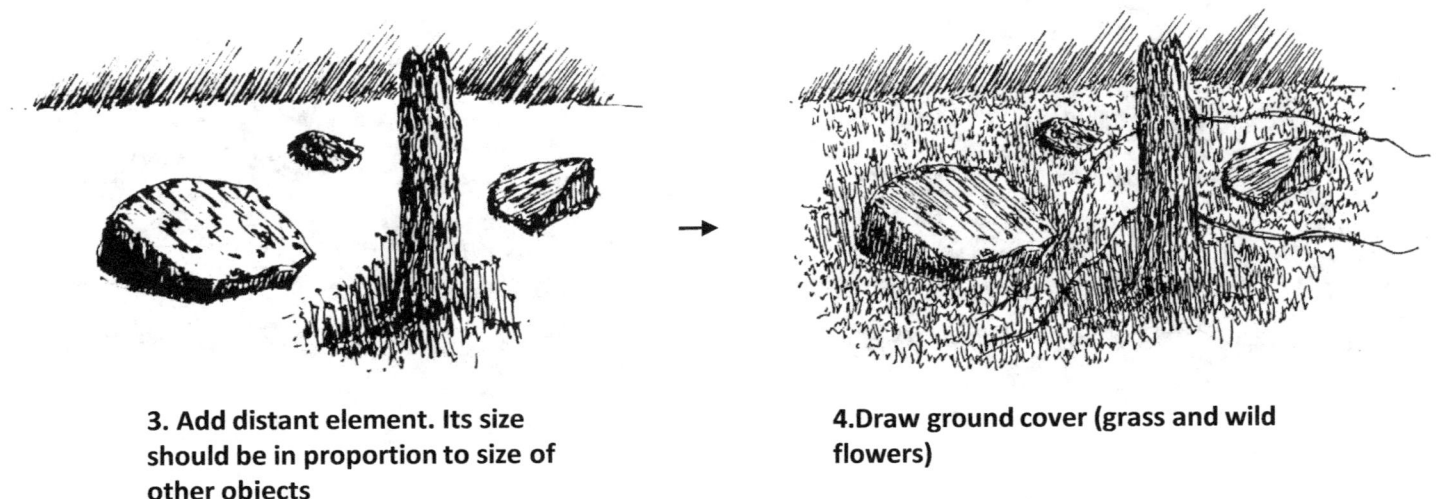

3. Add distant element. Its size should be in proportion to size of other objects

4. Draw ground cover (grass and wild flowers)

Trunks, Young trees, wooden posts etc. go very well with stones as foreground elements as we saw in some of drawings before. They are covered in other workbooks and I encourage you to consult them for learning to draw other elements as well. Pl. visit www.pendrawings.me/workbooks for more information.

## Typical Steps for a Landscape Composition :

In any small sized composition, a decision needs o be made regarding what is the focus of composition. In 'foreground' focus, the focus is on elements in the front in foreground closer to the viewer like in this drawing. Another option is to focus on distant horizons and plains with path leading to it as discussed next.

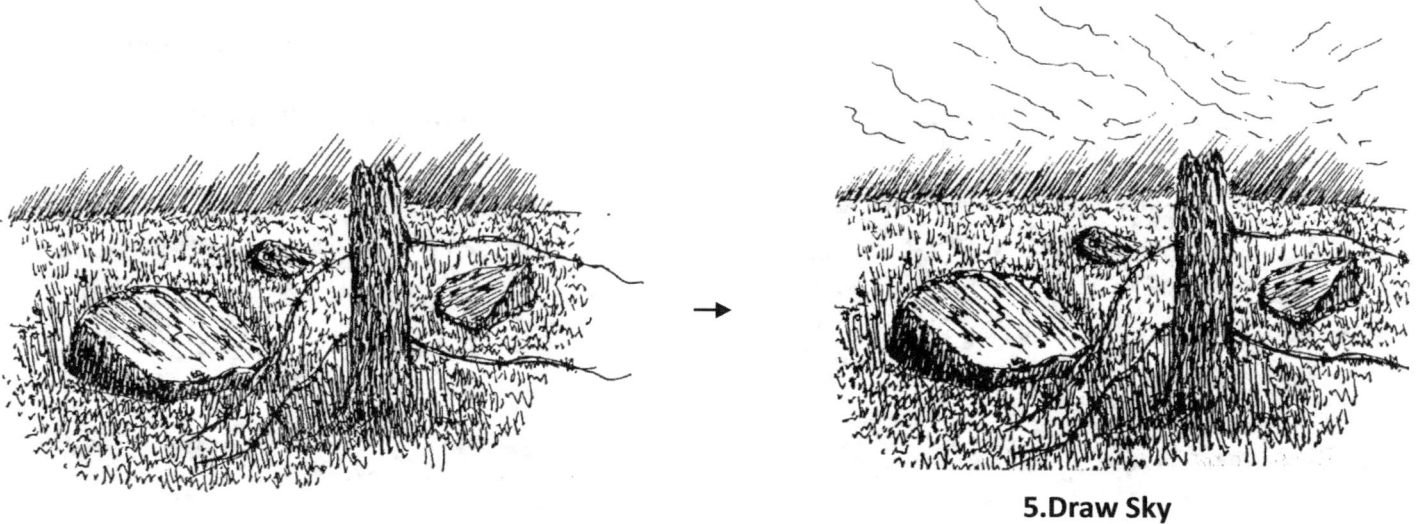

**5.Draw Sky**

By using different combinations of foreground elements and background elements, simple pleasing landscapes can be easily done from imagination. Use of Plain lines for middle ground is discussed later.

## Using Distant Horizon Focus:

Instead of focusing on foreground elements, another option is to use interesting horizon and plains as the main focus. Foreground elements can be added as well but they have to be smaller in size and hence aren't the focus. In vol 6. of my pen and ink drawing workbook (www.pendrawings.me/workbooks), I further discuss this in detail, specifically use of more interesting distant horizon and distant elements. By using information in these different workbooks together, you will have a complete understanding of the process.

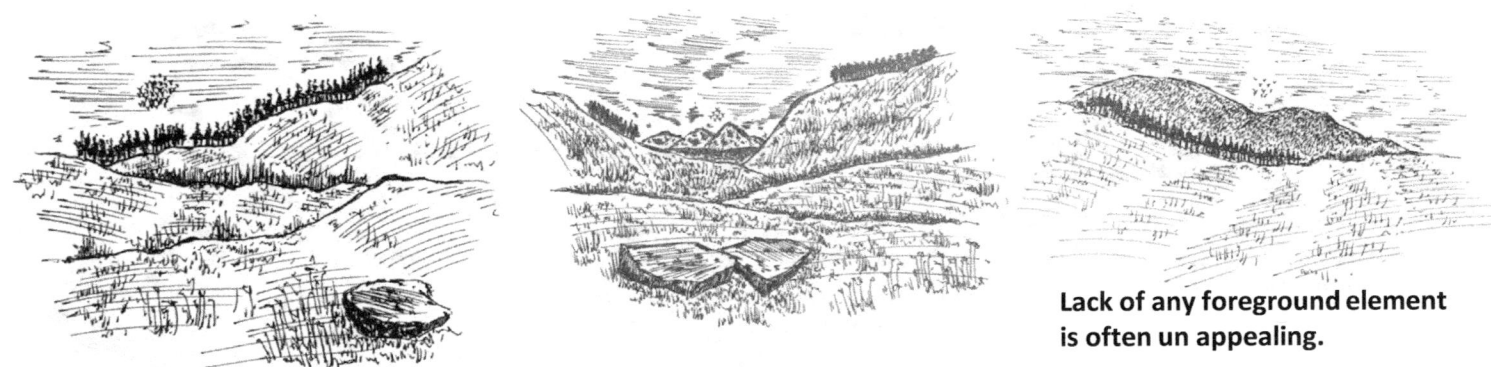

Lack of any foreground element is often un appealing.

Unlike the drawing in previous page, the foreground stones are not main focus here. They still provide a focal point and add to viewing interest, but it is the process of traversing from foreground to far distant view that the viewer enjoys mostly. Steps for creating such landscapes are discussed in detail in vol. 6 of the workbook.

## Keep Different Elements in Proportion:

It is important to have different foreground and background elements in proportion. If your composition is seeing far out in the distance, then it automatically implies that you are not closely focused on a nearby by element and that they are being seen from a distance. This implies that they wll be see and hence drawn smaller in size compared to when they are the main focus.

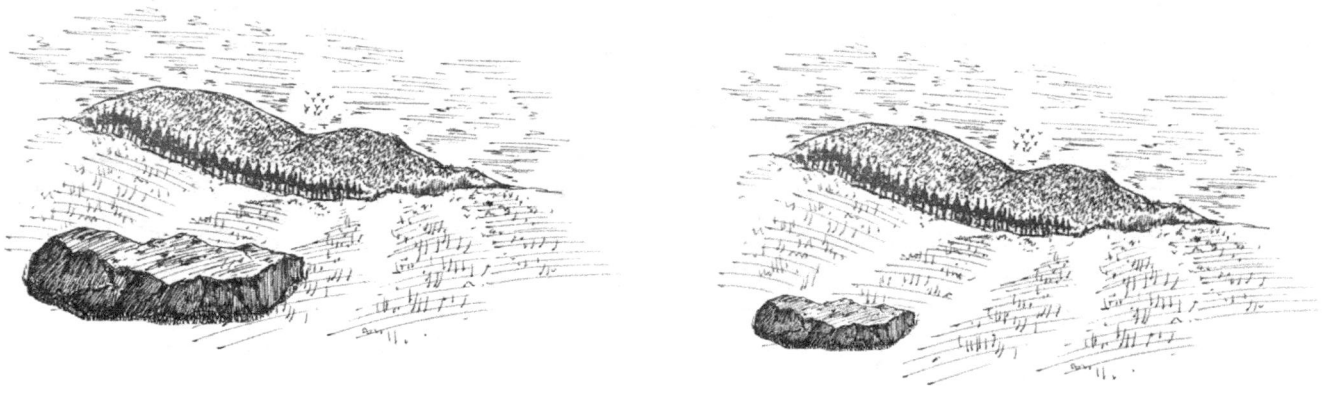

The drawing on the left looks odd as the foreground stone feel bigger than what it ought to be. Drawing on the right feels more 'natural' with stone smaller. There are no rules for relative sizes. Just make sure the drawing feels in 'proportion' and 'plausible'. Your eyes will tell you when it isn't.

## Incorporating Interesting Middle Ground:

As we saw earlier, in smaller landscapes, middle ground is often not expressed due to size limitation. In a bigger sized drawing, middle ground can be incorporated to give it more visual power. One way to do so is to create interesting middle ground plains using lines as shown below. This can be extended to foreground as well.

Use plain lines to create interesting surface irregularities. Distribute the plain lines to get a sense of balance across and use interesting shapes to add visual interest. Avoid any repetition and use of simple lines.

# Drawing Foliage on Plain Lines:

**Use following steps to draw foliage on the plain lines. Increase the size of foliage as it gets closer to viewer. Drawing foliage is covered in more detail in another volume in the series.**

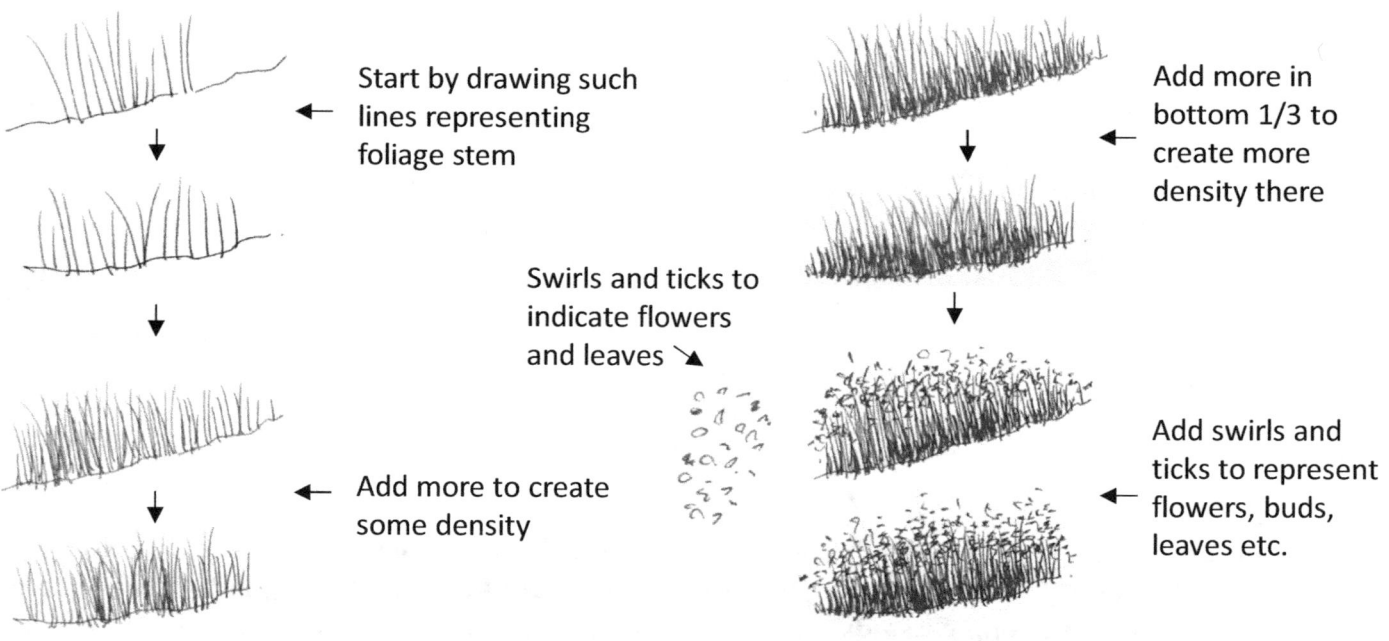

Start by drawing such lines representing foliage stem

Add more in bottom 1/3 to create more density there

Swirls and ticks to indicate flowers and leaves

Add more to create some density

Add swirls and ticks to represent flowers, buds, leaves etc.

## Adding Foliage to Plain Lines:

**Foliage per earlier instructions is drawn on the plain lines. This brings out the ground form. Per perspective, foliage is drawn increasingly bigger as it gets closer to the viewer (away from the horizon).**

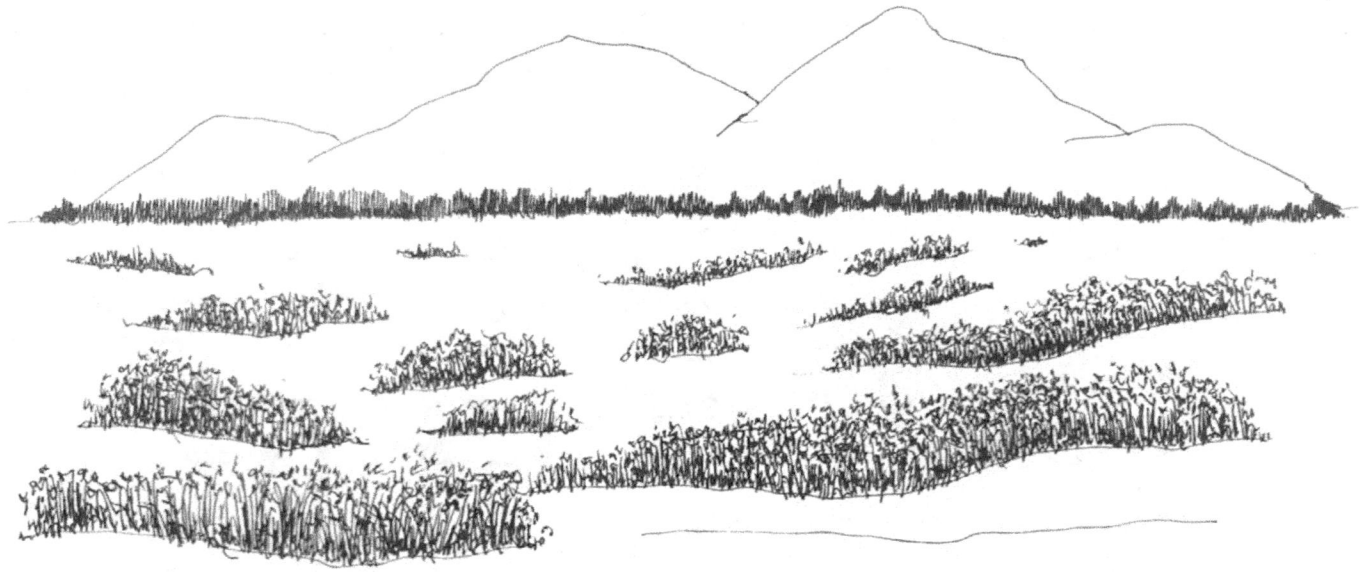

Notice how this is visually more pleasing than use of simple flat ground extending from front to back.

## Step by Step: Drawing Landscapes with Middle Ground and Coniferous Trees:

**A very pleasing landscape composition consists of drawing Pine trees along with foliage on interesting Plain lines spanning from foreground to background as discussed earlier.**

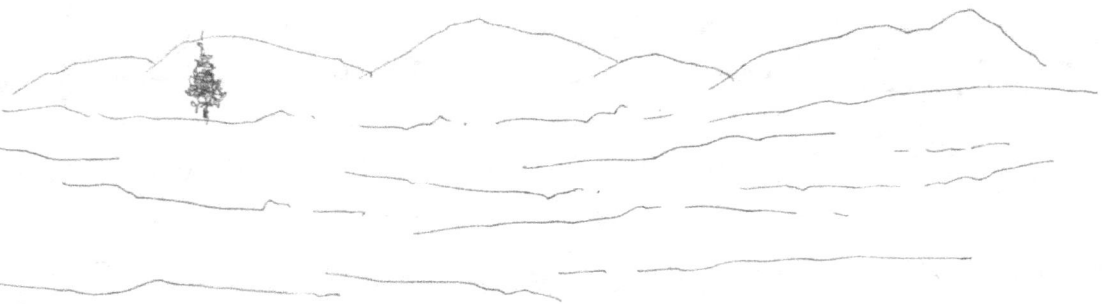

Start by drawing different  plain lines that gives a nice feel as our eyes travel to horizon. As the size of drawing is relatively bigger, we are able to express the plains in the middle ground.

## Step by Step: Drawing Landscapes with Middle Ground and Coniferous Trees:

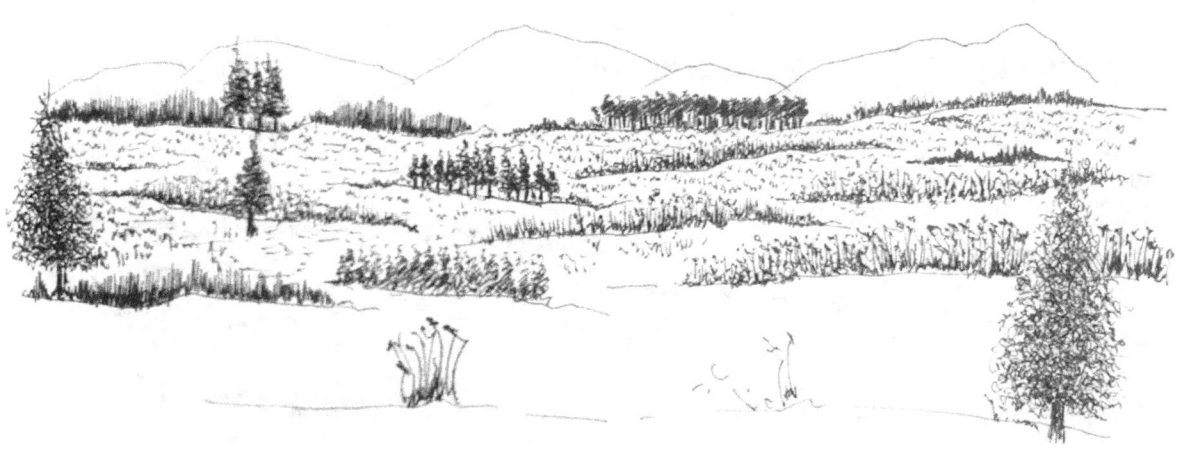

Add foliage and coniferous trees receding (becoming smaller) towards the horizon.

## Step by Step: Drawing Landscapes with Middle Ground and Coniferous Trees, Finished:

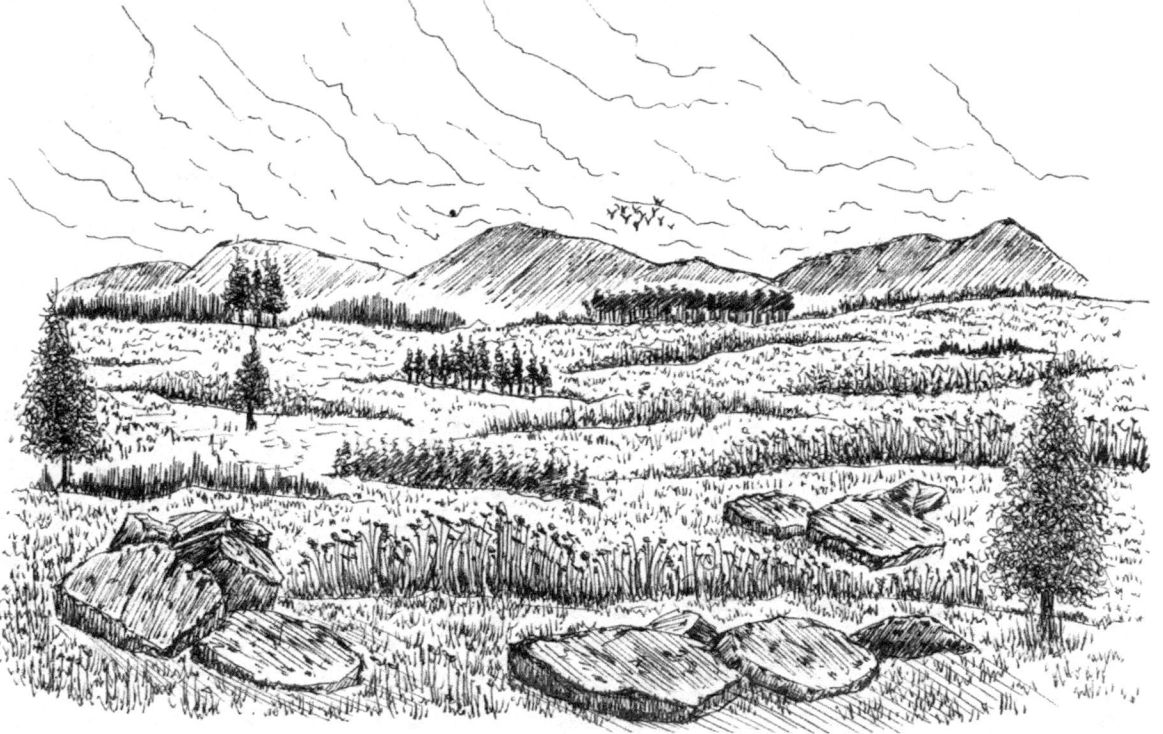

Finish by adding sky, other foreground elements, texturing mountains and adjusting tones to your likeness. Drawing mountains is covered in another workbook in the series.

**Here is another drawing using the same concepts:**

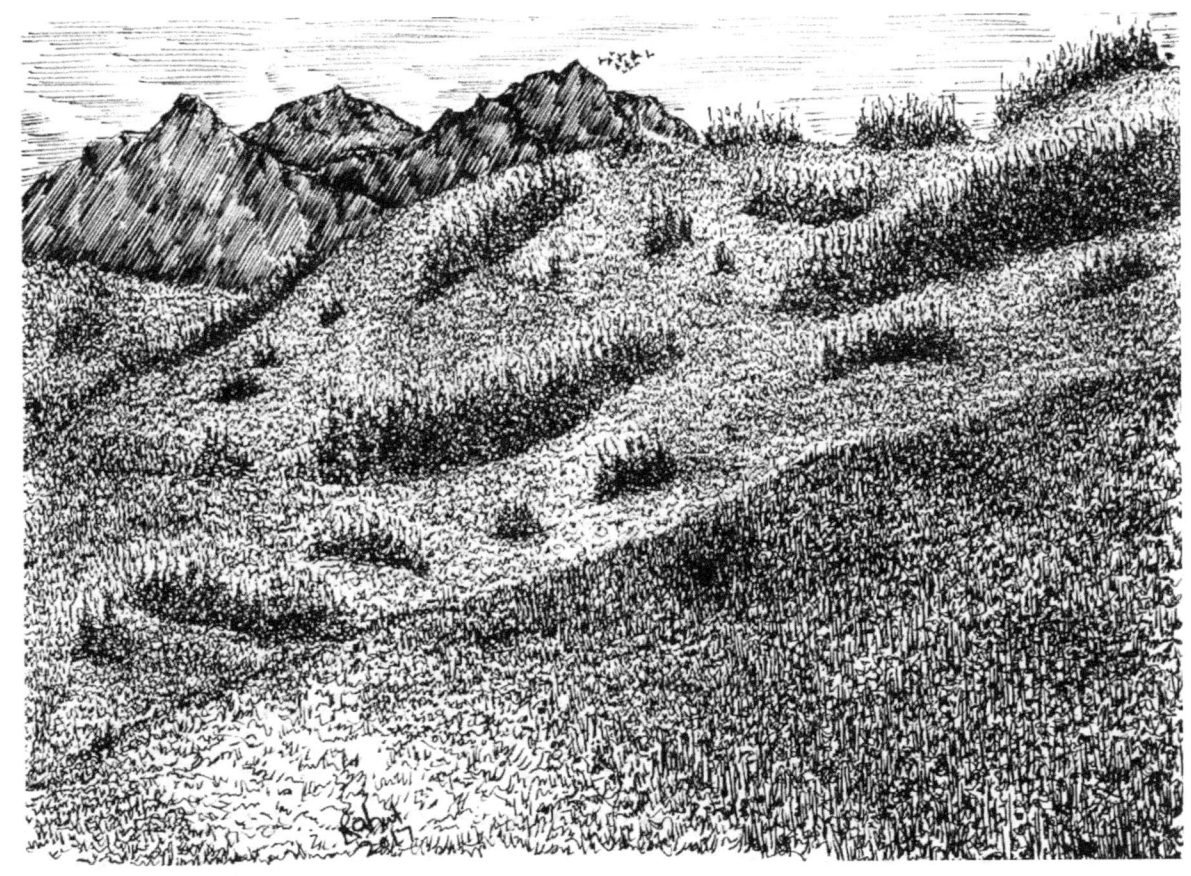

**Activity: Here is a starting point o draw a landscape per earlier instructions.**

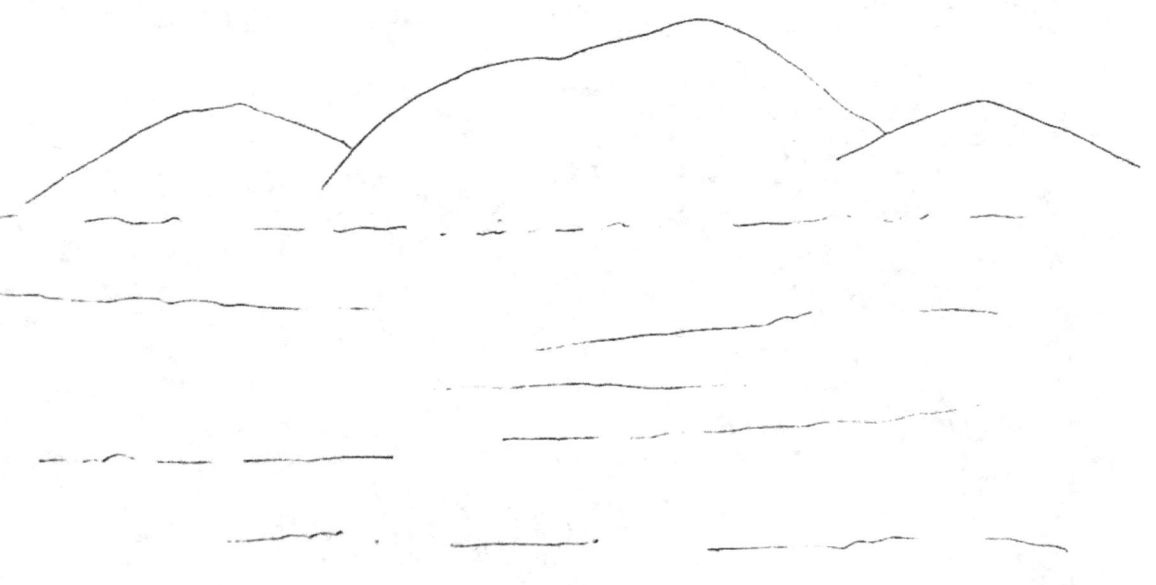

This completes this workbook but hopefully this is just the beginning of your pen and ink drawing adventure. You can visit my website for completely free tutorials and use other workbooks I have created to learn how to draw other elements of nature, like rocks, mountains etc. with pen and ink and create more interesting landscapes.

www.pendrawings.me/workbooks

Practice is key to improving. Carry a small pocket sketch book with you and a pen and try to draw something when ever you get some time. If you don't like your initial attempt, try again. Don't get discouraged.

Any comments, suggestions and feedback on improving contents of this workbook are most welcome. For more information on drawing landscapes with pen and ink, to learn more about my works and to reach me, please visit my website.

www.pendrawings.me/getstarted

Happy drawing,

Rahul Jain

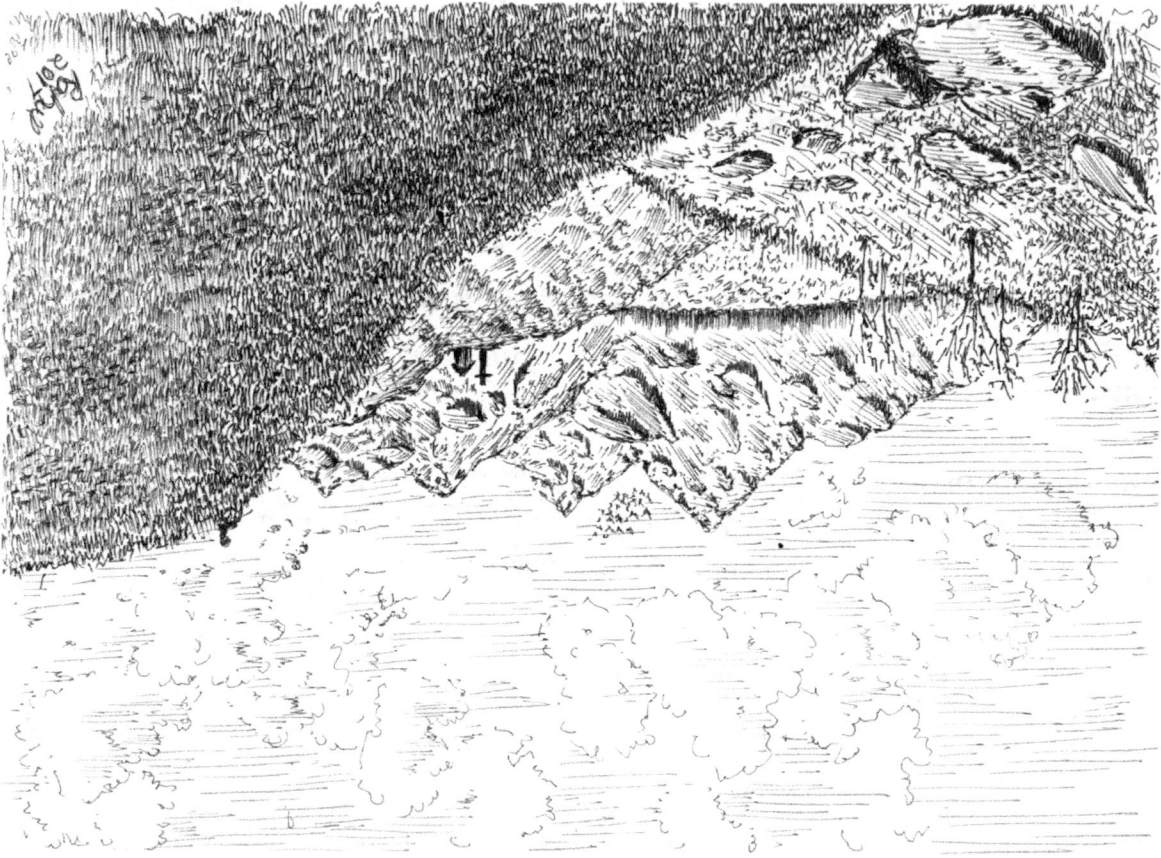

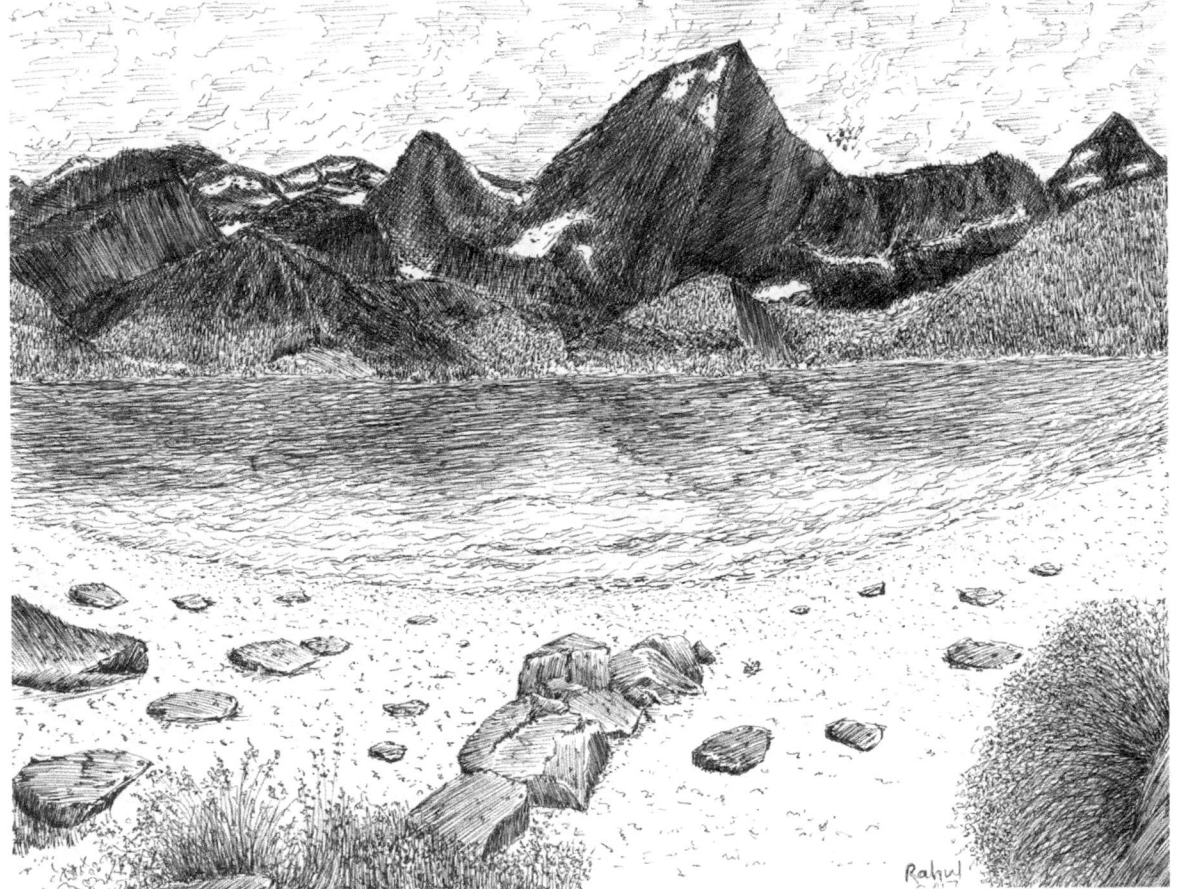

Rahul

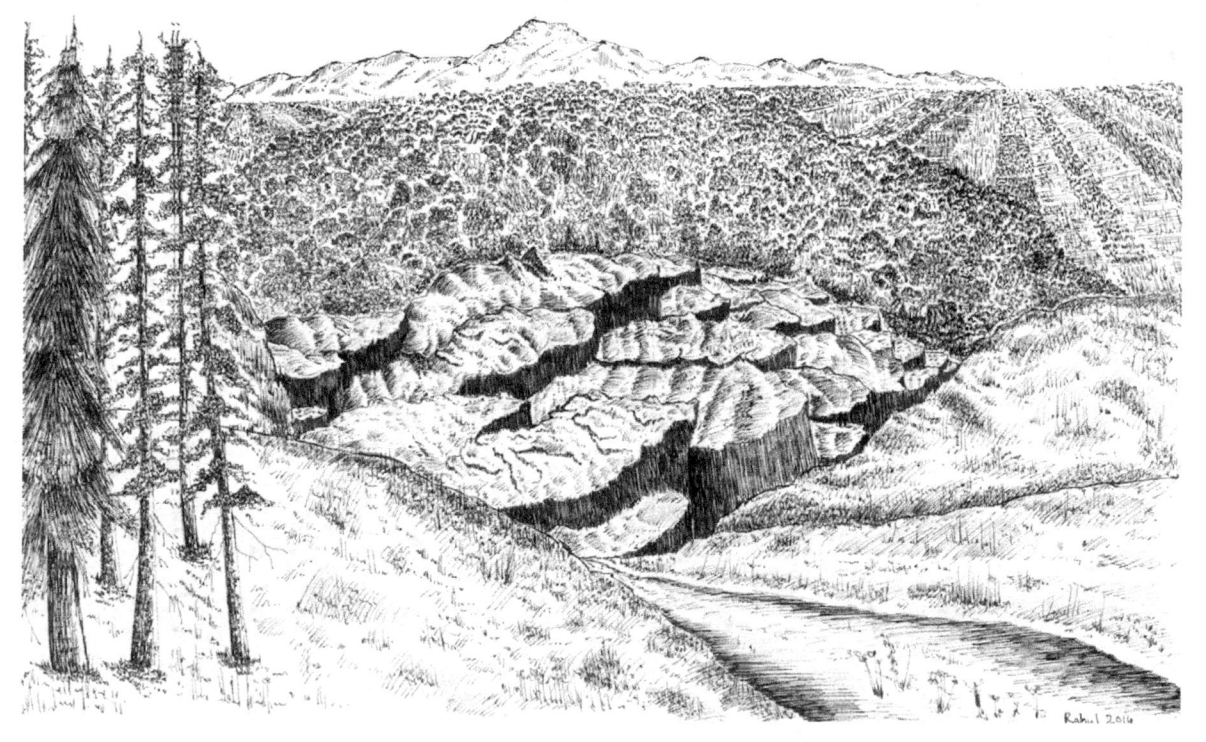

**Far, Far Away: Copyright: Rahul Jain**

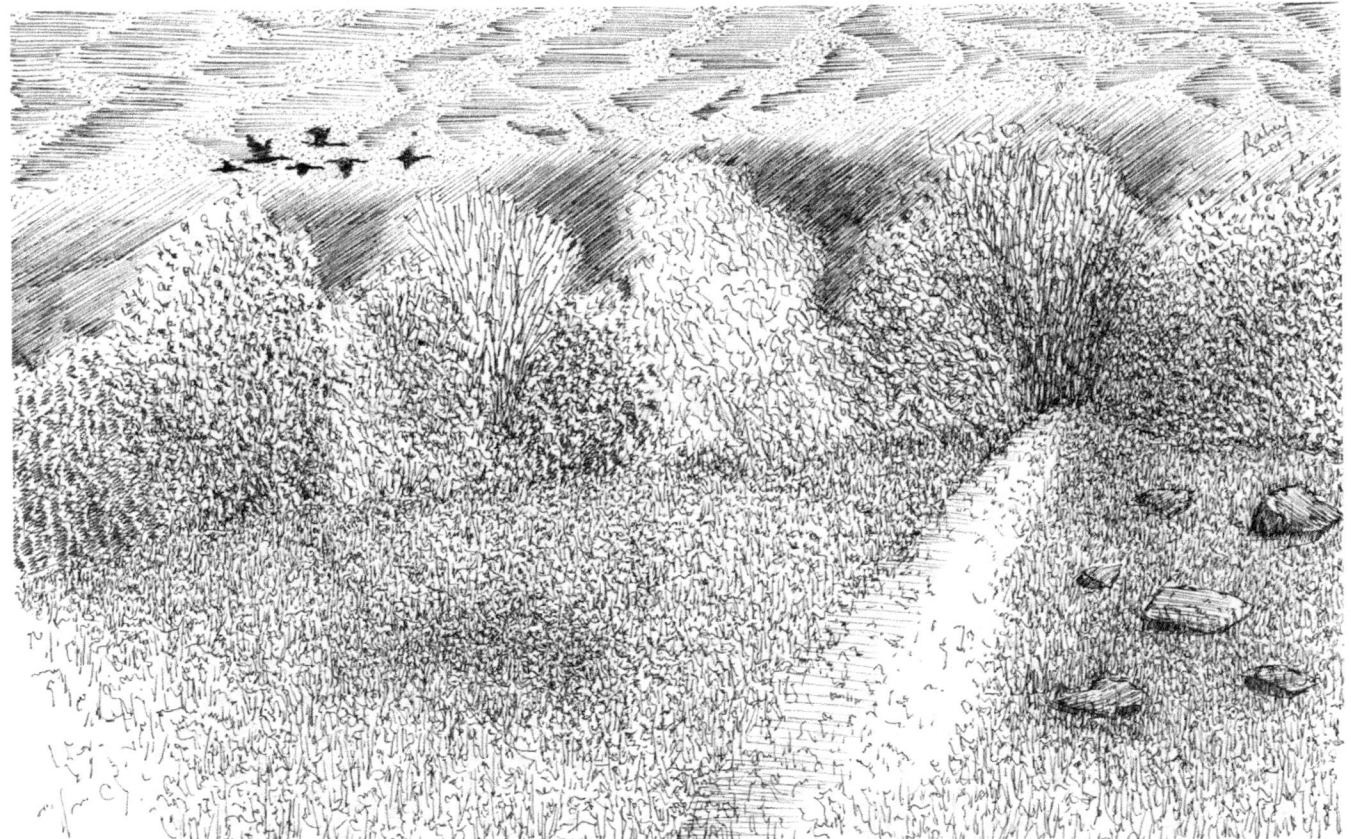

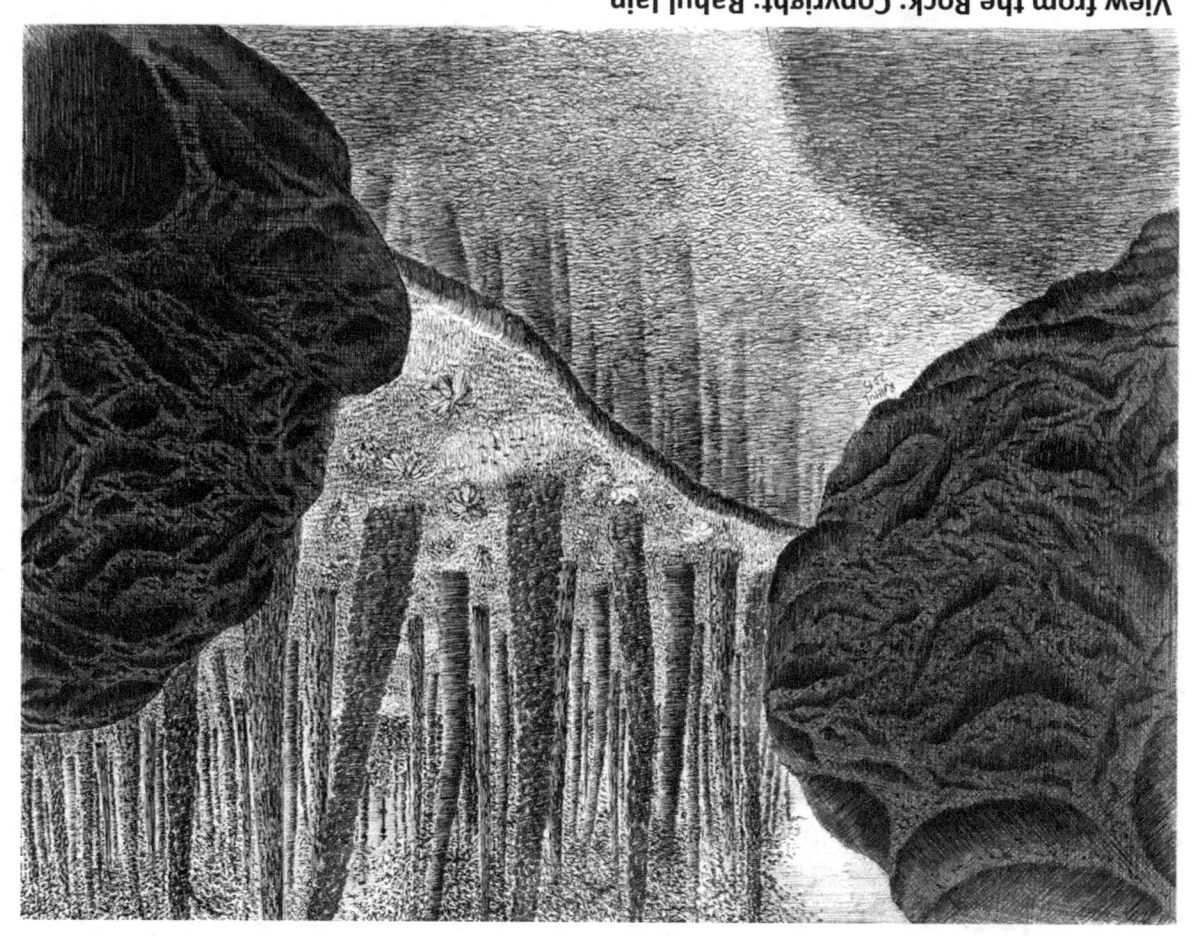

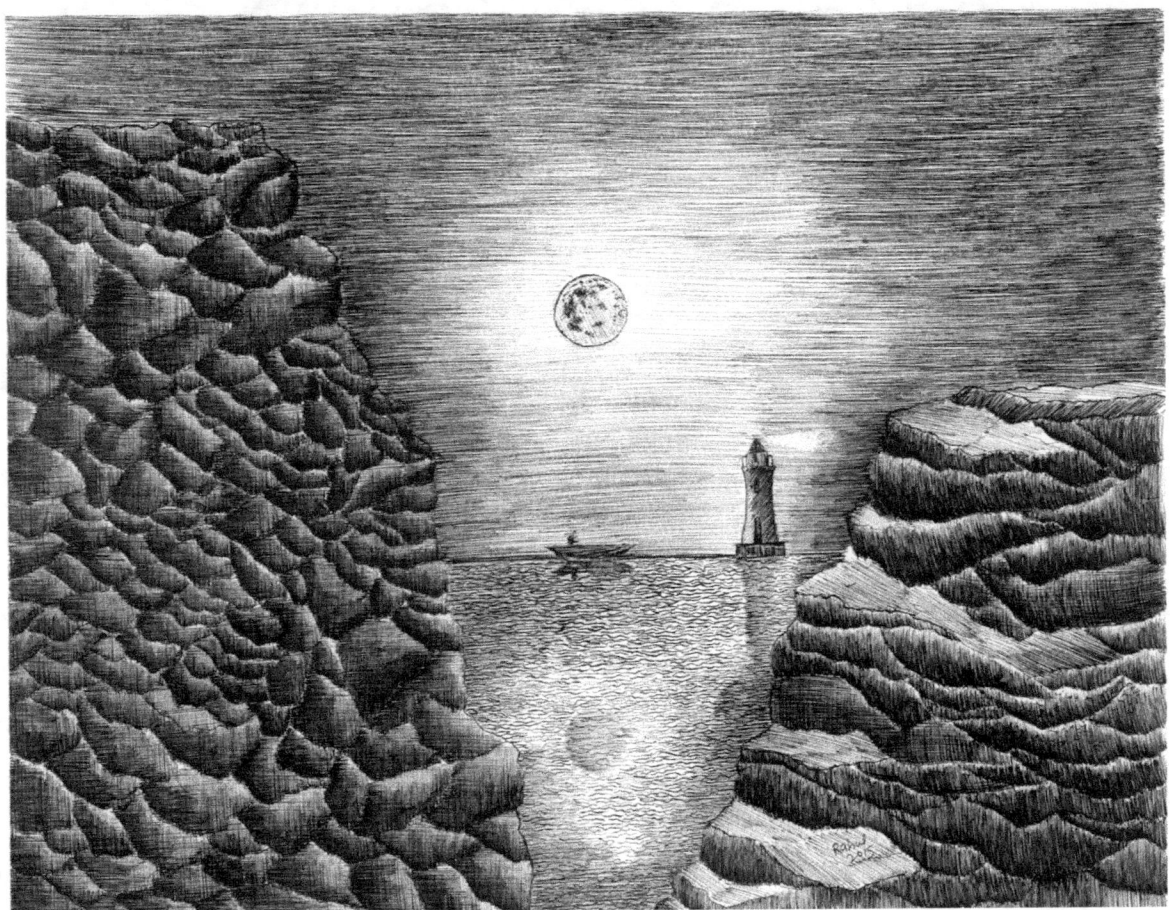

**A Beautiful Night: Copyright: Rahul Jain**